AF585503

# PRIVATE

## A GUIDE TO PERSONAL ART COLLECTIONS IN AUSTRALIA AND NEW ZEALAND

SKADI HECKMUELLER

DOTT PUBLISHING
ARTAND FOUNDATION

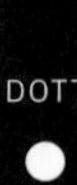

# CONTENTS

# FOREWORD

This book has emerged out of a personal passion. Being an ardent traveller, I have been exploring the world for many years. My wanderlust, combined with my interest in contemporary art, design and architecture, repeatedly prompted me to track down exciting art events and museums, not only in major art hubs, but also in unusual corners of the world. I have been privileged to see and experience many amazing exhibitions and projects. However, I have observed that my heart sings especially when I visit private art collections. The different personalities and motivations of the collectors, together with the often purposely-built edifices and carefully chosen properties, make these meeting places for lovers of art truly unique. Although a few of the private collections I have described are well-known institutions in their respective countries, the majority of these oases are practically unknown outside their region. To make visits to them more accessible and joyful, I have endeavoured to create a practical guidebook which includes many additional tips. However, I have to ask for your understanding that, due to the private nature of the collections and institutions, some details can change very quickly. It therefore is advisable to check the respective websites prior to your visit.

I hope the discovery of these art gems, on both sides of the Tasman Sea, gives you as much pleasure as it gave me.

Skadi

# AUSTRALIA

# NEW SOUTH WALES

# SYDNEY

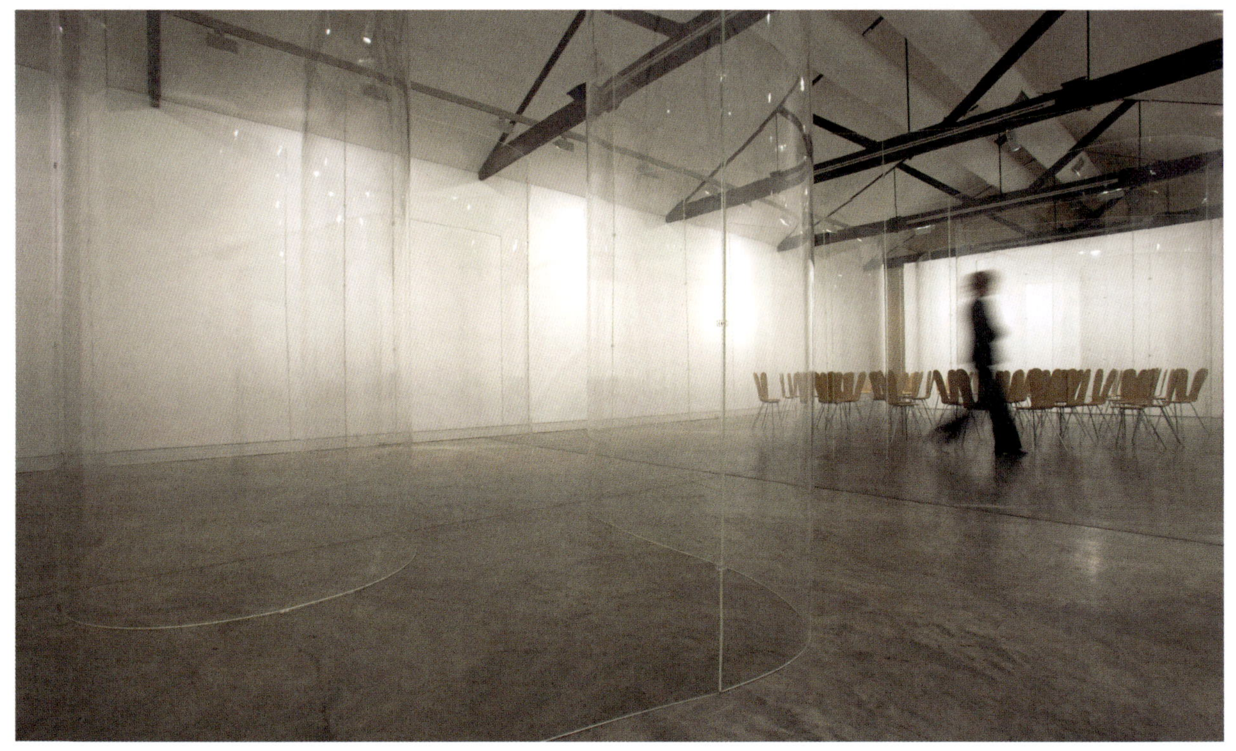

# SHERMAN CONTEMPORARY ART FOUNDATION (SCAF)

16–20 Goodhope Street
Paddington, NSW 2021

OPENING HOURS
Wednesday–Saturday 11am–5pm during exhibition times
Closed during January and February

Telephone: +61 (02) 9331 1112
info@sherman-scaf.org.au
sherman-scaf.org.au

Established in 2008 with Dr Gene Sherman AM as Director and Chairman, the Sherman Contemporary Art Foundation (SCAF) is a cultural jewel in Sydney's eastern suburb of Paddington. This philanthropic family enterprise provides an innovative and highly acclaimed forum for contemporary art, design, architecture and fashion. The foundation's beautiful minimalist gallery complex was repurposed by Andrew Andersons in 1991 and nowadays houses an exhibition space of 350 square metres, an outdoor Zen garden, a versatile theatre annexe, offices and, across the road, a contemporary cottage for resident artists and scholars designed by Alec Tzannes and Associates.

SCAF is built on twenty-one years of cutting-edge commercial exhibitions and artist representation by the Sherman Galleries (1986–2007) and presents work by internationally renowned visual practitioners from Australia, the Asia-Pacific region and the Middle East. Since 2008, the foundation has developed over twenty-five museum-quality projects and staged over 400 talks, forums, workshops and functions. Each year SCAF presents four projects accompanied by visually compelling, scholarly catalogues. Among the many artists who have created site-specific projects for the foundation are Ai Weiwei (China), Janet Laurence (Australia), Dinh Q. Lê (Vietnam), Kazuyo Sejima + Ryue Nishizawa /SANAA (Japan) and Tokujin Yoshioka (Japan). Others, including Yang Fudong (China), Fiona Tan (Indonesia/The Netherlands) and Jitish Kallat (India), have presented monumental existing works exhibited previously in China, Venice and London respectively. The year 2013 saw the inauguration of two ongoing series of interest, the Collection+ and the Fugitive Structures programs. Collection+ was conceived as a hybrid project with a specific cross-pollinating purpose. Some 800 works in The Gene & Brian Sherman Collection, which includes works by Do-Ho Suh, Shirin Neshat, Lily Kelly Napangardi, Bill Henson, Mike Parr, Guan Wei, Ai Weiwei and Cai Guo-Qiang are scrutinised and assessed by invited curators. Each curator then selects a single artist from the collection and researches other private collections nationally and internationally in order to identify and access significant related works by the same artist. These curatorial and research ventures have resulted in exciting museum-quality shows by Chiharu Shiota (Japan), Sopheap Pich (Cambodia), Pinaree Sanpitak (Thailand) and Shaun Gladwell (Australia).

Fugitive Structures, a series that aims to engage a wide audience with architectural thought and practice, is a collaborative initiative between SCAF and the architecture firm BVN. This annual competition invites emerging and early-career architects to design a small-scale temporary pavilion for SCAF's Zen garden. The interesting Crescent House, designed and built by Sydney-based architect Andrew Burns, was the first temporary pavilion to be installed. In 2014, the brief was amended to specify for that year alone that the structure would need to use the most progressive technology available at the time. The winner for the 2014 Fugitive Structures, the experimental architectural practice AR-MA, used advanced computer design to create the photogenic structure *Trifolium*. Tel-Aviv-based architects Sack and Reicher + Muller with Eyal Zur have been selected for Fugitive Structures 2015, and the Japan-trained Vietnamese architect Vo Trong Nghia has agreed to create the 4th Fugitive Structures Pavilion in 2016 to be installed in Brisbane at an architectural event before being reinstalled in SCAF's Zen garden.

Dr Sherman emigrated from South Africa with her young family in 1976. She has a specialised knowledge of art, literary theory, French and English literature. She sits on the board of several art organisations and regularly lectures on topics such as gallery management, exhibition-making, the art of collecting, philanthropy, private foundations, Australian and Asian contemporary artists, and contemporary Japanese

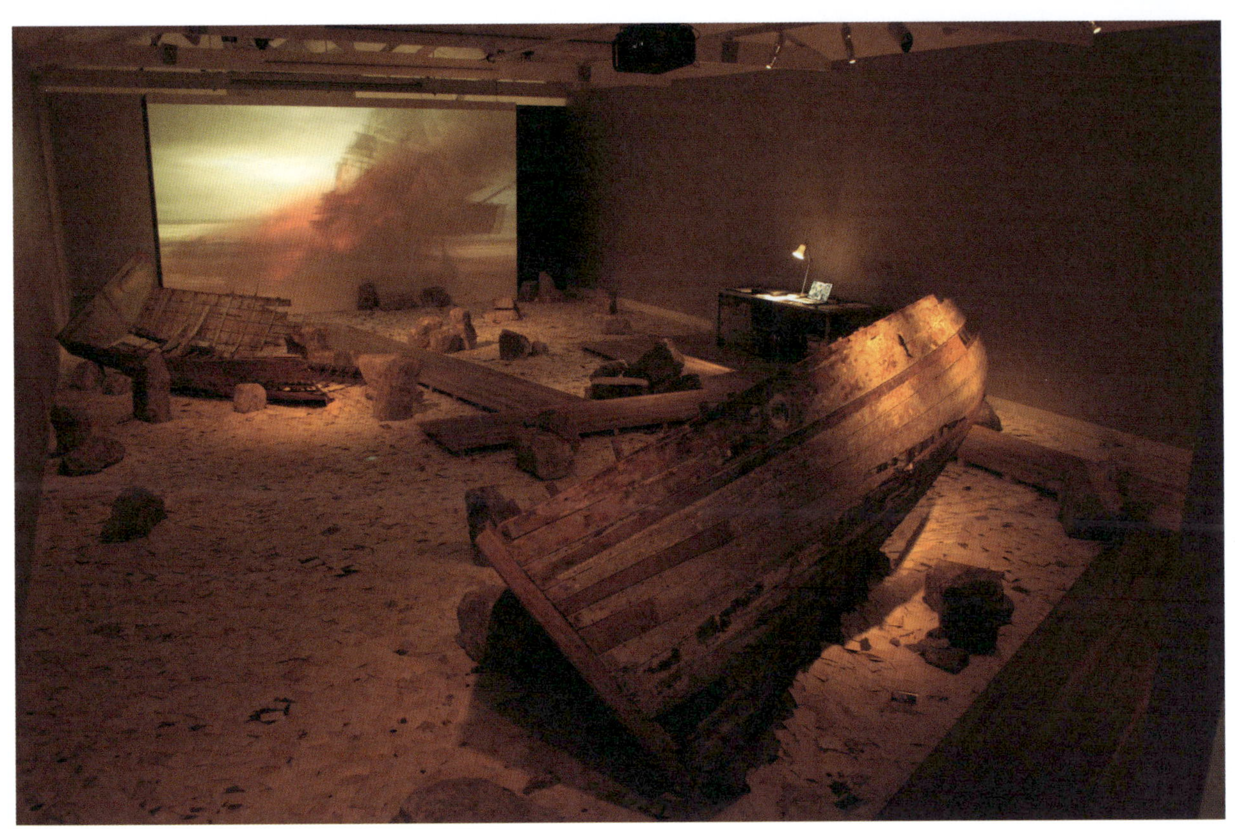

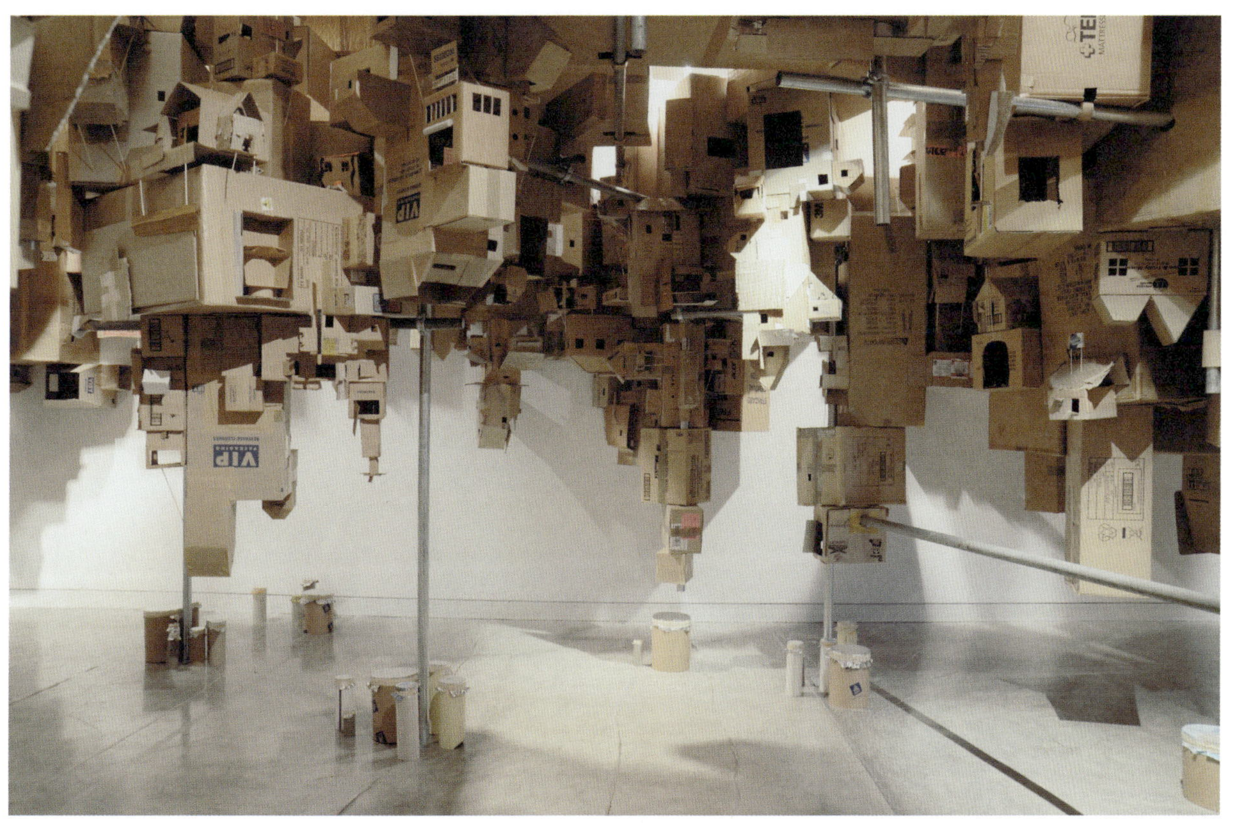

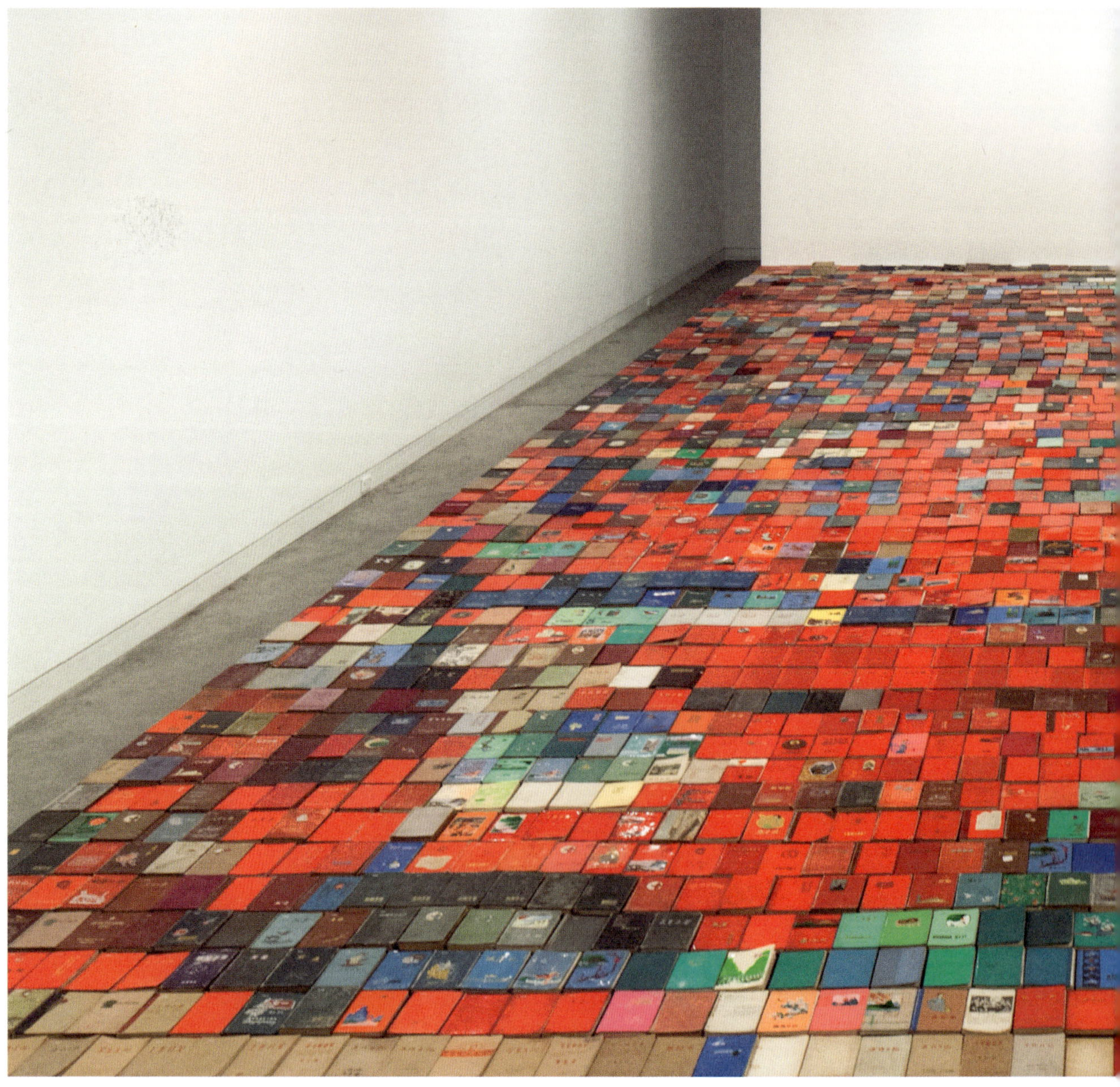

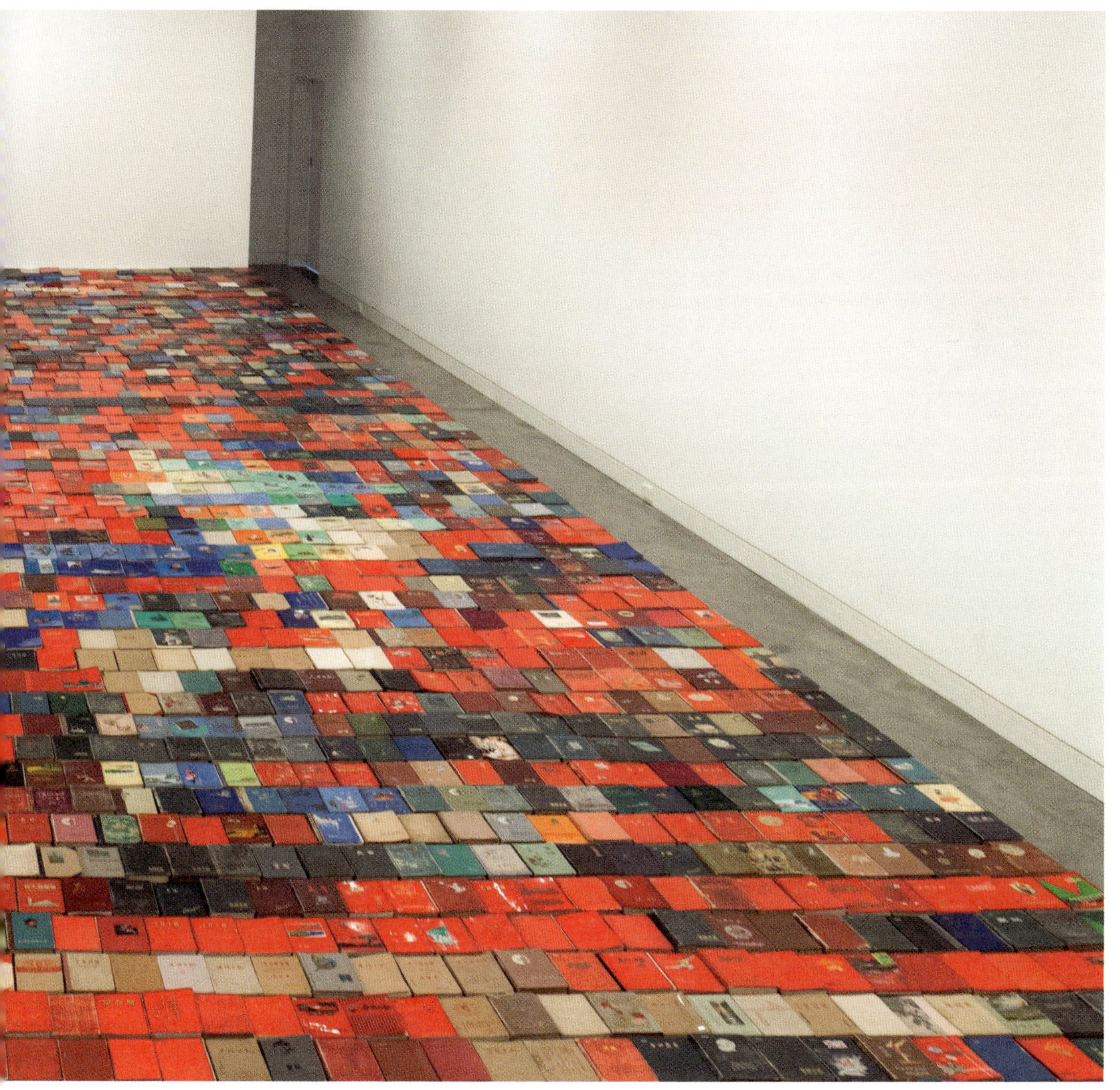

fashion. Dr Sherman was awarded the Chevalier de l'Ordre des Arts et des Lettres by the French Government (2003) and a Doctorate of Letters honoris causa by The University of Sydney (2008). She received the Member of the Order of Australia in 2010 for her cultural philanthropy and her support of emerging and established artists.

SCAF is generously supported by Dr Sherman's husband, Brian Sherman, the highly successful co-founder of the funds management group Equitilink and co-founder of the impressive animal protection group Voiceless. Together the couple support and collaborate with various national and international cultural, scientific and environmental institutions.

The Andrew Cameron Family Foundation is a valued supporter of Fugitive Structures, and the Nelson Meers Foundation has generously sponsored SCAF's Culture + Ideas program over many years.

VISITOR INFORMATION

**Admission Fees:** No entry charge

**Tours and other Events:** SCAF periodically initiates touring exhibitions in partnership with other institutions. In addition, projects are often mounted via differing level partnerships with international and national institutions.

SCAF offers a and diverse public program, which accompanies the various exhibitions. Culture + Ideas is a series of high-level talks and podium discussions which bring together top-tier creative practitioners, writers, chefs, filmmakers, environmentalists and scholars. Dr Sherman personally introduces every event. SCAF also organises film screenings and creative workshops for children.

**Access by car:** Leave the CBD in an easterly direction on Oxford Street, turn left onto Glenmore Road. Take the second exit at the roundabout and stay on Glenmore Road. At the roundabout, take the first exit onto Goodhope Street. SCAF is located on the left-hand side.

**Access by public transport:** Take the 389 City to North Bondi Bus from Circular Quay and other CBD bus stops to the 'Glenmore Road near Goodhope Street' bus stop. Turn left at the roundabout onto Goodhope Street.

**Extra Tips:** The Art Gallery of New South Wales is one of the most popular and active art museums in Australia. It features international and Australian art in impressive surroundings. It is also the home of over 200 exquisite works which have been generously gifted by John Kaldor, the founder of the acclaimed Kaldor Public Art Projects program, in 2011. It is the largest donation of art given to a public gallery in Australia's history and includes works by Robert Rauschenberg, Richard Long, Sol LeWitt, Jeff Koons, Christo, and Frank Stella (Art Gallery Road, The Domain). The art gallery also manages the Brett Whiteley Studio, which was the workplace and home of the renowned Australian artist (2 Raper Street, Surry Hills; open Friday–Sunday 10am–4pm). Gallery-goers will equally enjoy visiting the Museum of Contemporary Art (MCA), Australia's best-known museum dedicated to collecting and exhibiting the work of living artists (140 George Street, The Rocks). The MCA rooftop terrace café offers one of the greatest views in town. Also worth a visit, is Object, which has recently opened its new William Street creative hub, showcasing and supporting Australian design and craftsmanship (101–115 William Street, Darlinghurst).

Sydney features exquisite international art in public places. Worth a look is the Frank Stella installation in the lobby of Grosvenor Place (225 George Street), as well as the nearby sculpture by Alexander Calder, the Sol LeWitt mural and the tapestry by Joan Miró at the Australia Square complex (264 George Street). The late Harry Seidler, one of Sydney's most prominent architects, designed both of these iconic buildings. Quieter, but very impressive, is the marble installation *Touchstones* by Kan Yasuda at the Aurora Place plaza (corner of Phillip and Bent streets). Visitors to the Walsh Bay area might enjoy Jimmi Durnham's *Still life with stone and car,* which is owned by philanthropists Luca and Anita Belgiorno-Nettis.

Being one of the world's leading festival cities, Sydney offers an exciting art and cultural festival line-up. Lovers of the arts, architecture and design should check out the following: 'Sculpture by the Sea'; 'Sydney Festival'; 'Art and About'; 'Art Month Sydney' and 'Sydney Open'; as well as the websites for 'Sydney Biennale'; 'Sydney Writers Festival' and 'Sydney Film Festival'.

A visit to SCAF can be easily combined with a trip to the White Rabbit Gallery (refer to page 14) or an appointment to visit the Gordon Elliott Contemporary Art Collection (refer to page 22).

**Restaurant Tips:** Enjoy the extensive wine list and upmarket Italian small-dishes menu at the popular bar 10 William Street (10 William Street, Paddington). Queen Street, the leafy main road of nearby Woollahra, features several pleasant cafés with a somewhat European feel.

Page 14
Kazuyo Sejima + Ryue Nishizawa, *SANAA*, 2009
Acrylic and SANAA original rabbit chairs, dimensions variable
Courtesy Sherman Contemporary Art Foundation
Photograph Paul Green

Page 16
Dinh Q. Lê, *Erasure*, 2011
Single channel video, boat, found photographs, rocks, online archive, dimensions variable
Photograph Aaron de Souza

Page 17
Alfredo & Isabel Aquilizan, *In-Habit: Project Another Country*, 2012
Used transport cardboard boxes, packing tape, handcrafted cardboard houses, makeshift drums and sound, single channel video projection (The Badjao (Southern Philippines), 5:07 min), 5 LCD screen installations, dimensions variable
Photograph Jacob Ring

Pages 18-9
Yang Zhichao, *Chinese Bible*, 2009
3,000 found diaries, dimensions variable
Collection Gene & Brian Sherman, Sydney
Photograph silversalt photography

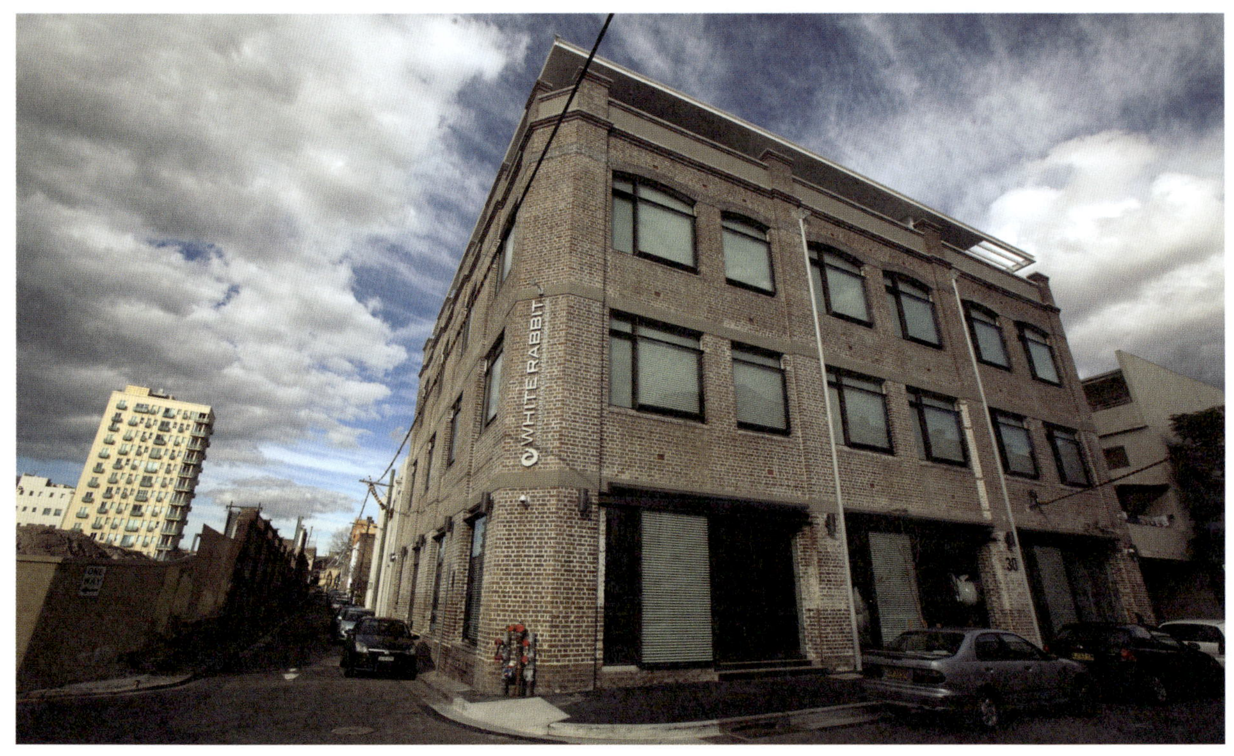


# WHITE RABBIT GALLERY

30 Balfour Street
Chippendale, NSW 2008

OPENING HOURS
Wednesday–Sunday 10am–5pm during exhibition time
(check website for closure dates)

Tel +61 (02) 8399 2867
info@whiterabbitcollection.org
whiterabbitcollection.org

Located in the newly gentrified Chippendale area, the White Rabbit Gallery was established in 2009 by the Neilson Foundation to share one of the world's most significant private collections of contemporary Chinese art.

Judith Neilson has been interested in art all her life. Born in Zimbabwe and schooled in graphic and textile design in South Africa, she worked as an art director in an advertising agency for nearly two decades before emigrating to Australia with her former husband, Kerr Neilson, the founder of Platinum Asset Management, in 1983. In 1999, on the spur of the moment, Neilson purchased a work by the Chinese artist Wang Zhiyuan at Sydney's Ray Hughes Gallery. When Wang returned to Australia a few years later to gain a Master's degree at the University of Sydney, Neilson convinced him to work with her. Through Wang and his artist friends, she was able to access what was then a largely untapped Chinese art market existing parallel to the artificially channelled and promoted one. Neilson has continued to visit artists' studios and selected galleries in China every three months or so since she started serious collecting in 2006.

Currently, the collection comprises well over 1000 works by almost 500 artists, although the number increases with dozens of new acquisitions each year. In addition to some of China's best-known artists, such as Ai Weiwei, Chen Haiyan, Zhou Xiaohu, Zhang Dali and Xu Zhen, the collection contains works by emerging talents such as Gao Rong, Bai Yiluo and Zong Ning. Neilson only acquires works that she finds visually and emotionally appealing and that have been created since 2000. The majority are produced in Beijing, where the enormous social changes are manifested in art in the most creative ways.

Called White Rabbit because it sounded friendly, the spacious, airy, inviting gallery was designed by Smart Design Studio, winner of the 2006 Royal Australian Institute of Architects Award for Architecture Conservation and Adaptive Re-use. Although the gallery has an exhibition space of about 2000 square metres on four floors (of which the top floor is accessible only by elevator), it can exhibit merely a fraction of the collection at any one time. To familiarise Sydney-siders and visitors with her vast collection, Neilson and her team replace the superb theme-oriented exhibitions at six-monthly intervals. The descriptions provided are always comprehensive, explaining not only the materials used but also the motives behind the artworks. Gallery attendants are all knowledgeable about the artists being exhibited and welcome enquiries from interested visitors. It is easy to understand why the White Rabbit Gallery has quickly emerged as one of Sydney's leading art attractions.

The gallery is funded by the Neilson Foundation, a philanthropic entity established by the Neilson family. The foundation became Principal Patron of the Biennale of Sydney in 2014.

VISITOR INFORMATION

**Admission Fees:** Free of charge

**Tours and other Events:** Free guided tours take place twice daily at 11am and 2pm. No booking necessary. The meeting point is the reception desk.

The reference library (located on the gallery's top floor) provides a large range of books on Chinese art, history and culture (open Wednesday to Sunday by appointment with the librarian).

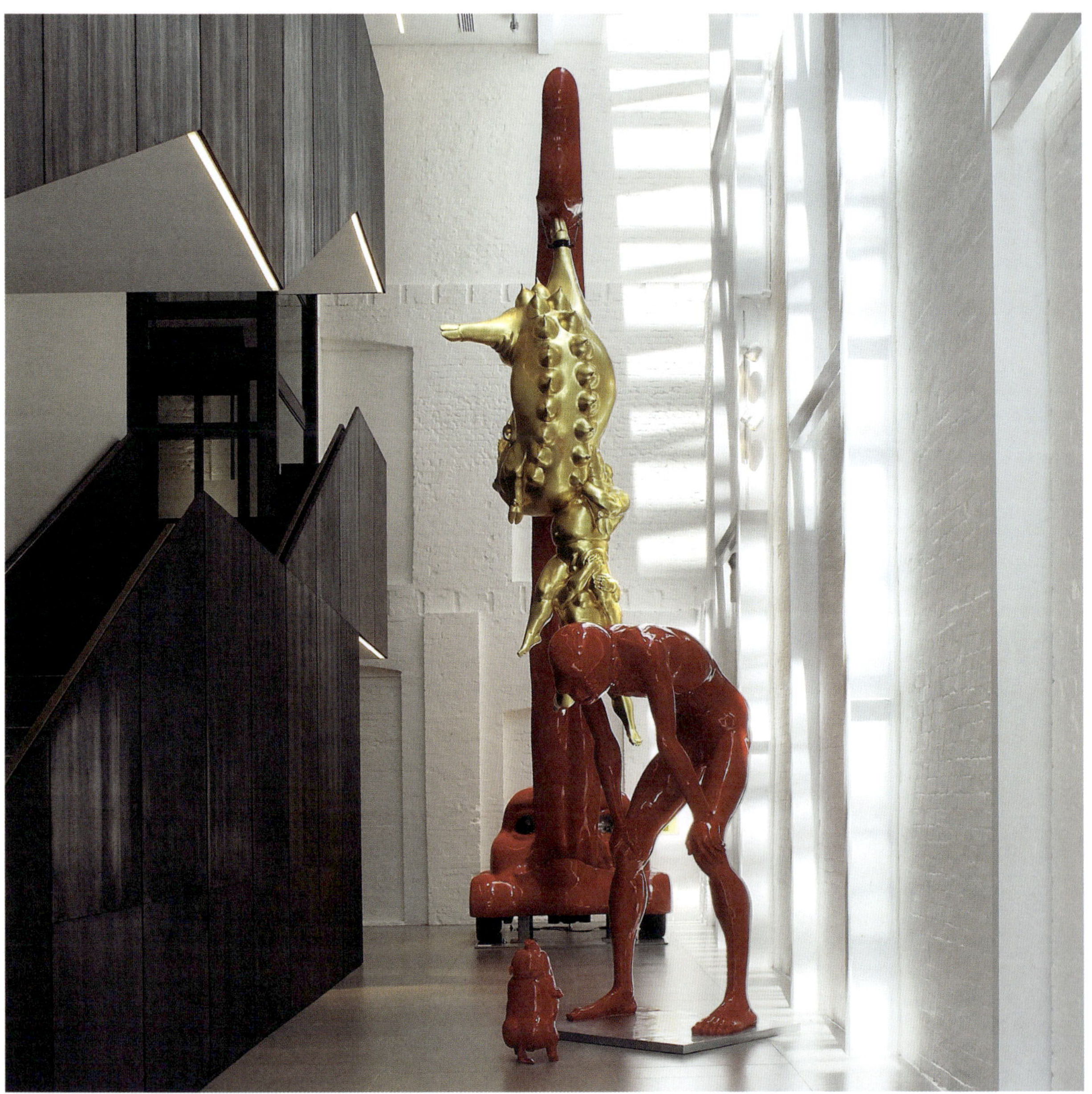

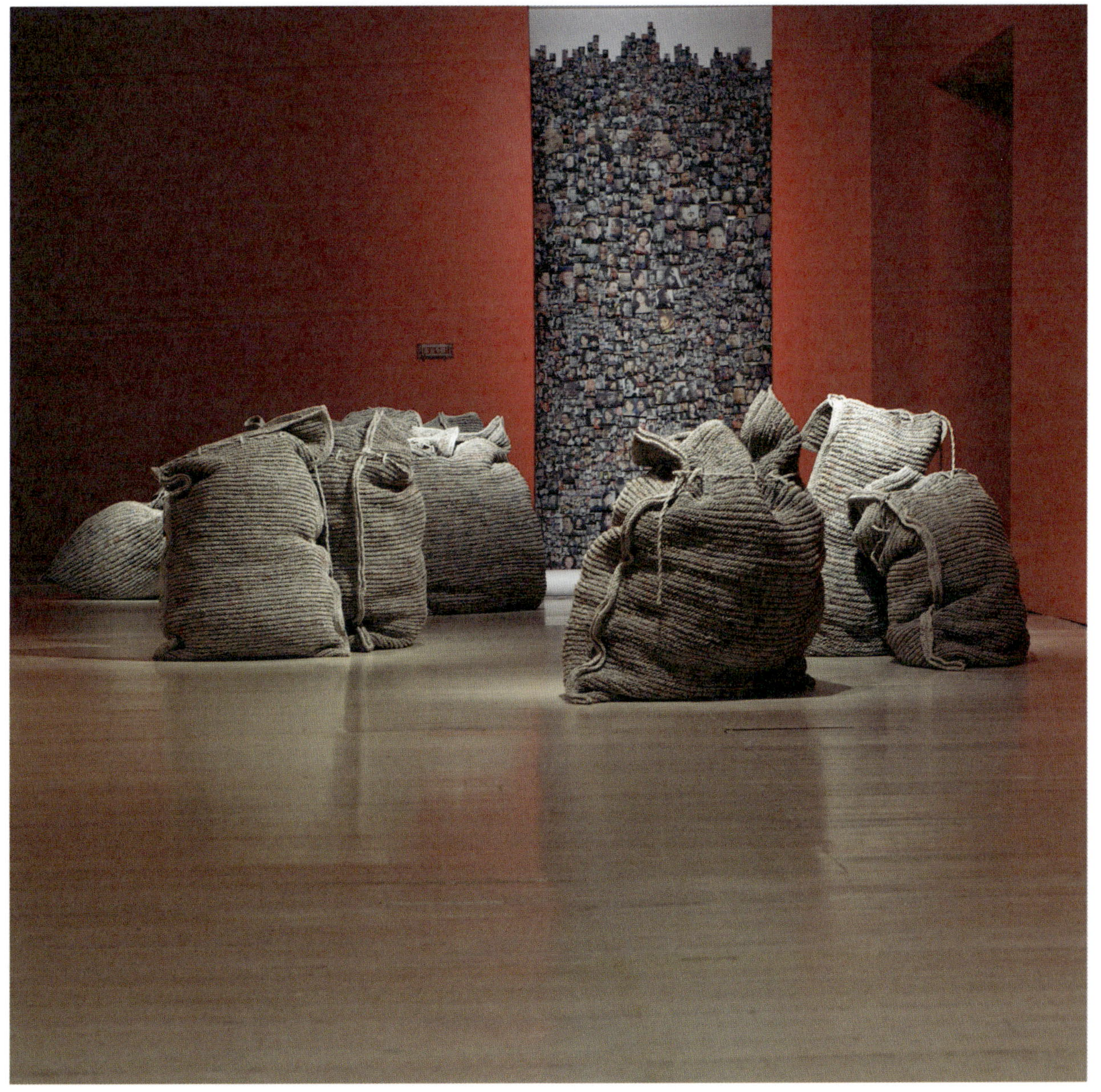

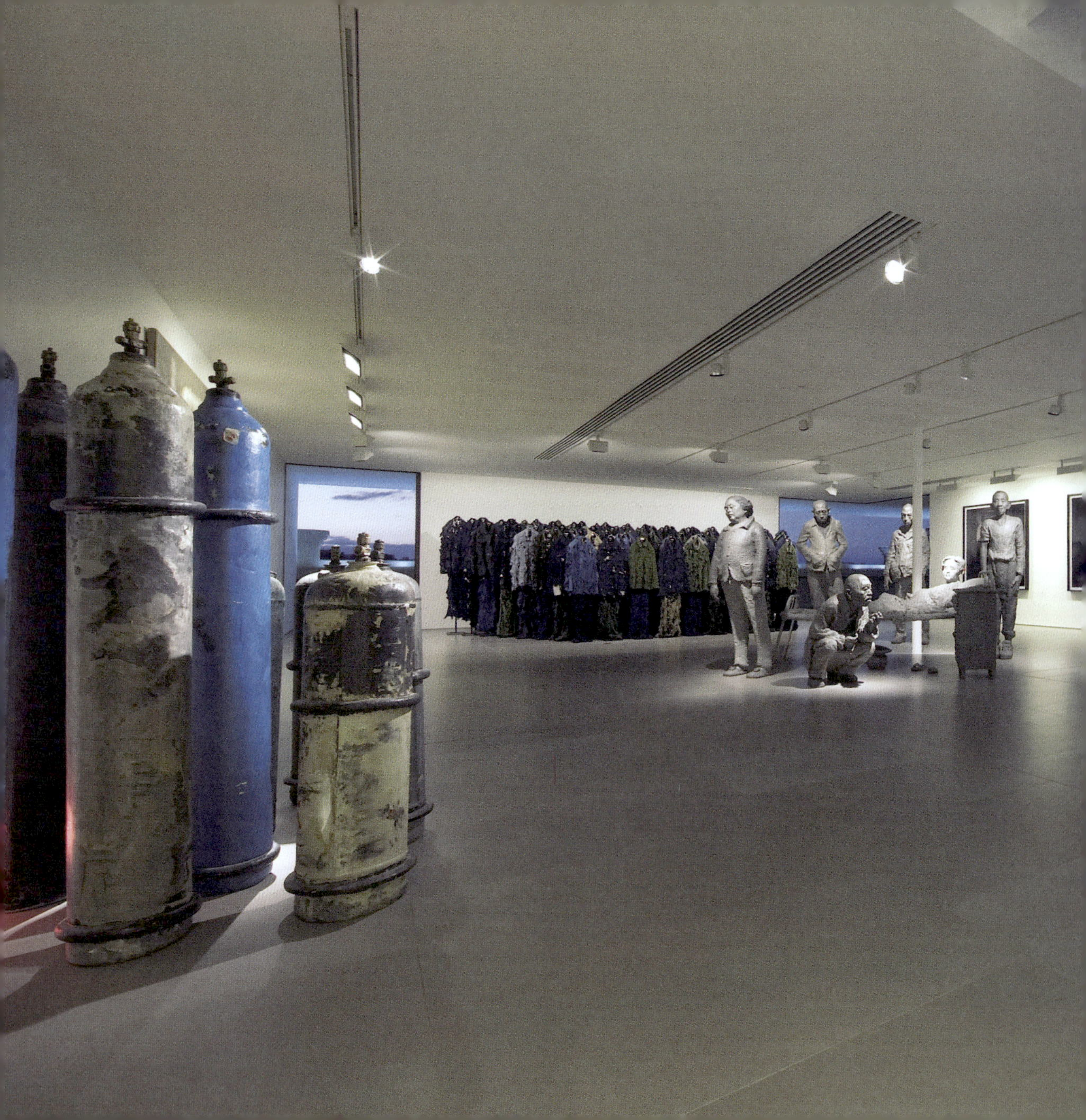

**Access by car:** Driving south on George Street, at Central Station continue onto Lee Street and Regent Street, turn right onto Queen Street and right again onto Balfour Street. The White Rabbit Gallery is located on the right.

**Access by public transport:** Arriving at Central Station, take the western exit (Ultimo, Chinatown, UTS), turn left into Lee Street/Regent Street and then right into Wellington Street, which leads to Balfour Street. There are also plenty of buses stopping on Broadway near Abercrombie Street. Heading west from the bus stop, walk straight from George Street across Central Park to Balfour Street.

**Extra Tips:** The Chippendale/Ultimo area is currently undergoing a huge transformation. The stimulating shopping and living quarter Central Park is the successful product of a global collaboration of architects and artists. Designed by Ateliers Jean Nouvel, One Central Park has been declared the 'Best Tall Building in the World' by the Council on Tall Buildings and Urban Habitat in 2014 (28 Broadway, Chippendale). Its smart food court terrace on Level 2 offers stunning views over the site and towards Sydney's most expensive public art installation. The attractive 13-metre high, wind-activated kinetic sculpture *Halo* was conceived by Jennifer Turpin and Michaelie Crawford, two of Australia's pre-eminent public artists. Architecture enthusiasts will equally enjoy visiting the recently completed Dr Chau Chak Wing building at the University of Technology Sydney, which was designed by Gehry Partners. The eastern facade of this amazing $180 million business-school building is made up of 320,000 custom-designed sandstone bricks, referencing Sydney's sandstone tradition (14–28 Ultimo Road, Ultimo).

A visit to White Rabbit can be easily combined with a trip to SCAF (refer to page 14) or an appointment at the Gordon Elliott Contemporary Art Collection (refer to page 28).

**Restaurant Tips:** White Rabbit serves exquisite Chinese teas and small snacks in a tranquil tea house on the ground floor. Sydney's foodies flock to the nearby upmarket yet casual-style Ester Restaurant and Bar (46–52 Meagher Street, Chippendale). Meat lovers will enjoy LP's Quality Meats (12–16 Chippen Street, Chippendale). Central Park's new $2 billion Kensington Street laneway precinct will accommodate three high-profile restaurants as part of the Unlisted Collection Sydney boutique hotel (Kensington Street, Chippendale).

Page 22
White Rabbit Gallery, exterior
Photograph Alex Craig

Page 24
Chen Wenling, *Red memory – asking God*, 2006
Bronze and vehicle duco, 77 x 33 x 27 cm

Chen Wenling, *Red memory – smile*, 2007
Bronze and vehicle duco, 290 x 120 x 200 cm

Chen Wenling, *Valiant struggle no.11*, 2006
Bronze, stainless steel, fibreglass, gold leaf, sound, vehicle duco, 363 x 355 x 70 cm

Page 25
Wang Lei, *Everything from nothing*, 2013
Newspaper, dimensions variable

Left
Qiu Xiaofei, *Cakravada Mountain no.2*, 2007
Fibreglass, acrylic, paint, sound, dimensions variable

Lu Zhengyuan, *Mental patients*, 2006
Fibreglass, dimensions variable

Sun Furong, *Nibbling up – tomb figures*, 2008
Cloth and mixed media, 180 x 800 x 500 cm

All images courtesy the artist and White Rabbit Gallery

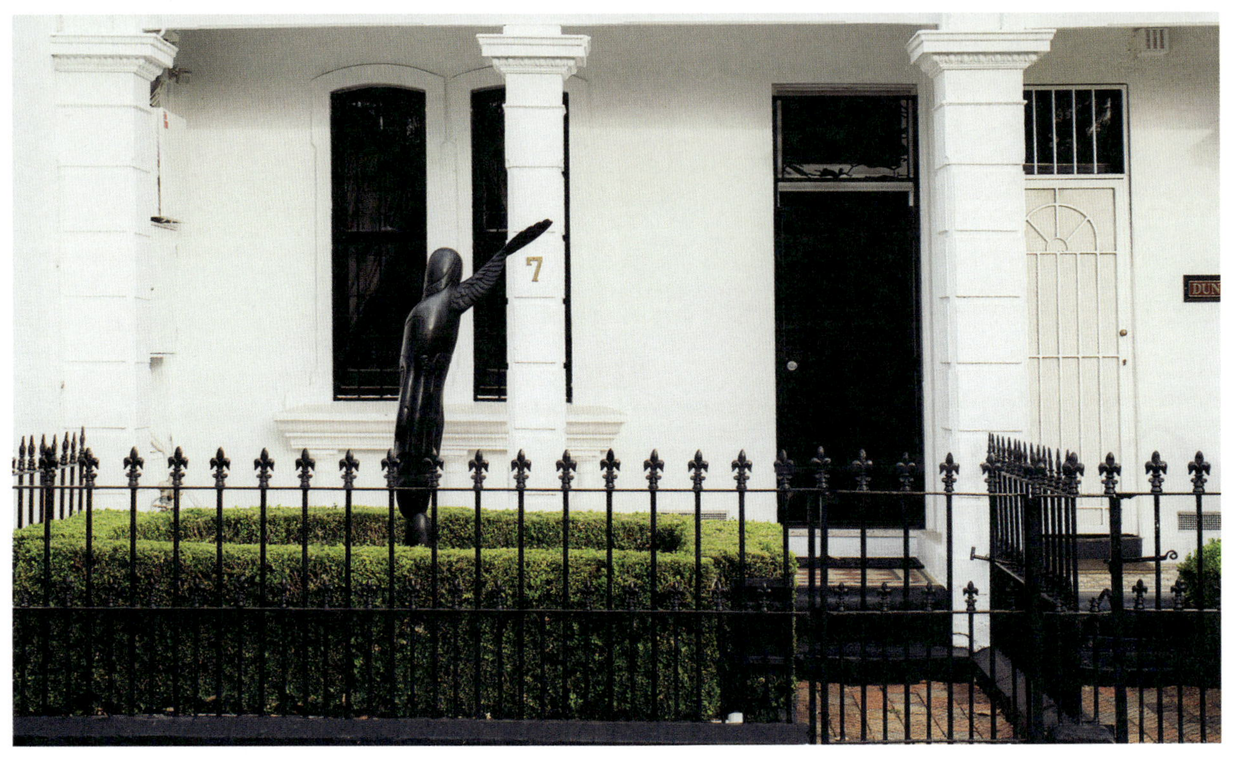


# GORDON ELLIOTT CONTEMPORARY ART COLLECTION

7 Bridge Street
Erskineville, NSW 2043

OPENING HOURS
By appointment only

Telephone: (+61) 0411 500 511
gordon@sydneyartwalks.com.au

Those who enjoy experiencing art in a domestic setting will enjoy visiting Gordon Elliott's classic Victorian terrace house in Sydney's inner-west suburb of Erskineville. Situated in a tiny forecourt you will find a large Terry Stringer sculpture together with a welded security door by Michael Snape – indicating that Elliott is a collector of humour as well as practicality.

When Gordon Elliott bought the house in 1997, he and his former partner decided to fill the walls with original artworks. Being a novice in the art market, Elliott's early acquisitions were 'pretty pictures that were pleasing to the eyes'. After the death of his partner, however, art became a welcome diversion and then an all-encompassing passion. He gained a Master of Art in Public Spaces in his spare time and now volunteers at art institutions. Elliott values the interaction and friendship with the artists he is following and always tries to buy several works from the same artist, preferably in different media. He has commissioned many works, either to fit into a particular spot in the house, or to celebrate a special occasion. To be able to afford major artworks by his favourite artists, Elliott often waits for a few years and puts the artworks on lay-by with his preferred galleries. This strategy, combined with the development of a good eye, has led to a very interesting collection of over 240 artworks by emerging and established artists. Well-known Australian painters Euan Macleod, Rick Amor, Michael Zavros, James Gleeson and John Coburn are represented in the collection with a wide spectrum of works. Many ceramic artworks, for instance by Australian artists Noel McKenna and Gwyn Hanssen Pigott, as well as by New Zealand and South African artists, are on display throughout the house. Former street artist 'Kill Pixie' is featured with ceramics and mixed media works on board. New Zealand art is well represented through Terry Stringer's clever bronze sculptures and Australian sculptor Clement Meadmore is equally admired and collected. Elliott has six works by renowned marble sculptor Alex Seton; *Courage*, displayed in the office, is particularly stunning. Emerging Sydney artist Todd Fuller's innovative hand-drawn animation is the only video work in the collection. Although he favours collecting works on canvas, Elliott made an exception by purchasing two small but very interesting works on paper by the renowned German artist Norbert Bisky, the preferred artist of former German foreign minister Guido Westerwelle.

The professional gallery hanging system upstairs enables a salon-style display of the vast majority of Elliott's collection. It will be interesting to observe where the new artworks, which have already been commissioned, will find a spot in this art-filled home.

VISITOR INFORMATION

**Admission Fees:** $15 (in cash)

**Tours and other Events:** Each visitor will be guided on a private tour throughout the house.

**Access by car:** Leave Sydney's CBD south on George Street, turn left onto Lee Street at Railway Square, continue onto Regent Street, continue onto Botany Road, turn right onto Henderson Road. Continue straight through three roundabouts to get to Railway Parade. Turn right onto Erskineville Road and take the first turn left onto George Street. Take the first left onto Victoria Street, which then becomes Bridge Street.

**Access by public transport:** Take the T3 Bankstown Train line (the all-stops service only) from Central Station or other CBD stations in the Liverpool or Lidcombe direction. Get off at Erskineville Station, turn right onto Erskineville Road/Swanson Street and immediately right again onto Bridge Street.

**Extra Tips:** Being extremely knowledgeable about public art, Gordon Elliott conducts very entertaining and informative sculpture walks throughout Sydney and beyond.

Visitors to Sydney might want to check out nearby Carriageworks, one of Australia's most exciting multi-arts centres. The stunning building, which is also open to the public during the day, frequently houses site-specific art commissions. Sydneysiders flock to Carriageworks to admire the international Sydney Festival/Carriageworks art project, which is usually on display annually from January to March.

A visit to Gordon Elliott Contemporary Art Collection can also be easily combined with a trip to the White Rabbit Gallery (refer to page 22) or a visit to SCAF (refer to page 14).

**Restaurant Tips:** Nearby Café Sofia serves excellent coffees and yummy café-style food (7 Swanson Street). The colourful Newtown district is full of funky cafés, ethnic restaurants and bookshops. The industrial areas of Alexandria and Roseberry form Sydney's latest café hub. The Grounds of Alexandria (Building 7A/2 Huntley Street, Alexandria), Bread & Circus Wholefoods Canteen (21 Fountain Street, Alexandria) and Kitchen by Mike (1/85 Dunning Avenue, Roseberry) all serve fantastic food in quirky environments.

Page 28
Gordon Elliott Contemporary Art Collection, exterior
Photograph Christopher Pearce

Right
Gordon Elliott Contemporary Art Collection, installation view

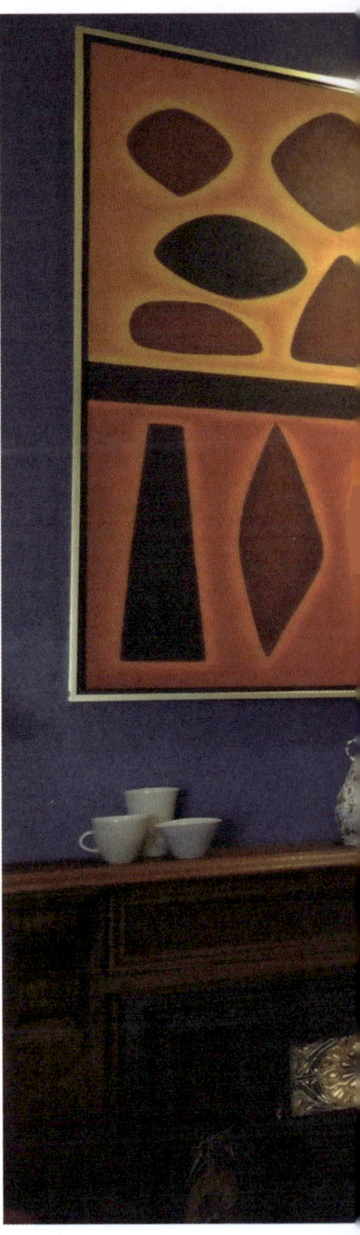

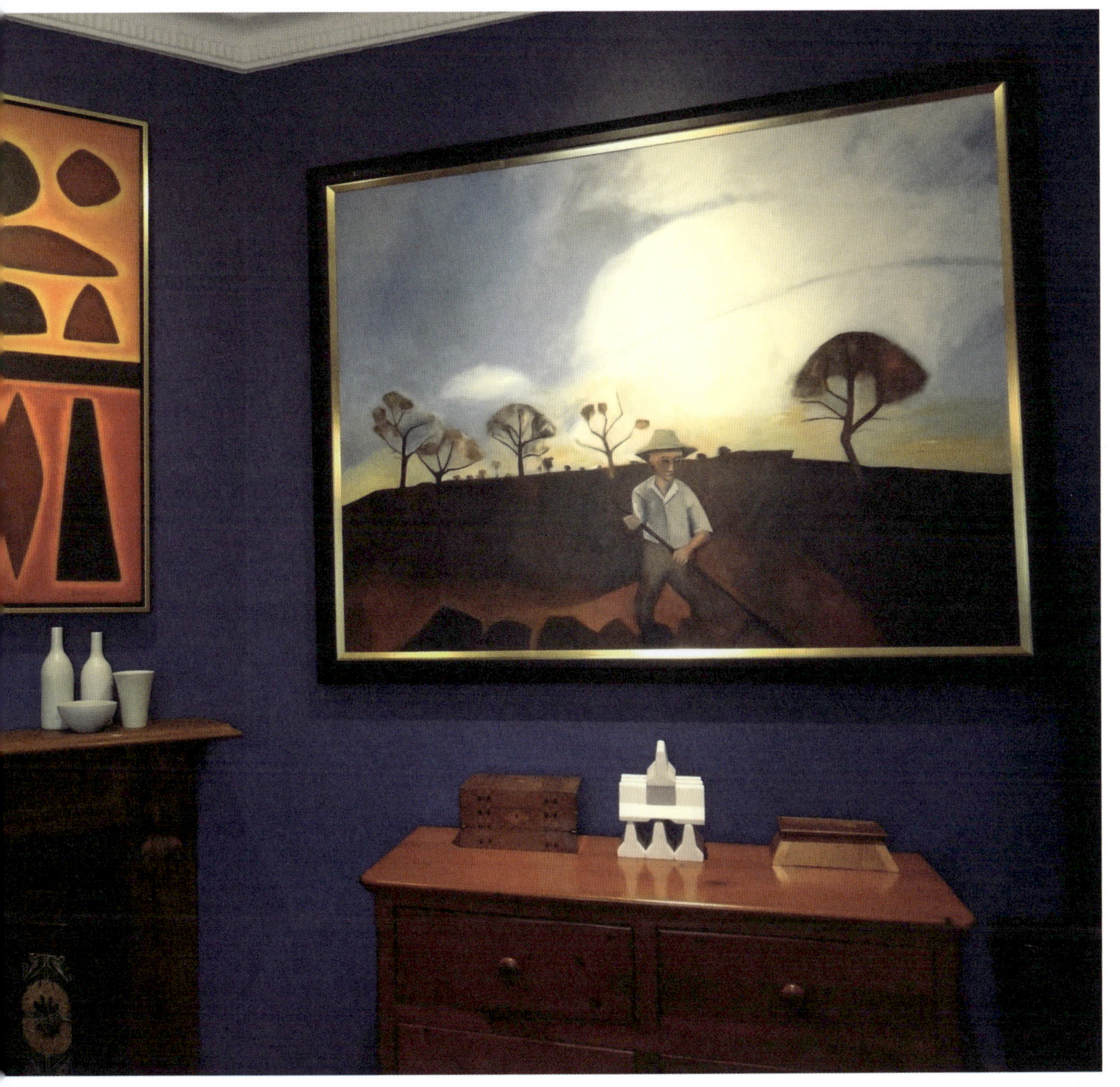

# RURAL

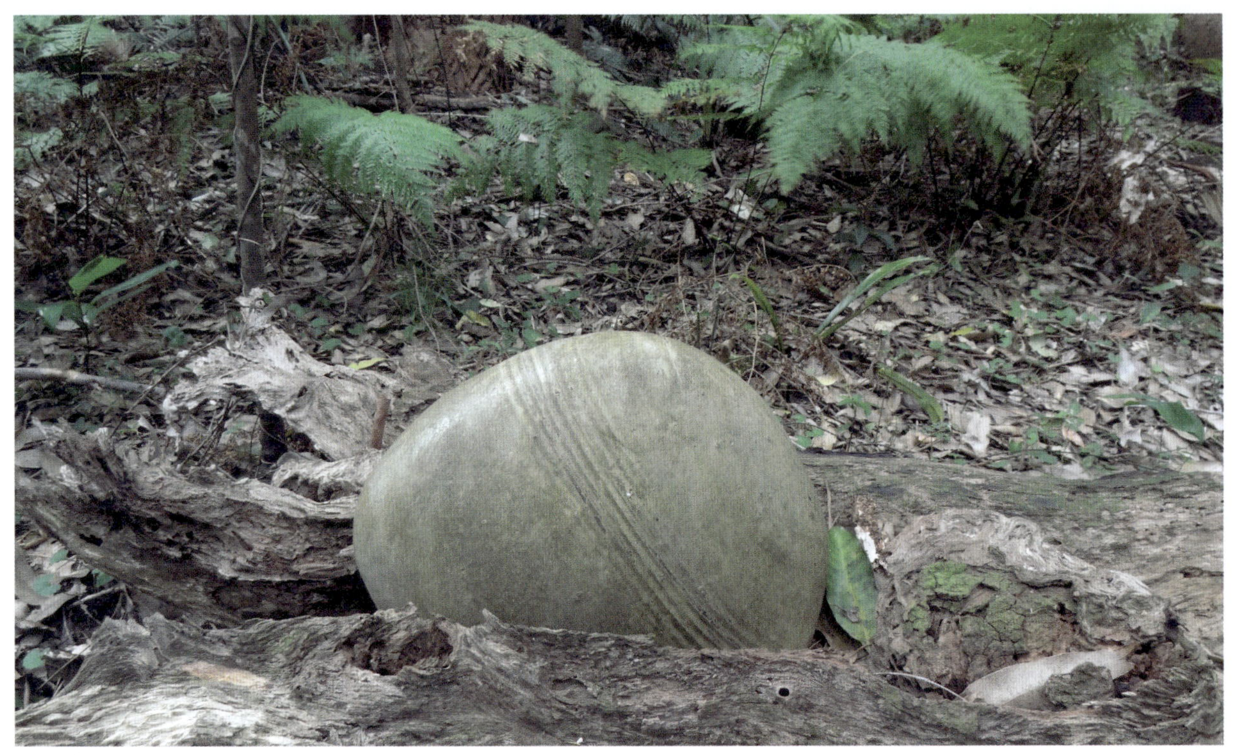

# WOMBARRA SCULPTURE GARDEN

57 Morrison Avenue
Wombarra, NSW 2515

OPENING HOURS
The first full weekend of each month 10am–4pm, and by appointment (please ring)

Telephone: +61 (02) 4268 2695
gaby@wombarra.com
wombarra.com

Hidden high in the lush Illawarra rainforest, the Wombarra Sculpture Garden is a fusion of art and nature. Well-known sculptor Gaby Porter OAM purchased this 4-hectare property with her engineer husband John Haymes from crime writer Peter Corris in 1997. Considerable work was needed to remove exotic plants and return the site to its original condition. When Porter and Haymes sold their warehouse in Surry Hills in 2009 what was first used as a holiday home and studio became their permanent residence. Having worked as a sculptor for over thirty years and held shows in the warehouse, Porter started organising outdoor exhibitions of her sculptures and those by other local artists. Slowly the idea grew that the sculpture collection could be a permanent fixture. Nowadays, the garden's giant trees provide a fitting canopy for over sixty sculptures that nestle amid the native vegetation. The works vary from large installations to small and whimsical sculptures, planned for different parts of the property. Styles range from abstract to figurative. A large variety of materials, including stone, bronze, ceramic mosaics, steel, local timber and concrete have been used to create the artworks. Several sculptures are made from leaves and twigs woven together with mesh and rope.

The majority of the artworks are by Gaby Porter herself, although sculptures by the late Anders Ousback (1951–2004), Anthony Buselli, Jozsef Paulini, Walter Auer, Roger Apte and Alex Forbes can also be found throughout the garden. Porter's latest installation is a 13-metre python, inspired by a dead snake found on her land. Being set on a fairly steep slope on the Illawarra escarpment, Porter began to use the logs and branches of dead trees to build the landscape and refers to herself as a 'bush-keeper' rather than a gardener. Several paths meander around the property, with steps, bridges and seating for moments of reflection. The Sculpture Garden is constantly evolving as trees and vegetation grow, the forest changes, and new sculptures are added, improved on or moved around. Being mindful that the disused Bulli Colliery runs beneath the property, this tribute to Porter's childhood adoration of nature showcases the planet's glorious abundance and ability to rejuvenate. Like good music, this garden is crafted to enrich the spirit. Gaby Porter was awarded the Medal of the Order of Australia (OAM) as a testament to the importance of her work.

VISITOR INFORMATION

**Admission Fees:** Adult/Child: $10/free

**Access by car:** Leave Sydney in south-easterly direction on the A36. Continue onto the Princes Highway, continue onto the M1 (signs for Helensburgh/Stanwell Park/ Metroad 1/Wollongong). Take the Route 10 exit towards Lawrence Hargrave Drive/Helensburgh/Stanwell Park. At the roundabout, take the 2nd exit onto Lawrence Hargrave Drive, turn right to stay on Lawrence Hargrave Drive and turn right onto Morrison Avenue (at the red brick church). The Wombarra Sculpture Garden is located on the left-hand side. Please park along the street.

**Access by public transport:** Take a South Coast Line 'Bondi Junction and Central to Bomaderry or Port Kembla' train to Wombarra Station. Turn left onto Morrison Avenue towards the hill. The Wombarra Sculpture Garden is located on the left-hand side (total travel time is about 1 hour 40 minutes).

**Extra Tips:** Those who are driving from Sydney can easily stop at the very interesting Hazelhurst Regional Gallery & Arts Centre (782 Kingsway, Gymea).

Drivers will also be able to visit Sydney's heritage-listed Royal National Park. The world's second-oldest national park is perfect for bushwalking, cycling, surfing, or

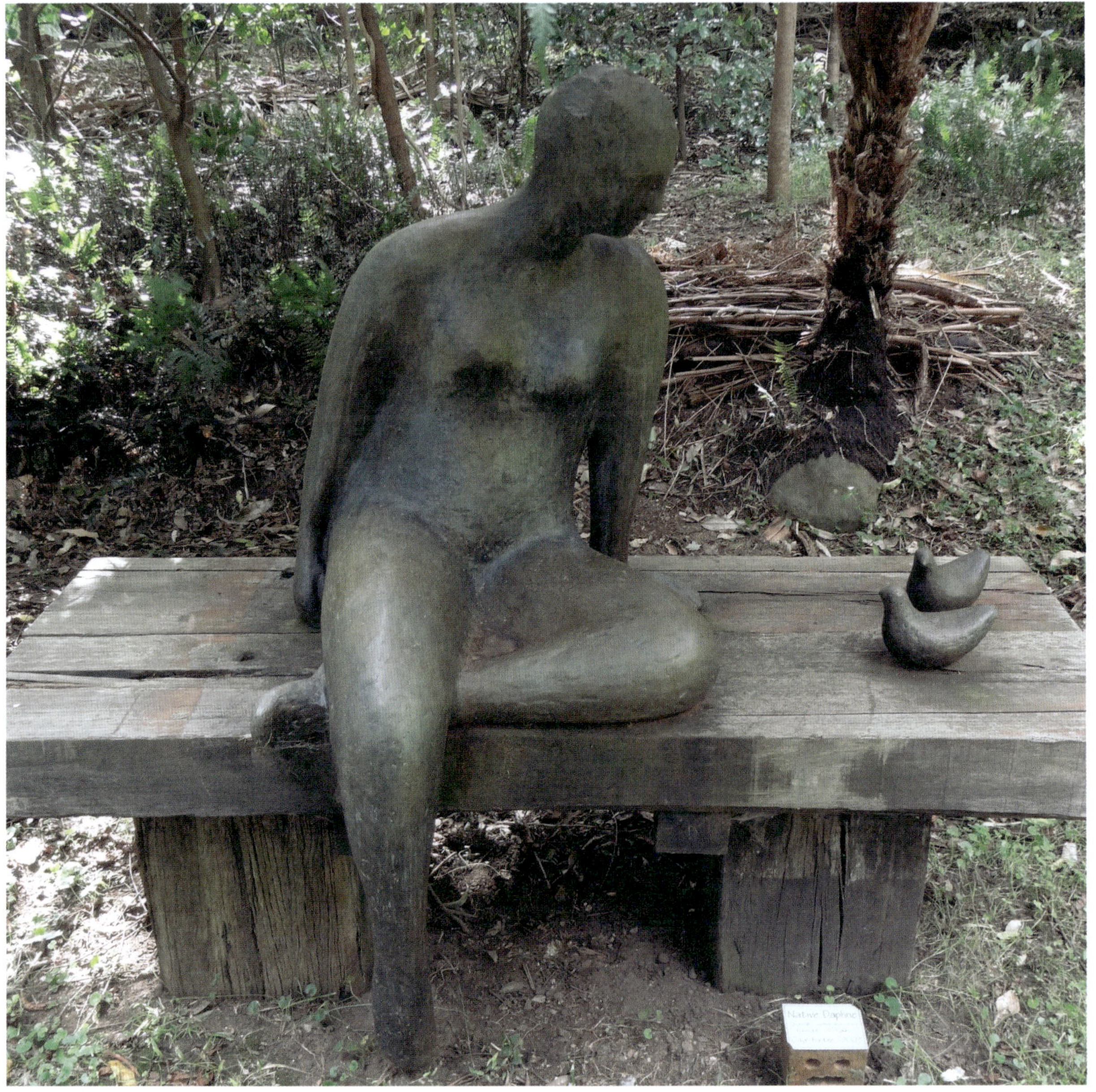
Native Daphne

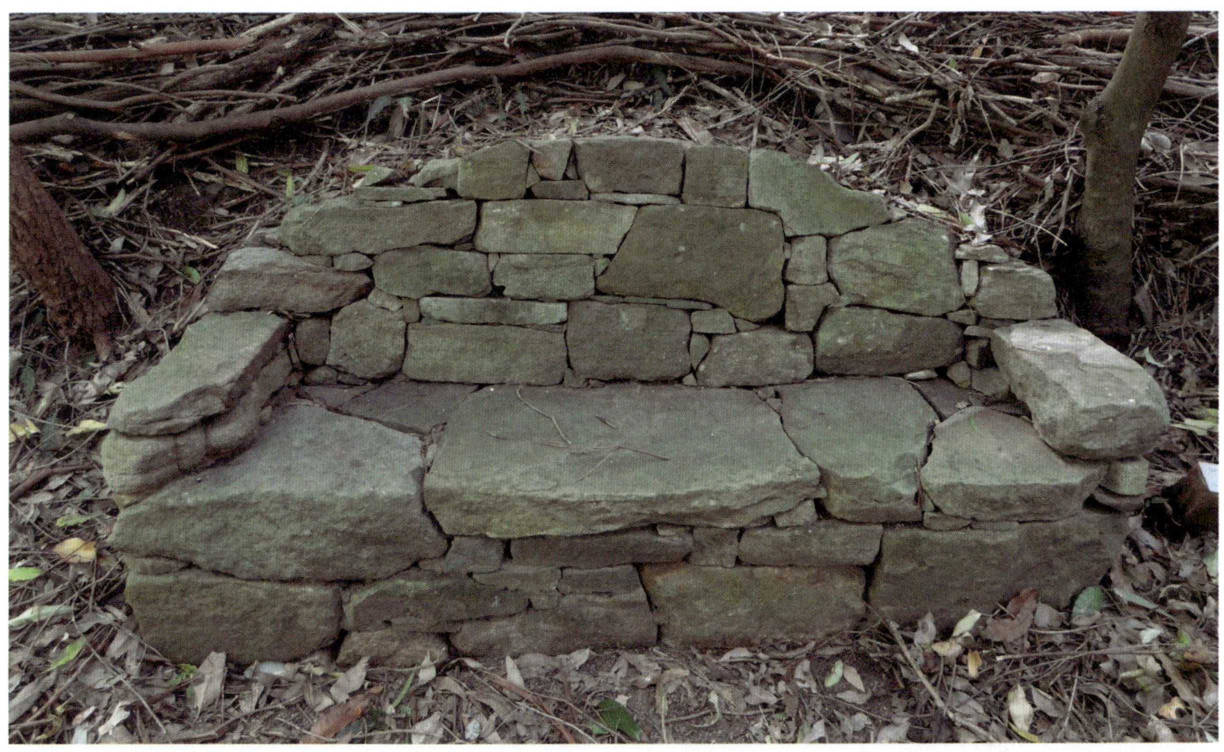

picnicking. There are several interesting bushwalks available in the Wombarra area. Located south of Wombarra, Tourism Wollongong offers maps and great tips for the entire region (Southern Gateway Centre, Princes Highway, Bulli Tops).

The commercial Defiance Sculpture Park will exhibit a large number of outdoor sculptures by prominent and emerging artists at their new location in the Southern Highlands.

**Restaurant Tips:** Fine dining can be enjoyed at Samuels Restaurant (382 Lawrence Hargrave Drive, Thirroul; (02) 4268 2244). Located in a former butcher's shop, the whimsical Fireworks Café offers creative food for breakfast, lunch and dinner (40 Moore Street, Austinmer). City West Café Restaurant serves a fantastic homemade breakfast (76–78 Market Street, Wollongong; open on Saturdays until 1pm but closed on Sundays). Being part of the coffee-roasting company Delano, Kafe Restaurant has the best coffee in Wollongong (85 Montague Street, Wollongong).

Pages 34 and 36-7
All images courtesy Wombarra Sculpture Garden

# VICTORIA

# MELBOURNE

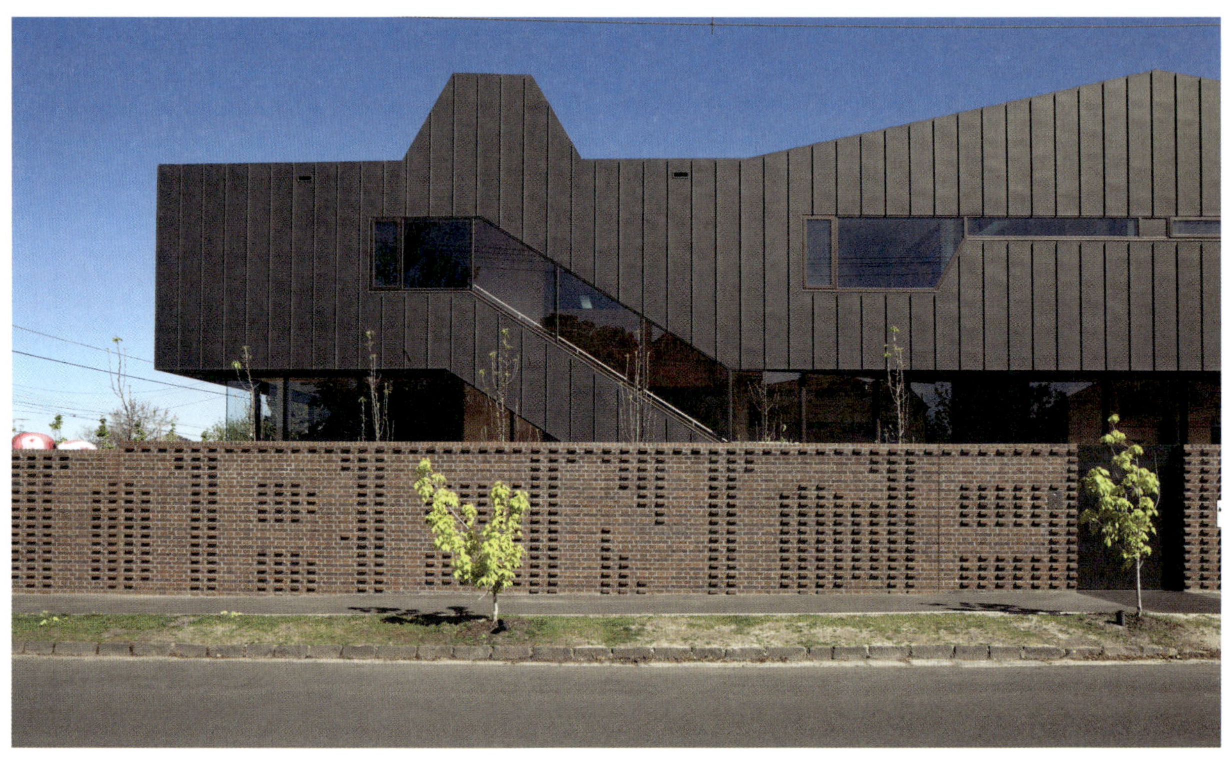

# LYON HOUSEMUSEUM

219 Cotham Road
Kew, VIC 3101

OPENING HOURS
Designated Mondays, Tuesdays and Sundays each year

Telephone: +61 (03) 9817 2300
museum@lyonhousemuseum.com.au
lyonhousemuseum.com.au

Aficionados of contemporary Australian art and architecture will delight in this hybridised gem, which brings together art and living while combining the concept of public and private in a unique setting.

The Lyon Housemuseum and its collection were inspired by a long history of private art collections displayed in residential settings and made available for public viewing. These include Sir John Soane's Museum in London, New York's Frick Collection, the Peggy Guggenheim Collection in Venice and the Reed Collection at Melbourne's Heide Museum of Modern Art (refer to page 66). Originally conceived in 2000, after five years of planning and two years of construction, Corbett Lyon and his wife and co-collector Yueji finally moved into their dream home with their young family in 2008. Corbett, an admirer of the Italian Renaissance architect Andrea Palladio, is the co-founder of award-winning Melbourne architectural firm Lyons.

The Housemuseum is designed around a two-storey 'white cube' at the front of the building and a two-storey 'black box' at the rear. The 'white cube' is the most gallery-like space of the house. It is used for exhibiting paintings, sculpture, large-scale installations and for family living. The entire building is anchored by a stunning artwork. Howard Arkley's massive 17-panel work *Fabricated rooms* is on permanent display in the formal dining room above the 'white cube' on the second floor. At the Venice Biennale in 1999, where the work was exhibited after Corbett and Yueji Lyon purchased it, Arkley spoke with Corbett about expanding the installation to become an in-the-round experience. The artist's early death a few months later put paid to these plans. The 'black box' houses video works and doubles as the home cinema room for Corbett and Yueji's teenage daughters. Other family living areas flow around these spaces and accommodate further artworks, architectural drawings and artefacts intermixed with the domestic settings of the house. The ground floor spaces open out onto a series of landscaped private courtyards and sculpture gardens. Between the kitchen and the 'black box', a small music room auditorium featuring a built-in digital and hybrid organ features a permanent installation by Indigenous artist Brook Andrew.

The living room is the home of a 'cabinet-of-curiosities' that the Lyons' daughters 'curate' from a collection of their travelling souvenirs inside an opened cupboard. The Victorian ash timber ceiling and wall panels of the room itself are digitally printed with thousands of words from the four family members and the textured wallpapers and decorative surfaces of earlier private museums. A bird's-eye (or Google Earth) view of the building reveals the project initials 'LHM' written onto the garden's landscape design, and the names of Cotham and Florence streets on which the corner plot sits are emblazoned in 2-metre-high letters in brickwork on the boundary wall. The attention to detail and the craftsmanship throughout is most impressive and, in 2010, the building won the Australian Institute of Architects' highest award for residential architecture, the Harold Desbrowe-Annear Award.

The Lyon Collection was established in 1990 following Corbett's visit to the art dealer Georges Mora at Tolarno Galleries, who advised him to invest in contemporary Australian art. The first works in the collection were *Nude in a landscape* by Linda Marrinon and *Orange building site* by Louise Forthun. Now in its twenty-fifth year, in addition to many works by Howard Arkley, the Lyon Collection includes large bodies of works by many of Australia's internationally recognised contemporary artists, including Patricia Piccinini, Callum Morton, Daniel von Sturmer, and Shaun Gladwell, who coincidentally have all represented Australia at the Venice Biennale. Today, the collection comprises over 300 paintings, sculptures, large-scale installations and video artworks by over

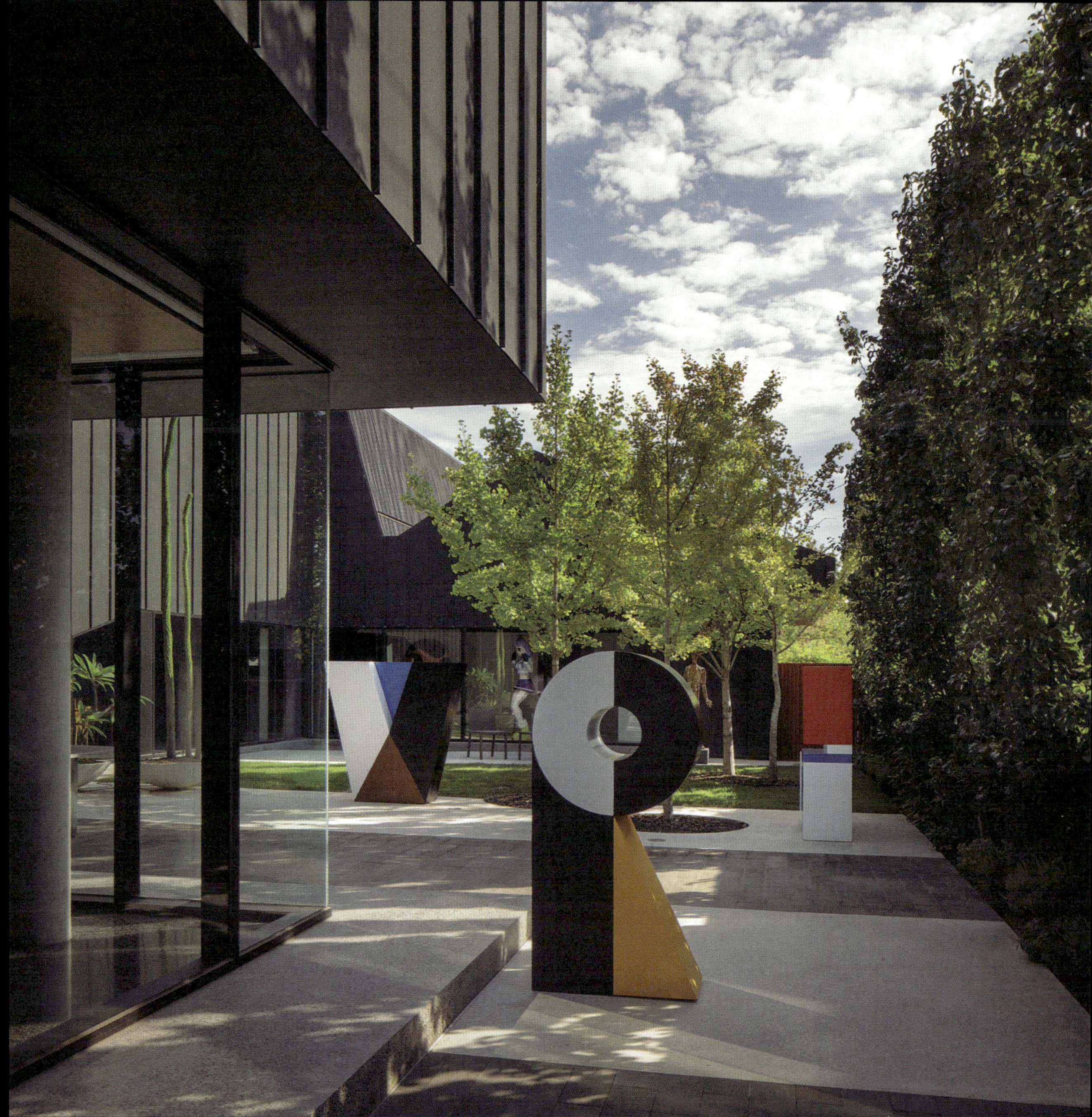

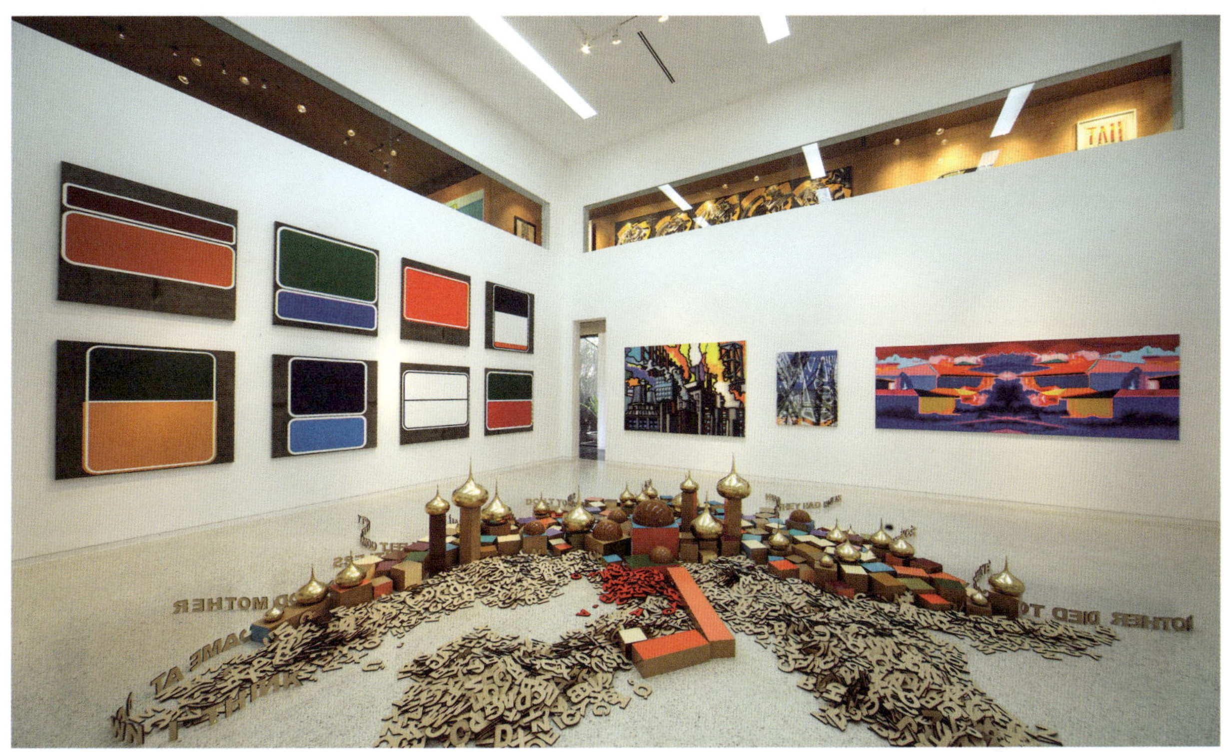

forty artists, all sourced exclusively on the primary market. Selected works from the collection are displayed within the Housemuseum, which extends over a floor space of 1,350 square metres, for two years. The entire family takes part in the buying process and curates the new hanging during the Christmas holidays each alternate year.

The future holds an interesting prospect for the Lyon Collection and its admirers. Phase two of the Lyon project foresees a small publicly endowed museum on the adjacent property to be operated in parallel to the Housemuseum, but with regular visiting hours. The family envisions donating the Lyon Collection, the neighbouring parcel of land and the funds for a new building to ensure that the public is able to enjoy the collection into the future. The last phase would be the merger of the public and the private museum into a single museum entity.

VISITOR INFORMATION

All visits to the Housemuseum must be pre-booked.
Please refer to the website for details of visiting dates/times.

Visitors are guided in a group by a member of the Lyon family. The tour lasts 1 hour and 15 minutes.

**Admission Fees:** The family requests a donation of $22 for guided tours and $40 for talks and events

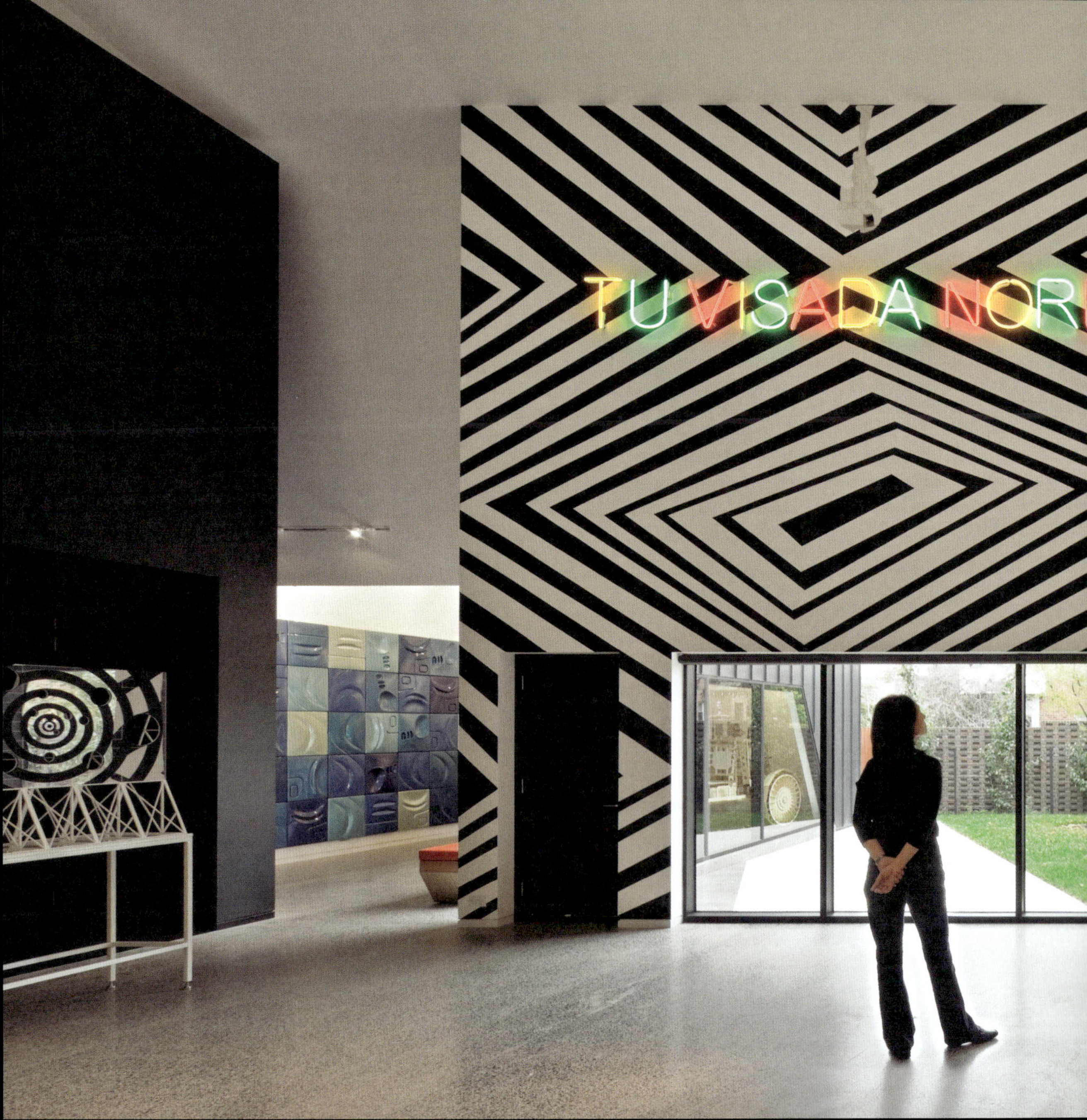
TU VISADA NOR

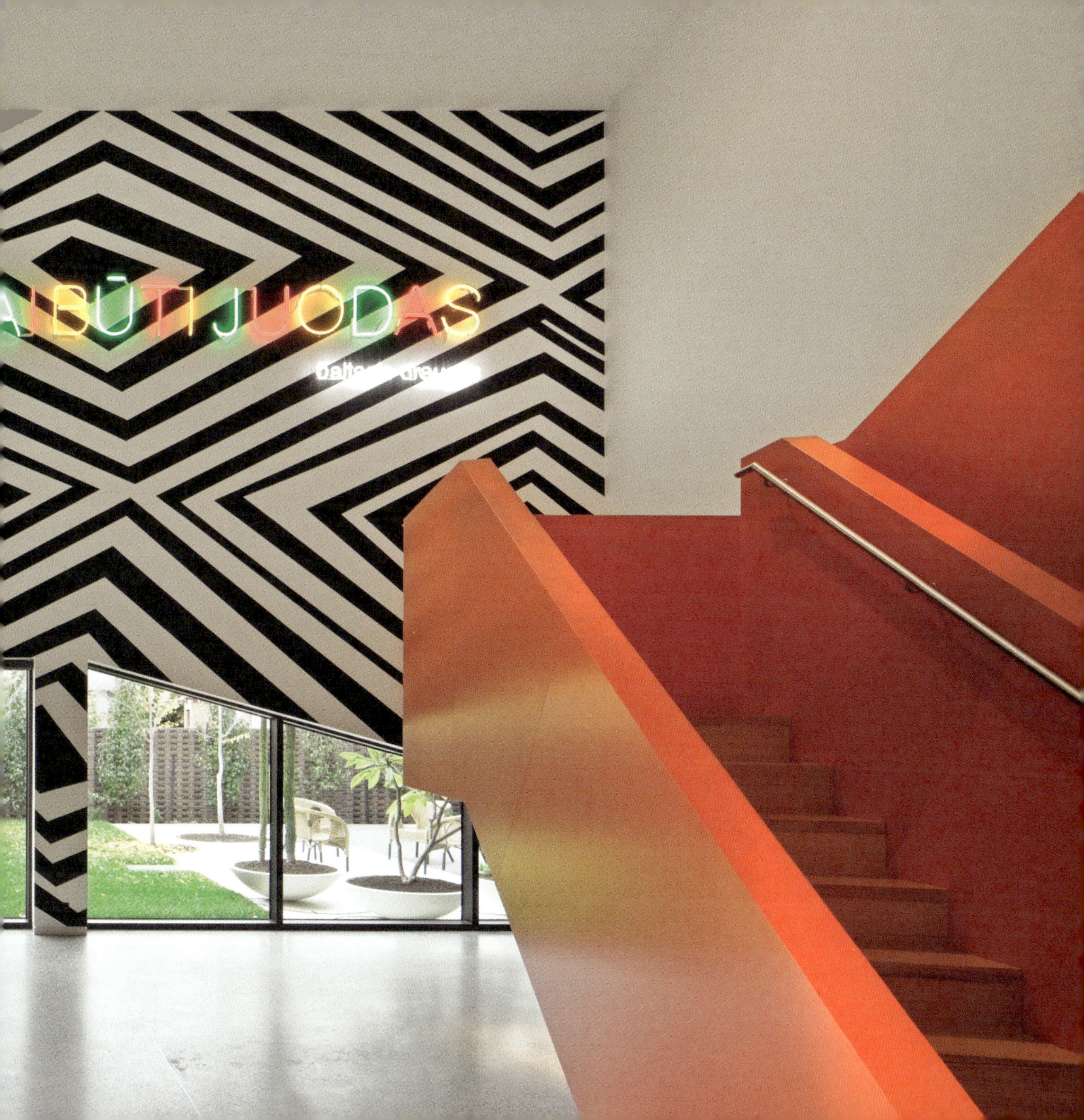
BŪTI JUODAS

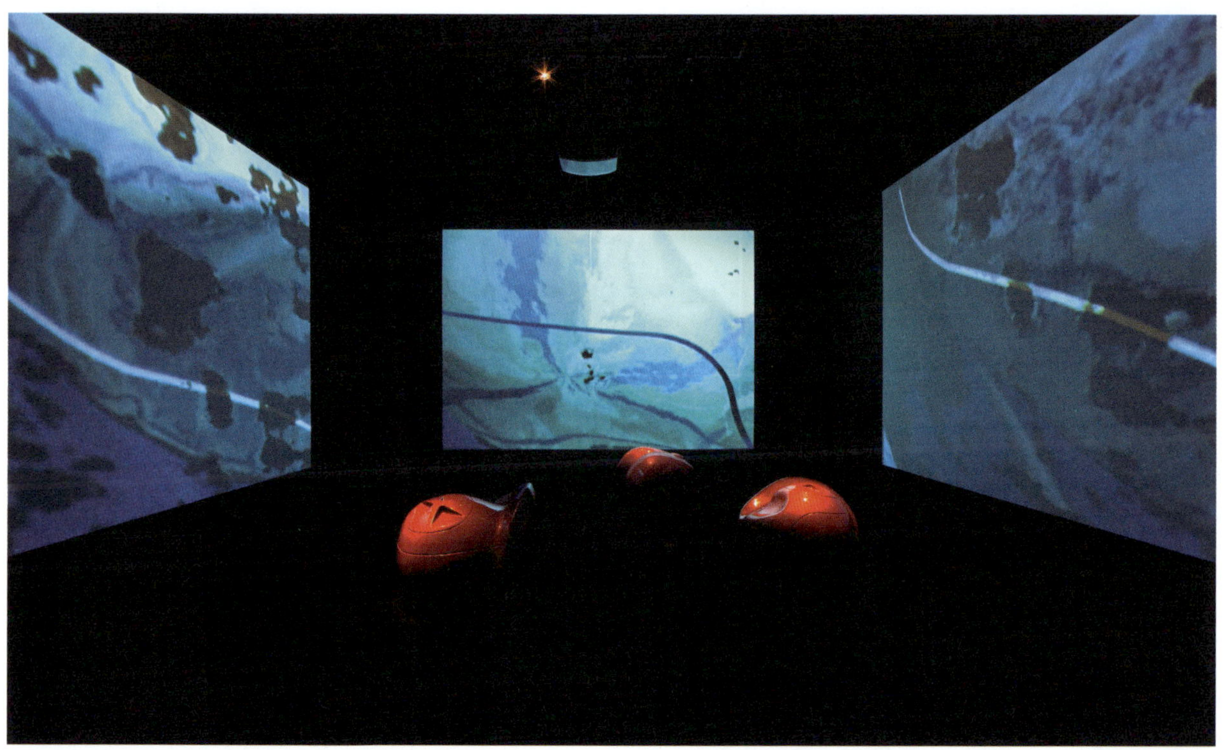

**Tours and other Events:** The Lyon family sponsors an annual series of art and architecture talks and music events, which are held in the music room of the house. Early bookings are essential due to the high demand (refer to website).

**Access by car:** The house is located 8 km east of Melbourne in the residential suburb of Kew.

**Access by public transport:** Take Tram 109 from Collins Street in the CBD (or from Docklands) in an easterly (Box Hill) direction to Stop 39 (Thomas Street/Cotham Road).

**Extra Tips:** If the visit to the Housemuseum is scheduled for a Tuesday or a Sunday, visitors with private transport could easily extend their journey to the Heide Museum of Modern Art (refer to page 66).

While in the Melbourne CBD, art gallery-goers might want to check out the National Gallery of Victoria (180 St Kilda Road; Tuesdays closed, aside from special exhibitions), the Australian Centre for Contemporary Art (111 Sturt Street; refer to website for opening days), The Ian Potter Centre: NGV Australia (corner Russell and Flinders streets; Mondays closed), The Ian Potter Museum of Art, the University of Melbourne's highly commended art museum (on Swanston

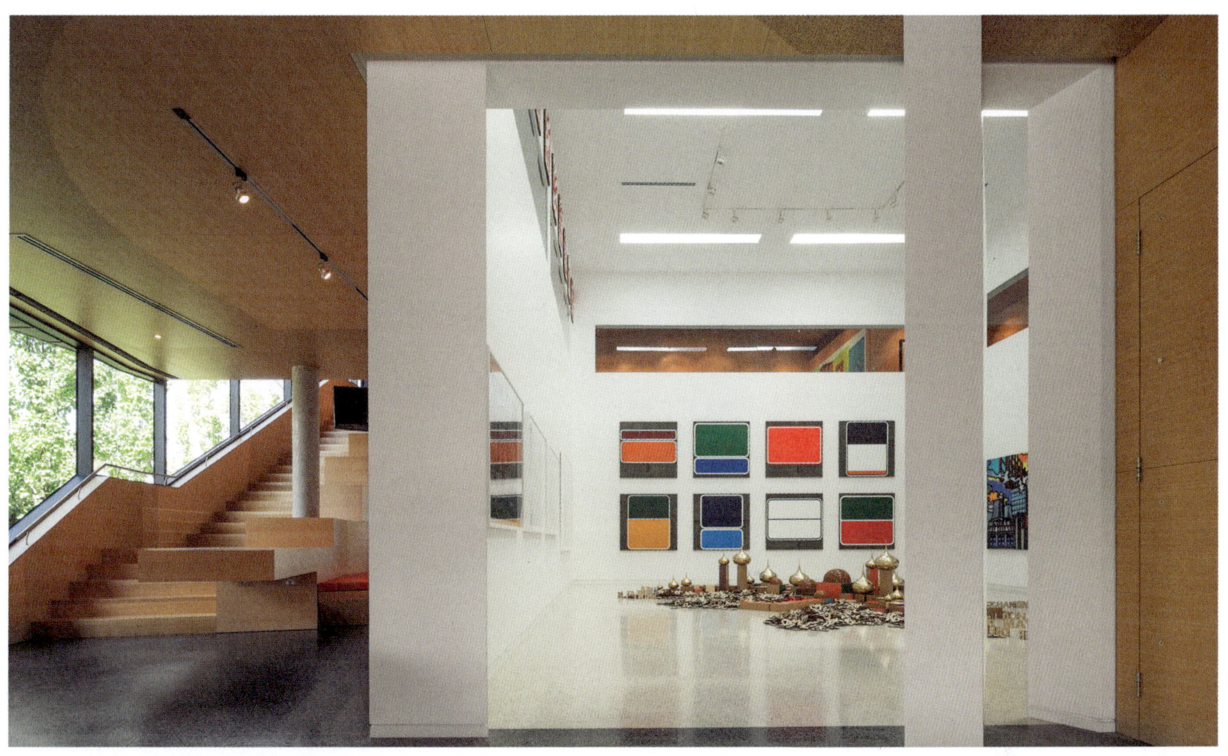

Street between Faraday and Elgin streets; Mondays closed) as well as Gertrude Contemporary, one of the city's leading hubs for presentation and production of contemporary art (200 Gertrude Street, Fitzroy; Sundays and Mondays closed).

Melbourne is known as one of the world's great street art capitals. To see some of the city's best street art locations, either wander through the small laneways between Collins Street and Flinders Lane opposite Federation Square or join the expensive but inspiring Melbourne Street Art Tour, which is run by street artists.

**Restaurant Tips:** Located near the Lyon Housemuseum, the Snow Pony serves hearty lunches and great coffees (95 Whitehorse Road, Deepdene; Stop 43 on Tram 109).

Pages 42 and 46-8
Lyon Housemuseum
Photograph Dianna Snape

Pages 44-5 and 49
Lyon Housemuseum
Photograph John Gollings

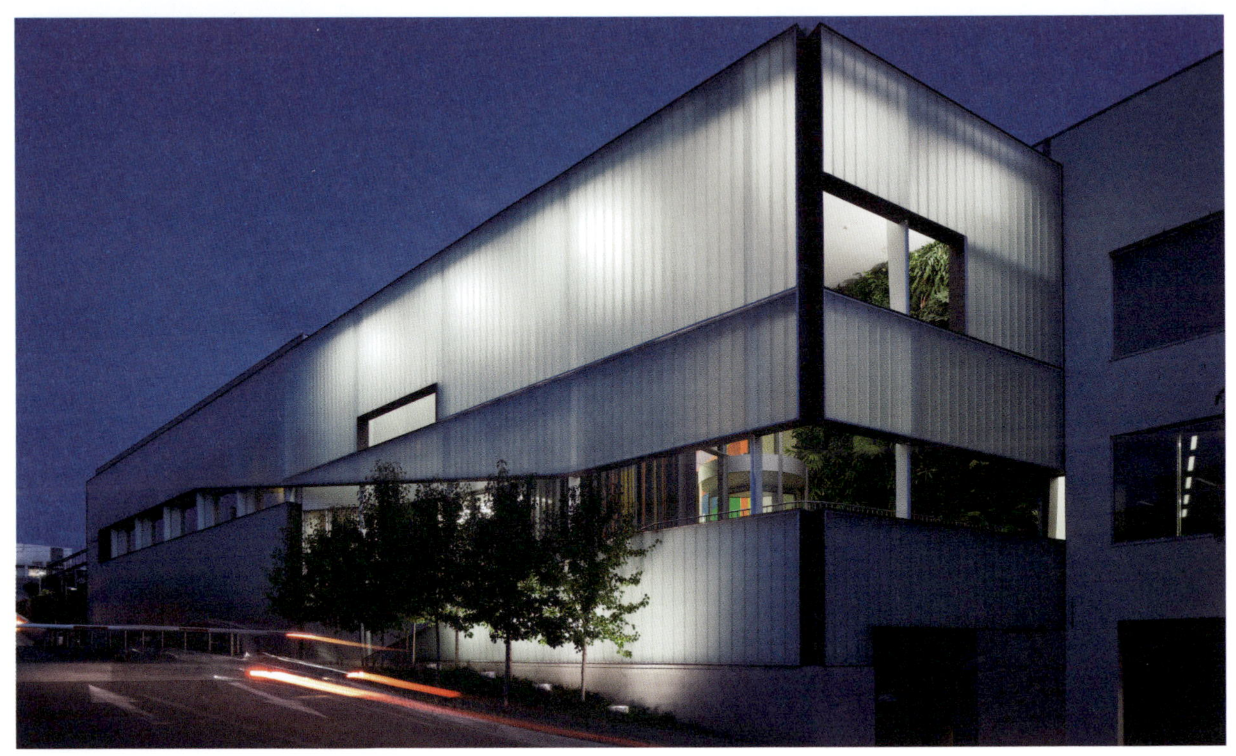

# COLLECTION OF NAOMI MILGROM AO

Sussan Headquarters
11 Palmer Parade
Cremorne, VIC 3121

OPENING HOURS
By appointment only

Telephone: +61 (03) 9413 2184

An exciting private collection of international contemporary art is found at the Sportsgirl/Sussan Headquarters in the Melbourne industrial suburb of Cremorne. Sussan Group owner and Executive Chair, Naomi Milgrom AO, commissioned Durbach Block Jaggers Architects to transform three existing buildings into a corporate office that is also an art gallery. The refurbishment won the Australian Institute of Architects' prestigious National Award for Commercial Architecture in 2009.

The calibre of this extraordinary art collection is signalled by the rainbow installation *Our magic hour* by Swiss artist Ugo Rondinone on the roof of the building. At ground level, a living garden sculpture by horticulturalist and marine biologist Mark Paul greets visitors entering the building. The light-filled reception area features a carved wooden bench designed by the architects and Sol LeWitt's large colourful wall-drawing *Bar of color within a square*, which was commissioned in 2008 and installed over four weeks. A site-specific ceiling light-work by Sydney artist Jonathan Jones guides visitors down a few steps into the main exhibition space. Accessed through an enormous sliding door, the 10-metre-high art space is dominated by Richard Long's powerful terracotta mud wall-painting *One circle leads to another*. This beautiful space is also visible from the first floor executive area. Apart from the site-specific installations, the artworks are moved regularly throughout the building. Milgrom and her team try to facilitate at least two exhibitions a year and there is also provision for showing video works in a media room. Visiting curators are sometimes invited to create exhibitions in this space.

Venturing through the different office and communal spaces, it becomes clear that the display of contemporary artworks and the connection with nature played an important role in the design. The offices are built around a linear central courtyard, conceived as a 'forest' and planted with an informal arrangement of sixty, mature silver-birch trees. The colourful boardroom features a commissioned artwork by the German artist Thomas Demand, whose wallpaper curtains cascading from ceiling to floor creates a theatrical surround for his photograph and for the viewer.

A Rosalie Gascoigne assemblage was one of the first artworks that Milgrom acquired while working at Joseph Brown Gallery in Collins Street during a university semester break. Nowadays, there are over 300 artworks in the collection spanning: photography, paintings, works on paper, sculpture, video art and tapestry. Milgrom collects predominantly contemporary art by international artists, among them Adrián Villar Rojas, Tatiana Trouvé, Tacita Dean, Bernd and Hilla Becher, Gillian Wearing, Monika Sosnowski, Danh Vo, Miwa Yanagi, Kara Walker, Richard Prince, Wolfgang Tillmans, Andreas Gursky and William Kentridge. When Milgrom forms an affinity with an artist, she often collects them in depth and follows their career closely.

The Naomi Milgrom Foundation (NMF) was established in 2014 to initiate and support public art, design and architecture projects. One such project is the curated MPavilion, a temporary architectural commission inspired by the temporary pavilions erected each summer next to London's Serpentine Galleries. Internationally renowned Australian architect Sean Godsell was commissioned to design the inaugural MPavilion. The site-specific structure is the first of a series of four to be installed in the Queen Victoria Memorial Gardens in Melbourne.

Naomi Milgrom is a pivotal figure in the Australian retail and fashion industries, a distinguished philanthropist, and leader and mentor to a wide range of arts, education and scientific organisations. She was awarded an AO (Officer of the Order of Australia) in 2010 and an Honorary Doctorate of Business from RMIT University in 2011.

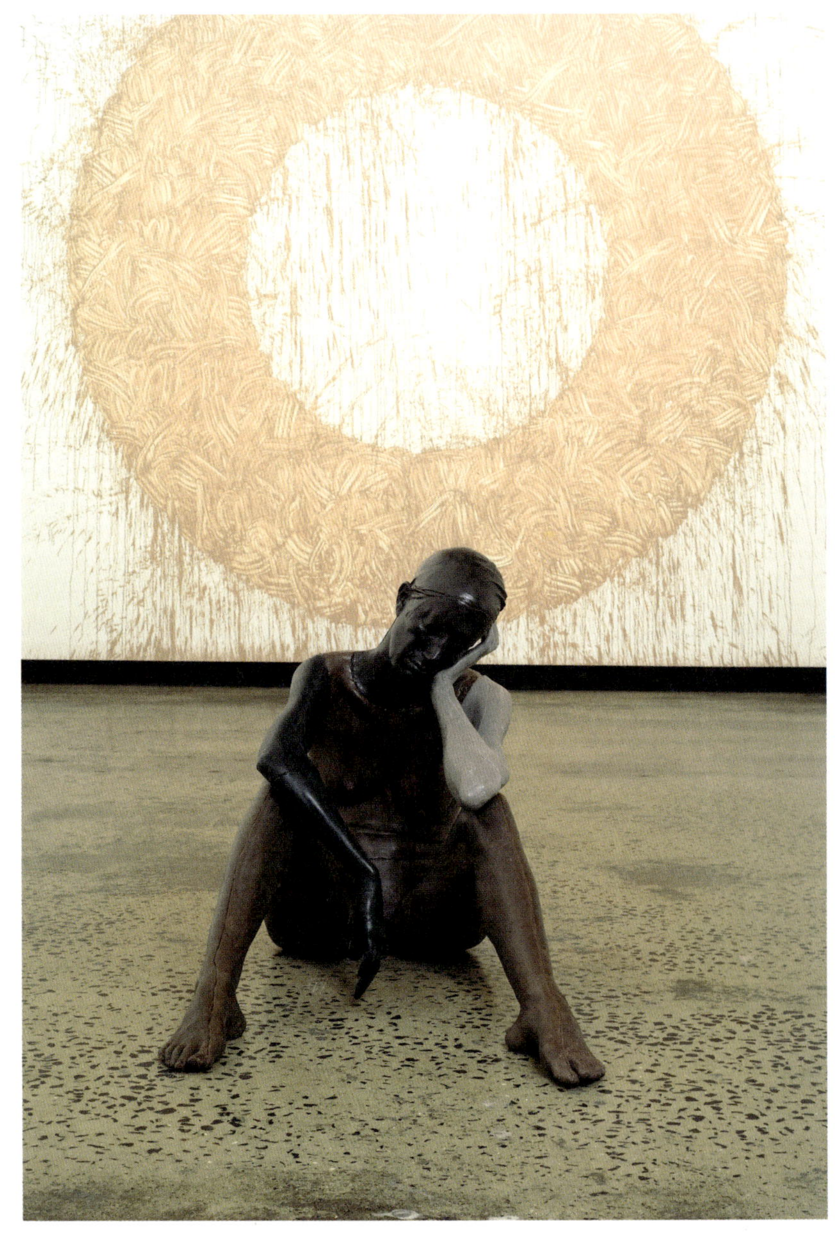

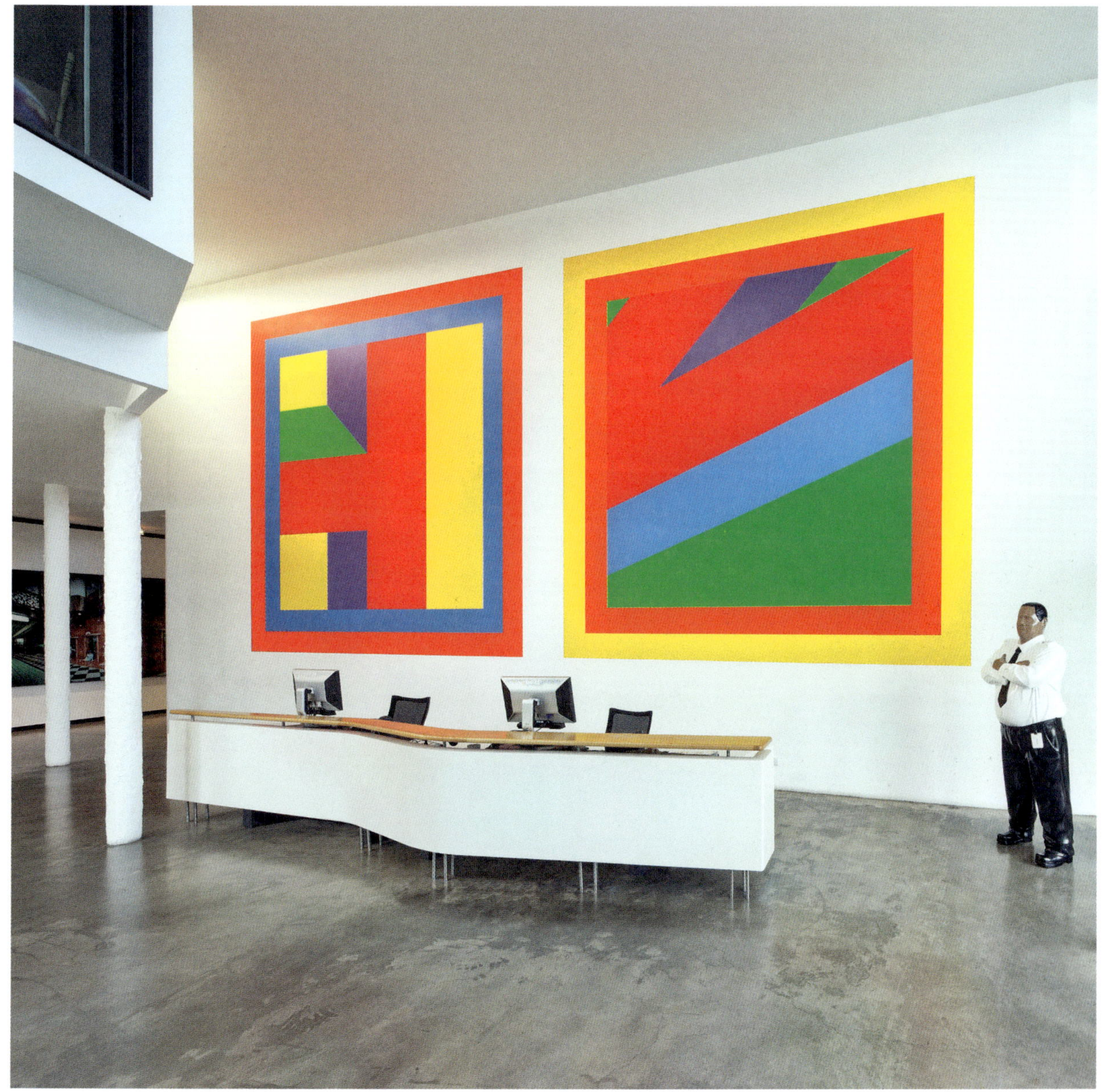

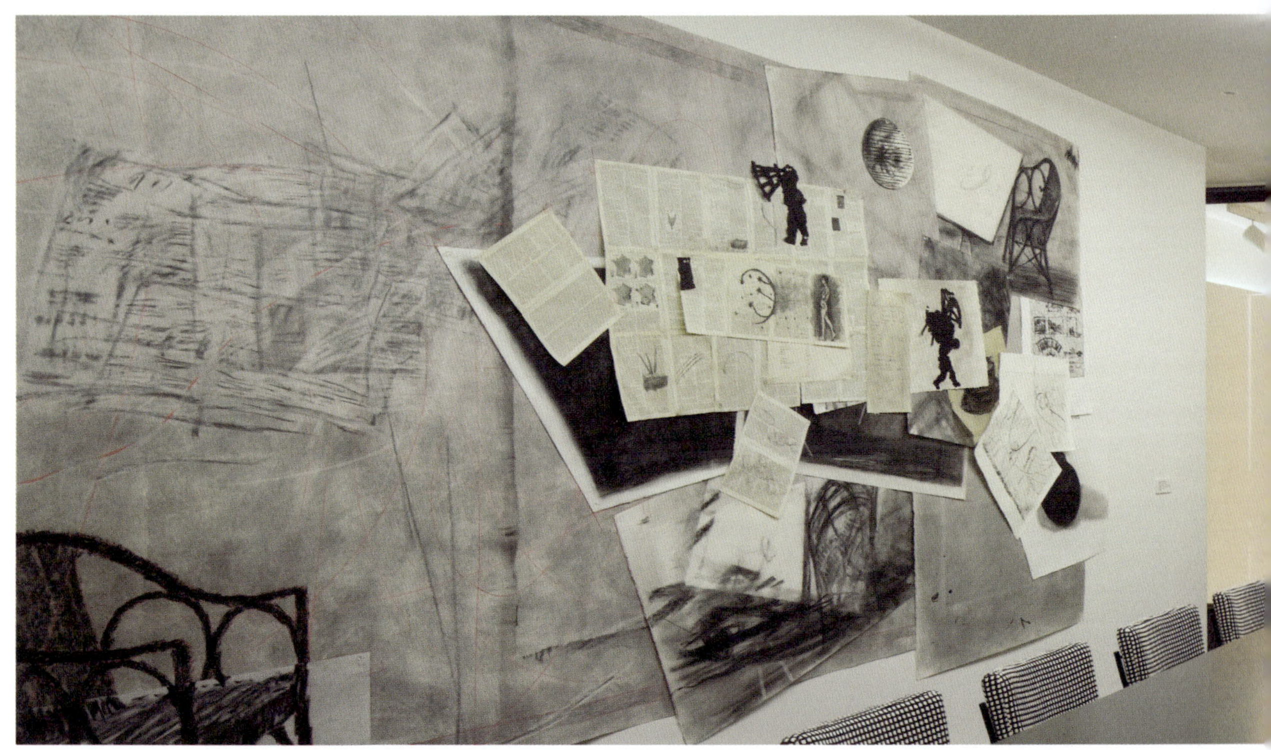

VISITOR INFORMATION
The collection can be visited on designated days during the year and through association with particular art and cultural events.

**Admission Fees:** Free of charge

**Access by car:** Leaving Melbourne's CBD, head south on Exhibition Street, continue onto Batman Avenue, continue onto the M1, take the Church Street exit, turn left onto Church Street, turn left onto Balmain Street and left again onto Palmer Parade.

**Access by public transport:** From Flinders Street Railway Station, take the train towards Blackburn. Get off at East Richmond Railway Station. Turn right onto Church Street, right again onto Balmain Street and turn left onto Palmer Parade. Sussan Headquarters is located at the end of the road on your left-hand side.

**Extra Tips:** A visit to Sussan Headquarters can be easily combined with a trip to the Ten Cubed Collection (refer to page 56), the TarraWarra Museum of Art (refer to page 72), or an appointment at the Lyon Housemuseum (refer to page 42).

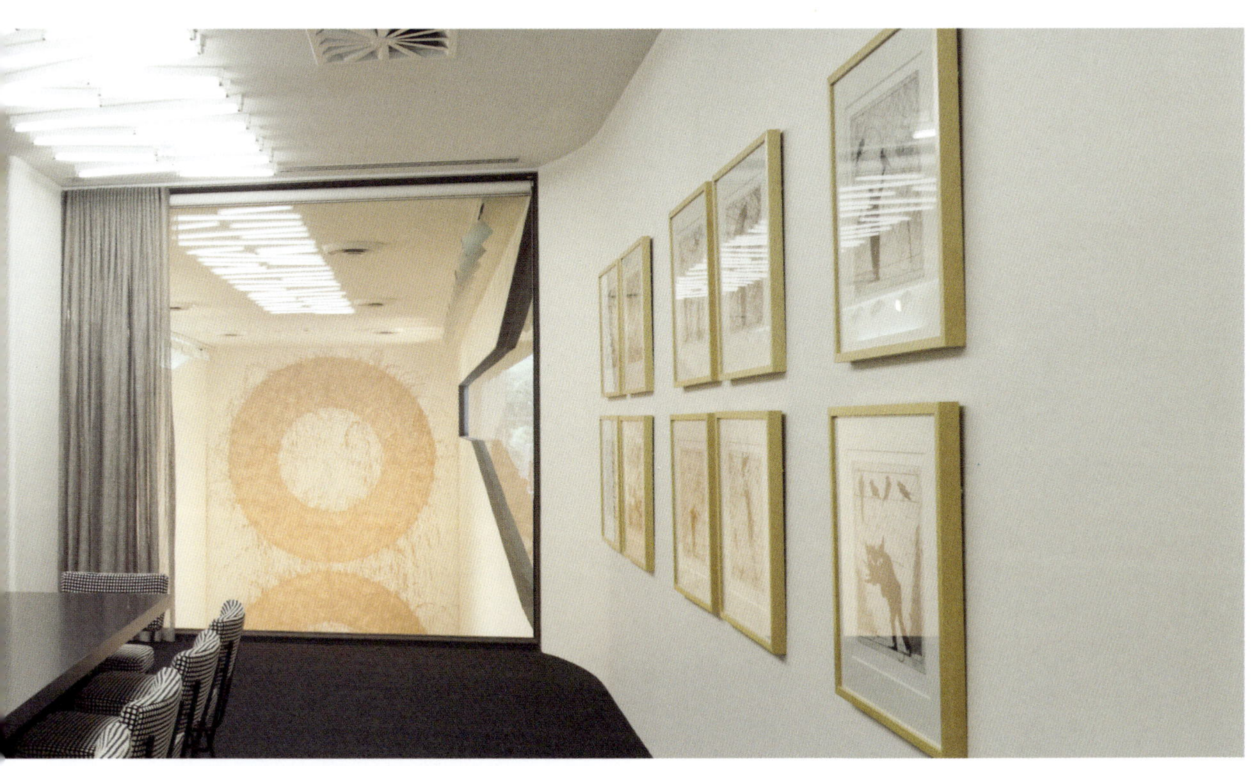

**Restaurant Tips:** Authentic Italian pizza and pasta as well as good coffee can be enjoyed at Baby Café and Pizzeria (631–633 Church Street, Richmond). Kong, Chris Lucas's latest queue-magnet, serves Asian fusion cuisine (599 Church Street, Richmond). 7 Grams offers superb coffee and café style lunches (505 Church Street, Richmond). The small and unassuming 3 Lives Café serves great coffee, sweet treats and interesting Korean fusion dishes (76 Chestnut Street, Cremorne).

Page 50
Naomi Milgrom AO Collection, exterior
Photograph Peter Bennetts

Page 52
Ugo Rondinone, Richard Long
Photograph John Brash
Page 53
Sol LeWitt, Michael Parekowhai
Photograph Ben Wrigley

Pages 54–5
William Kentridge
Photograph Peter Bennetts

All images courtesy Naomi Milgrom AO Collection

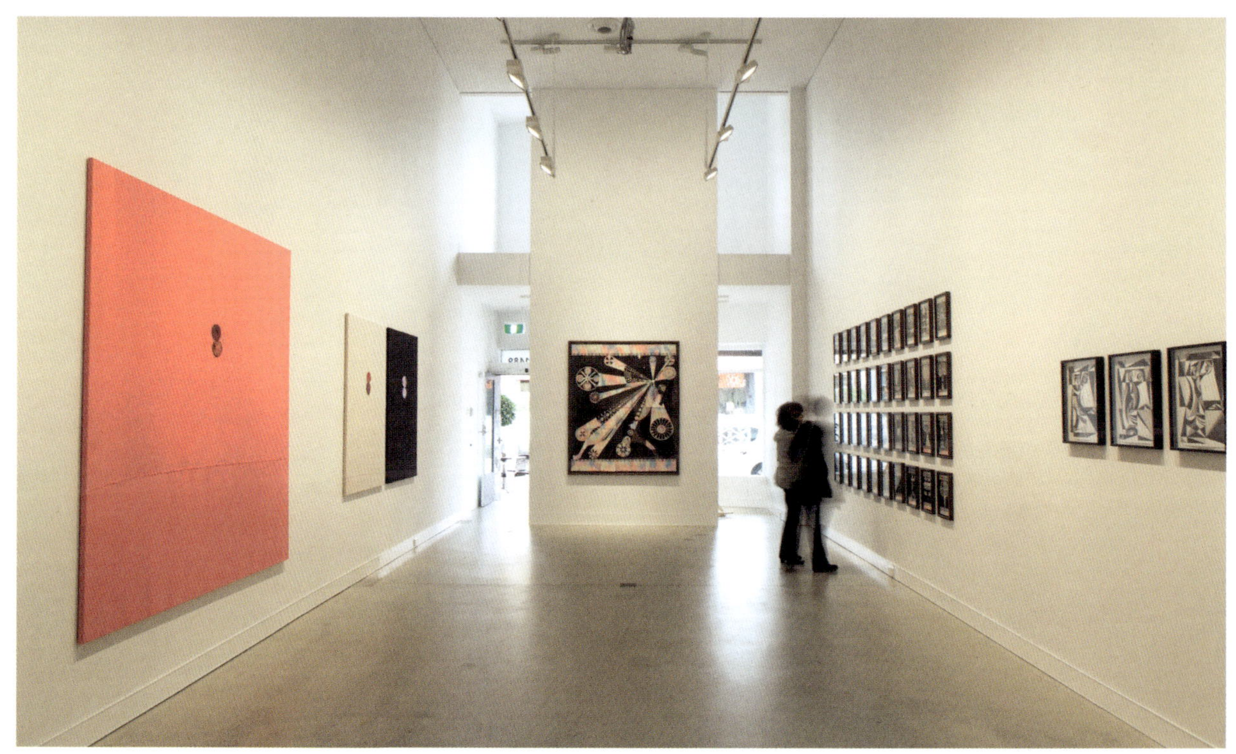

# TEN CUBED COLLECTION

1489 Malvern Road
Glen Iris, VIC 3146

OPENING HOURS
Tuesday–Saturday 10am–4pm

Telephone: +61 (03) 9822 0833
info@tencubed.com.au
tencubed.com.au

A visit to Ten Cubed will reveal more than an architecturally designed interior. The converted terrace houses a private collection of contemporary art that is quite literally a treasure in an unassuming inner-city suburb of Melbourne.

Executive Director, philanthropist Dianne Gringlas and her family have collected art for many years, but it was not until 2010 that she and her sister-in-law, former barrister turned curator Ada Moshinsky, decided to formalise their passion for contemporary art and established Ten Cubed, a collecting concept unique in the Australian art world.

Setting themselves a time-frame of ten years, they determined to collect the work of ten artists in depth, initially anticipating that this would involve at least ten works by each artist – hence the name Ten Cubed.

It was always their intention to make the works available for loan to public galleries, but in 2013, the Gringlas family decided to open their privately funded gallery space to showcase the Ten Cubed collection to the public. The collection has grown rapidly and now includes over 170 artworks. Dianne and Ada admit that they have acquired work by more than ten artists along the way, although the focus on selecting and exhibiting a core group of ten remains true to the original concept.

Artists selected to be part of the core collection must demonstrate a sustained commitment to their practice, intellectual and technical rigour and, most importantly, produce work that has an aesthetic and conceptual appeal to both Dianne and Ada. After all, this is a private collection and part of the allure of watching it evolve is to see how the personal taste and eye of the collector is reflected in the art acquired.

The eight artists currently represented in the core collection are Pat Brassington, Jonathan Delafield Cook, Alasdair McLuckie, Anne-Marie May, David Rosetzky, Tim Silver, Daniel von Sturmer and David Wadelton.

The patronage shown by Ten Cubed extends not only to the artists but also recognises the integral role played by their representing galleries in the infrastructure of the industry. The symbiotic relationship between artist, gallery and collector is acknowledged and celebrated through the collaborative approach taken to each non-commercial exhibition mounted at Ten Cubed.

Visitors to Ten Cubed are greeted in the vaulted exhibition space of the Atrium Gallery. Upstairs in the Collection Lounge, art books, catalogues and magazines may be perused while visitors enjoy a curated selection of artworks in a more casual setting. Paintings, drawings and photographs not out on loan or exhibition are displayed on racks in the catalogued storeroom, and tours for individuals and small groups are available on request. The staff are only too happy to share their knowledge of the collection.

Ten Cubed is a collection in progress, and the next five years will see not only the announcement of the final two artists but a continuing program of more exciting exhibitions, publications and art events.

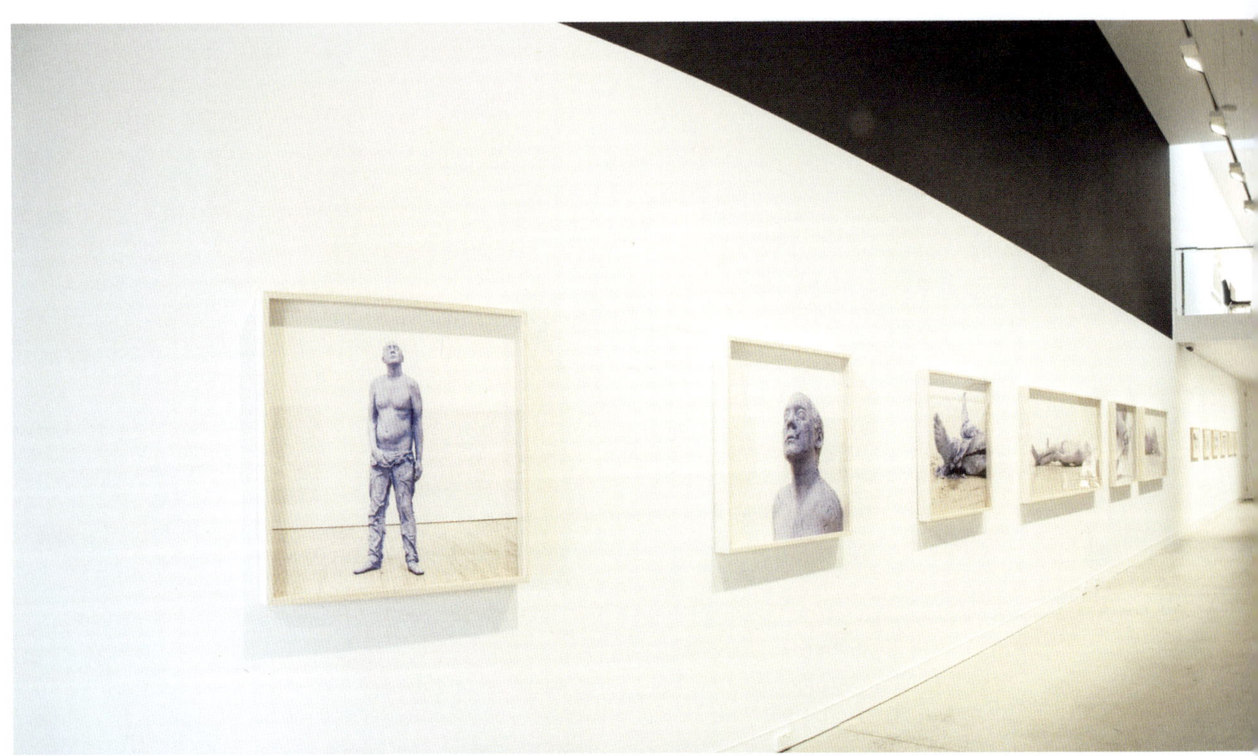

VISITOR INFORMATION

**Admission Fees:** Free of charge

**Tours and other Events:** The Ten Cubed Collection holds school group tours, collectors tours and other events, including the occasional floor talk and great opening drink parties.

**Access by car:** Leave Melbourne's CBD in an easterly direction on the M1, take the exit towards Toorak, merge onto Toorak Road/State Route 26, turn left onto Milton Parade, turn right onto Tooronga Road and turn left again onto Malvern Road. Ten Cubed Collection is located on your left-hand side. Parking is available along Malvern Road and in adjoining streets.

**Access by public transport:** From Flinders Street Station, take the train towards Glen Waverley. Get off at Tooronga Railway Station (Malvern). Turn right onto Tooronga Road and then turn left at Malvern Road. Or take Tram 72 tram towards Camberwell from Federation Square/Swanston Street. Get off at Stop 47 Tooronga Road/Malvern Road (Malvern). Continue on Malvern Road. Ten Cubed Collection is located on the left-hand side. The Driver's Bus Line route 624 bus runs between Kew and Oakleigh along Tooronga Road (alight at Malvern Road). Refer to Public

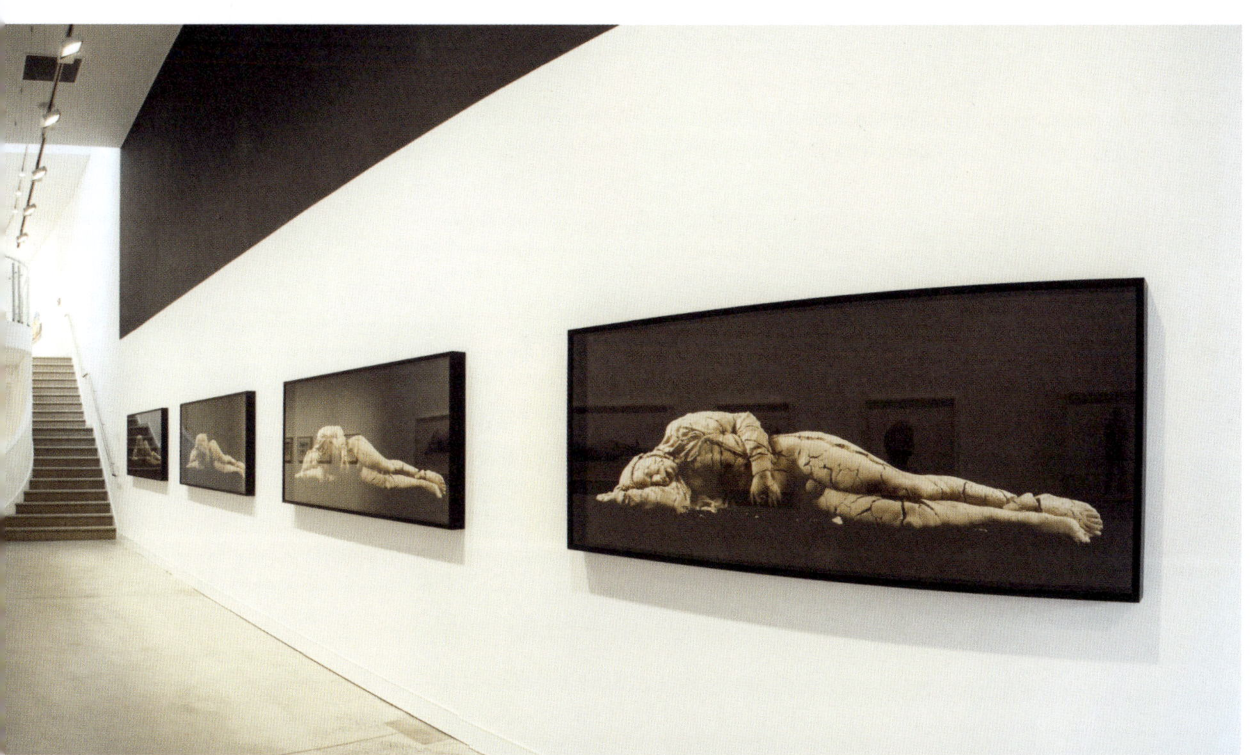

Transport Planner for the different transportation means and time schedules.

**Extra Tips:** A visit to the Ten Cubed Collection can be easily combined with a trip to The Duldig Studio (refer to page 60), the Heide Museum of Modern Art (refer to page 66) or with an appointment on a Tuesday at the Lyon Housemuseum (refer to page 42).

**Restaurant Tips**: The very popular café Mr Foxx, which is located next door to the Ten Cubed Collection, serves great coffee and a wide selection of tasty dishes (1491 Malvern Road). The seasonally dictated food, gorgeous treats as well as excellent coffee can be enjoyed at the cute Platform Espresso (1529 High Street, Glen Iris). Golden Child serves amazing food in a great setting (1–3 Bardolph Street, Glen Iris). The enoteca Chaucer Cellars offers a fantastic wine list and wholesome café style meals in a quiet atmosphere (155 Burke Road, Glen Iris).

Page 56
Alasdair McLuckie, installation view, Ten Cubed Collection
Photograph Jeremy Blode

Pages 58-9
Tim Silver, installation view, Ten Cubed Collection
Photograph Jeremy Blode

All images courtesy Ten Cubed Collection

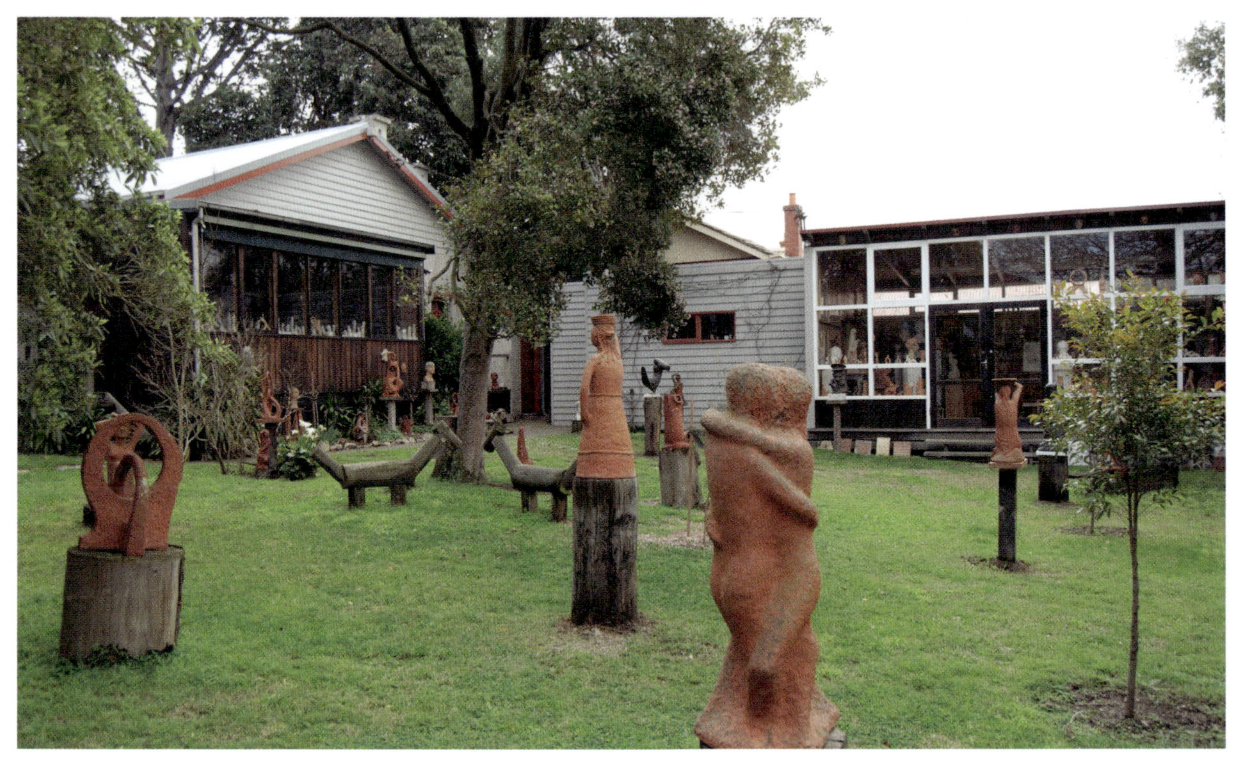

# THE DULDIG STUDIO

92 Burke Road
Malvern East, VIC 3145

OPENING HOURS
Tuesdays and Thursdays 1pm–3pm,
other weekdays by appointment
Every second Saturday of each month 1pm–3pm
Closed on public holidays and during January
Groups can be accommodated by appointment only

Telephone: +61 (03) 9885 3358
enquiries@duldig.org.au
duldig.org.au

One would not necessarily assume that a visit to this relatively small house museum in a residential street in Malvern East, south-east of Melbourne, would powerfully invoke the feelings of a different time and place. This time capsule holds many fascinating stories and showcases sculptures, ceramics and drawings, mainly by Karl and Slawa Duldig as well as a collection of custom-made art-house Viennese furniture. Karl Duldig (1902–1986) was born in the Polish part of the old Austrian Empire and moved to Vienna with his family in 1914. He was a student at the University of Applied Arts from 1921 to 1925 where he studied for three years under the noted and highly regarded mentor, Austrian sculptor Anton Hanak (1875–1934). Hanak was a member of the Secessionist Group and a friend and professional colleague of the architect and designer Josef Hoffmann. Karl Duldig met Slawa Horowitz (1902–1975), who was a private student of Hanak, for the first time in their teacher's studio. A rare photograph of Hanak and his students in 1924, including Karl and Slawa, is today one of the Duldig Studio's prized possessions, along with original Hanak drawings he gave to his two students. Karl and Slawa went on to study at the Academy of Fine Arts and were married in 1931. Two years earlier, Slawa Horowitz had taken out worldwide patents for her invention of the first foldable umbrella, called Flirt. The approved patent application and a prototype of Flirt are on display in the Duldig Studio. The umbrella went into production in Austria and Germany and Slawa received royalties until 1938. She used the first royalties to commission Sigmund Jaray, a distinguished Austrian firm of furniture designers and craftsmen, to design the furniture for the flat she and Karl had set up in the Engzingergasse in Vienna.

After their graduation, both artists worked on private commissions and exhibited regularly in the Künstlerhaus and the Secession. Their daughter Eva was born shortly before the annexation of Austria by Nazi Germany in 1938. A bizarre set of circumstances prompted Karl's hasty departure from Austria to Switzerland, from where he managed to organise visas for his family.

Back in Vienna Slawa cleverly avoided the imminent impoundment of the family's precious works of art, furniture and other personal possessions by simulating evidence that a 'sale' had taken place. She then carefully organised their packing and storage for possible future transportation. Once in Switzerland, Slawa sold all the rights to her umbrella invention to Austrian manufacturer Brüder Wüster for 1000 Reichmarks. The family then sailed for Singapore where Karl and Slawa set up a successful art school and Karl completed major commissions for the Sultan of Johore and Aw Boon Haw, the Tiger Balm king. However, as they held German passports all family members were classified as 'enemy aliens' and the British colonial authorities deported them to Australia in 1940.

After arriving in Sydney on the *Queen Mary*, the Duldigs were herded onto a train to remote Tatura, in northern Victoria, where they were interned for the next eighteen months. In the camp, Karl turned to sketching and used an axe to carve firewood into sculptures, as he had no other tools. When Karl was able to voluntarily join the Australian Military Forces he even turned potatoes he was peeling for the army kitchens into small carvings. Some of these have been cast into bronze and can be seen today at the Duldig Studio. The family eventually settled in Melbourne and formally became Australian citizens in 1946. Karl and Slawa discovered that Slawa's sister, Rella, had managed to salvage their precious works of art and furniture by declaring them as her own and transporting them to France. These were eventually shipped to Melbourne.

Karl and Slawa contributed immeasurably to the cultural life of Melbourne, particularly by stimulating an appreciation

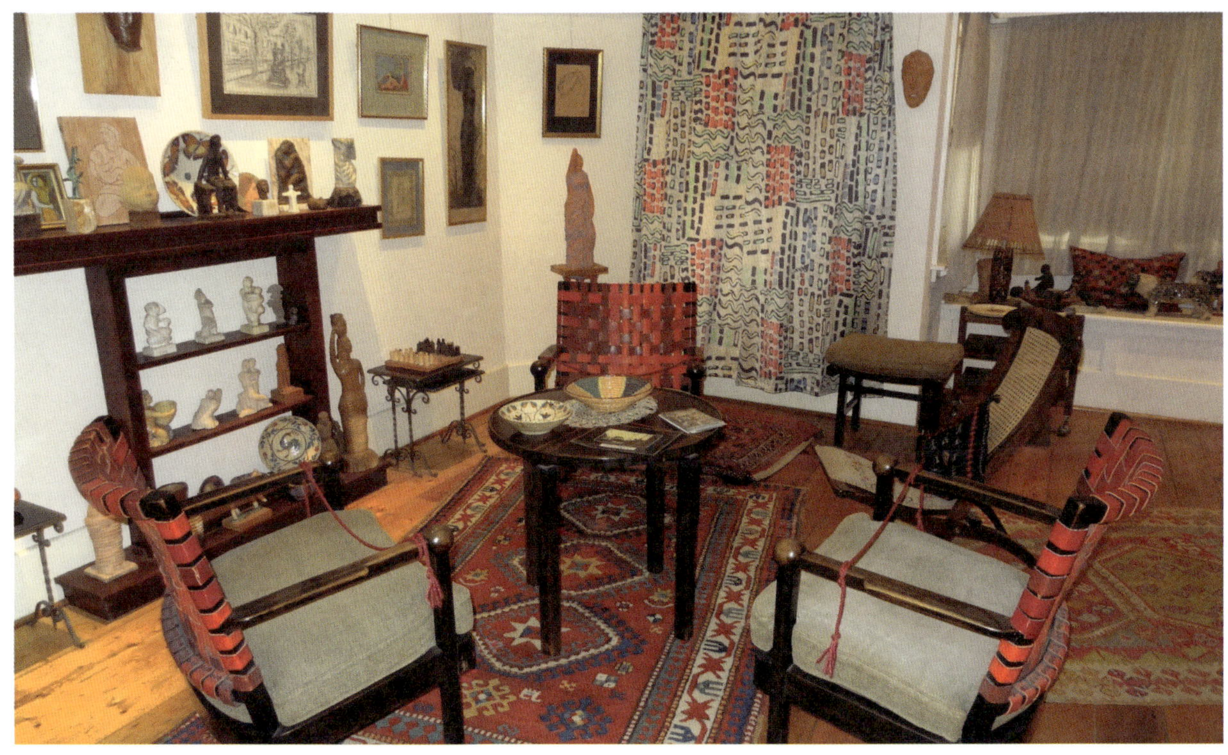

of modern sculpture in Australia. They both worked as art teachers at prestigious Melbourne grammar schools, while simultaneously establishing a small ceramics business. Later Karl completed a number of ceramic relief murals which were commissioned by private and public patrons. He also exhibited regularly with the Victorian Sculptors' Society and in private and public galleries. Karl and Slawa's home became a place of learning and culture where their generous and artistic spirit can still be sensed today. When Eva travelled to France to compete in the French Tennis championships, her mother's sister revealed a store of sculptures that had remained hidden in her cellar. Over the next four decades, these works of art were returned to the family in Melbourne. One of the most precious 'rediscovered' sculptures was *Mask*, 1921, one of Karl's earliest student works, which Slawa had so carefully packed for storage before she fled Vienna. It and many other masks can be seen in the house, artist's studio and sculpture garden. Slawa first voiced the idea for the Duldig Studio in the early 1970s. Karl died in 1986, gifting the collection to his daughter Eva, who is ardent about sharing her parents' legacy. She oversaw the renovation of the original house and the addition of a new gallery space between 1994 and 1996. Fortunately, Karl's atmospheric studio has been pretty much left as it was for decades, with old tools, a small stove, a kiln and rows and rows of sculptures in diverse materials from different creative periods on display. The Duldig Studio collection encompasses about 1500 sculptures as well as hundreds of paintings, ceramics, drawings and decorative art pieces. Annually changing exhibitions from the permanent collection are on display in the new gallery space. The remaining rooms and the delightful sculpture garden remain intact and can be seen in their original enchanting setting.

Eva established Duldig Gallery Inc. in 2002 as a 'not-for-profit, tax-exempt and gift recipient public museum and art gallery' administered by an independent committee.

VISITOR INFORMATION

**Admission Fees:** Adult/Concession: $20/$10

**Tours and other Events:** When the museum is open, the Duldig Studio conducts exhibition tours daily at 2pm (free of charge with entry ticket). Please refer to the website for special events.

**Access by car:** The Duldig Studio is located about 10 km south-east of Melbourne's CBD.

**Access by public transport:** From Flinders Street Railway Station/Federation Square, take Tram 5 towards Malvern getting off at Stop 52: Burke Road/Wattletree Road. After turning right (south) on Burke Road, The Duldig Studio can be found across the street from the Central Park Road/Burke Road T-junction.

**Extra Tips:** The Monash University Museum of Art (MUMA), which was designed by Kerstin Thompson Architects as part of the Caulfield campus, holds one of the most significant and adventurous collections of contemporary (post 1960s) Australian art outside the state galleries (900 Dandenong Road, Caulfield East).

**Restaurant Tips:** Nearby, Our Kitchen Table café offers hearty stews and curries, homemade cakes and slices in a homely, welcoming atmosphere. They also offer temptations to take away (134 Burke Road, East Malvern).

Pages 88
Karl Duldig

Left
Karl & Slawa Duldig

All images courtesy The Duldig Studio

# RURAL

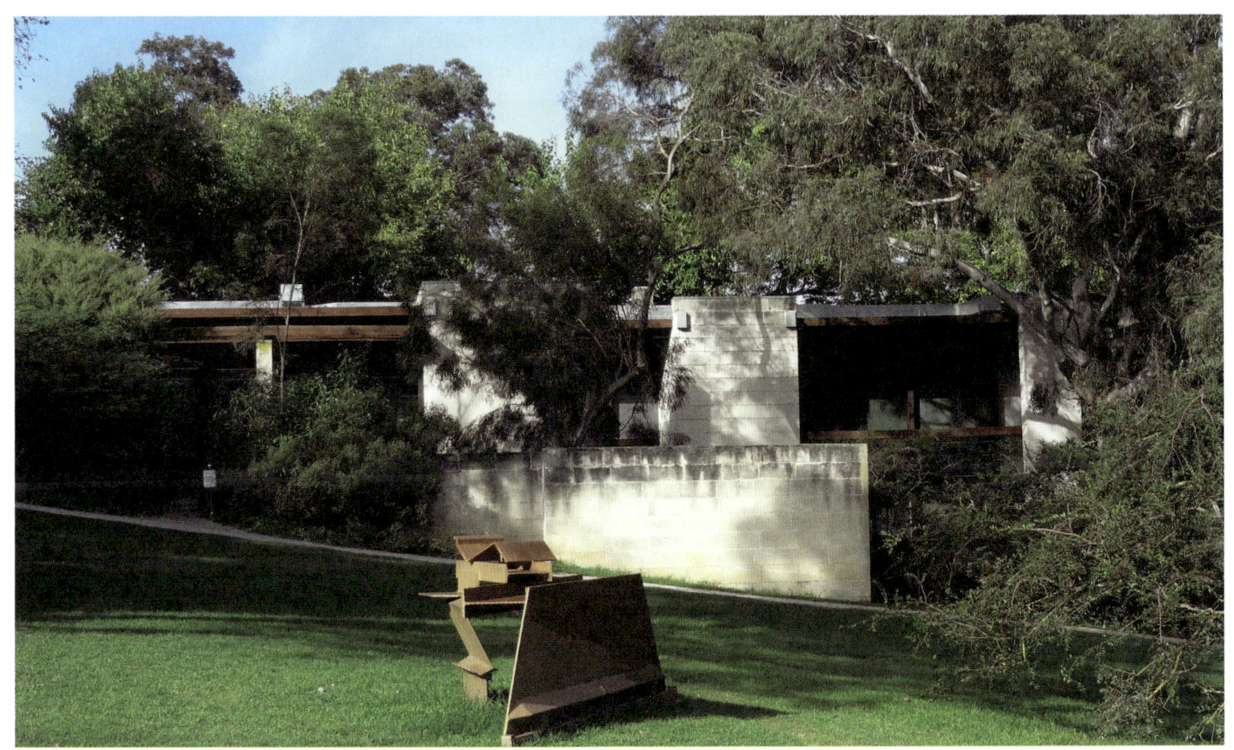

# HEIDE MUSEUM OF MODERN ART

7 Templestowe Road
Bulleen, VIC 3105

OPENING HOURS
Tuesday–Sunday 10am–5pm

Telephone: +61 (03) 9850 1500
info@heide.com.au
heide.com.au

Heide, as it is still affectionately known, offers an inspiring, educational and insightful experience of modern and contemporary art, architecture and landscape on a variety of levels. It is regarded as one of Victoria's most interesting art institutions.

Named after the nearby township of Heidelberg, Heide began life as the home of John and Sunday Reed who, in 1934, purchased the neglected 6-hectare dairy farm in what is now Melbourne's suburb of Bulleen. Being passionate environmentalists, the Reeds renovated the weatherboard farmhouse in a French provincial style, transformed the run-down and virtually treeless farmland into gardens and informal parklands, and established a Provençal-inspired kitchen garden for what was to become a largely self-sustaining lifestyle. The 1940s were a watershed in the development of modern art and the Reeds quickly became central to the evolution of Melbourne's progressive modernist art and literature through their establishment of a comprehensive art collection as well as an extensive library and particularly through their moral and financial support of like-minded individuals. In these years, the Reeds launched the careers of artists now considered major figures in Australian art – Arthur Boyd, Sidney Nolan, Albert Tucker, Joy Hester, John Perceval and Danila Vassilieff – today collectively known as the Angry Penguins, after the avant-garde journal published by the Reeds and the writer Max Harris. Nolan, who lived at Heide intermittently for almost a decade until 1947 and who developed a particularly close relationship with Sunday, painted his famous 'Ned Kelly' series in the dining room. Romantically inclined visitors might want to visit the small Heart Garden at Heide I, a recreated enclosed heart-shaped bed, which Sunday Reed originally established in 1949 in memory of her long love affair with Sidney Nolan.

In 1956, the Reeds established the Gallery of Contemporary Art (GCA) in Tavistock Place, Melbourne. It served as a venue for exhibitions of the Contemporary Art Society, an art organisation of which John was a founding member and president. Two years later, with the assistance of friend and entrepreneur Georges Mora, they re-launched the gallery as the Museum of Modern Art and Design of Australia (MoMADA), which can be seen as the precursor to Heide and which operated until 1966. To form the basis of the museum, the Reeds donated 163 works to MoMADA during this period, which have since entered the Heide Collection.

Amassing a large collection of the contemporary art of their time, and extending their interest in modernism, in 1963 the Reeds commissioned architect David McGlashan with the design and construction of a second, modernist home on the Heide site as a 'gallery to be lived in'. Parallel to the building construction, the Reeds also established a second kitchen garden nearby. The light-filled, iconic Heide II, which is mainly constructed of Mount Gambier limestone, won the Royal Australian Institute of Architect's prize in 1968 and is today considered to be one of the finest examples of modernist architecture in the state. It remained the Reeds' home until 1980, when they sold the building, most of the adjoining property and 112 artworks from their collection to the Victorian State Government. Seeing their vision fulfilled, they moved into the renovated Heide I in the same year and bequeathed a further 388 works to the newly established 'Heide Park and Art Gallery'. The public museum opened its doors in November 1981, shortly before the death of John and Sunday in December, ten days apart.

Attached to Heide II, a dedicated gallery building (Heide III), designed by Andrew Andersons of Peddle Thorp Architects, was opened to the public in 1993. The museum's name was changed to Museum of Modern Art at Heide only to be re-named 'Heide Museum of Modern Art' in 1999. The museum underwent a further redevelopment in 2005–06 which included the addition of several outdoor sculptures, landscaping and redesign of the gardens, construction of a new education centre and the extension of the Heide III building by O'Connor + Houle Architecture.

Part of the allure of Heide is the element of surprise in discovering the numerous different spaces and artworks on the property, which reflect such a diverse range of art periods. The core of the Heide Collection was assembled over five decades by John and Sunday Reed. They supported artists who came up with new and radical ideas and techniques. They bought works that ranged from expressionist to realist and from figurative to abstract. Initially, they acquired works by artists spearheading the modernist movement in Australia, such as Moya Dyring and Sam Atyeo. In the 1950s and 1960s, they collected works which reflected their cultural activities and friendships of that period. Artworks by Charles Blackman, Mike Brown, Robert Dickerson, Mirka Mora, Fred Williams and other artists found their way into the collection during this exciting period. During the 1970s, the Reeds began to collect the work of a younger generation of artists, mainly contemporaries of their adopted son Sweeney Reed (son of artists Joy Hester and Albert Tucker), such as Sydney Ball, Col Jordan and Les Kossatz, as well as works by Sweeney Reed himself. The Heide Collection has since expanded through many additional gifts as well as the inclusion of four significant collections – the Museum of Art and Design of Australia Collection, the Baillieu Myer Collection of the 1980s, the Barrett Reid Bequest and most recently the Barbara Tucker Gift. Heide's constantly growing collection nowadays holds over 3000 artworks. Heide's current collecting priorities are to expand the presentation of living Australian artists and to commission new works for the sculpture park.

The museum offers a very substantial exhibition schedule of up to twelve different shows per year. Works from the original Heide Collection as well as archival material are mainly displayed in the atmospheric rooms of Heide I. Heide II features works form the Heide Collection by modernist artists associated with Heide's history as well as more recent acquisitions. The Central Galleries in Heide III present Heide's three major exhibitions throughout the year. Changing exhibitions of works by Albert Tucker and his peers are displayed in the Albert & Barbara Tucker Gallery. The Kerry Gardner & Andrew Myer Project Gallery feature site-specific installations by emerging artists. The changing program of exhibitions draws from individual artists, private and public collections, as well as from the Heide Collection. Although the focus is on Australian art, international artists have always been a part of the program at Heide. Among others, visitors were able to enjoy exhibitions of works by Pablo Picasso, Henry Moore and Louise Bourgeois in the past.

There are over thirty sculptures dispersed over the 6-hectare site. Two sculptures were purchased from the Reeds by the Victorian Government to establish the museum collection: David Tolley's *Man/woman*, c. 1966, and Ronald Upton's *Three forms,* 1964. Since that time all sculptures in the grounds have been acquired by the museum separately through purchase (using funds donated for acquisition) and donation. The Anish Kapoor sculptures in the forecourt of Heide III were purchased through the Georges Mora Foundation with funds donated by the Victor Smorgon Charitable Trust in 1993, and the stunning Inge King sculpture *Rings of Saturn*, 2005–6, was commissioned through the Heide Foundation with significant assistance from Lindsay and Paula Fox in 2005.

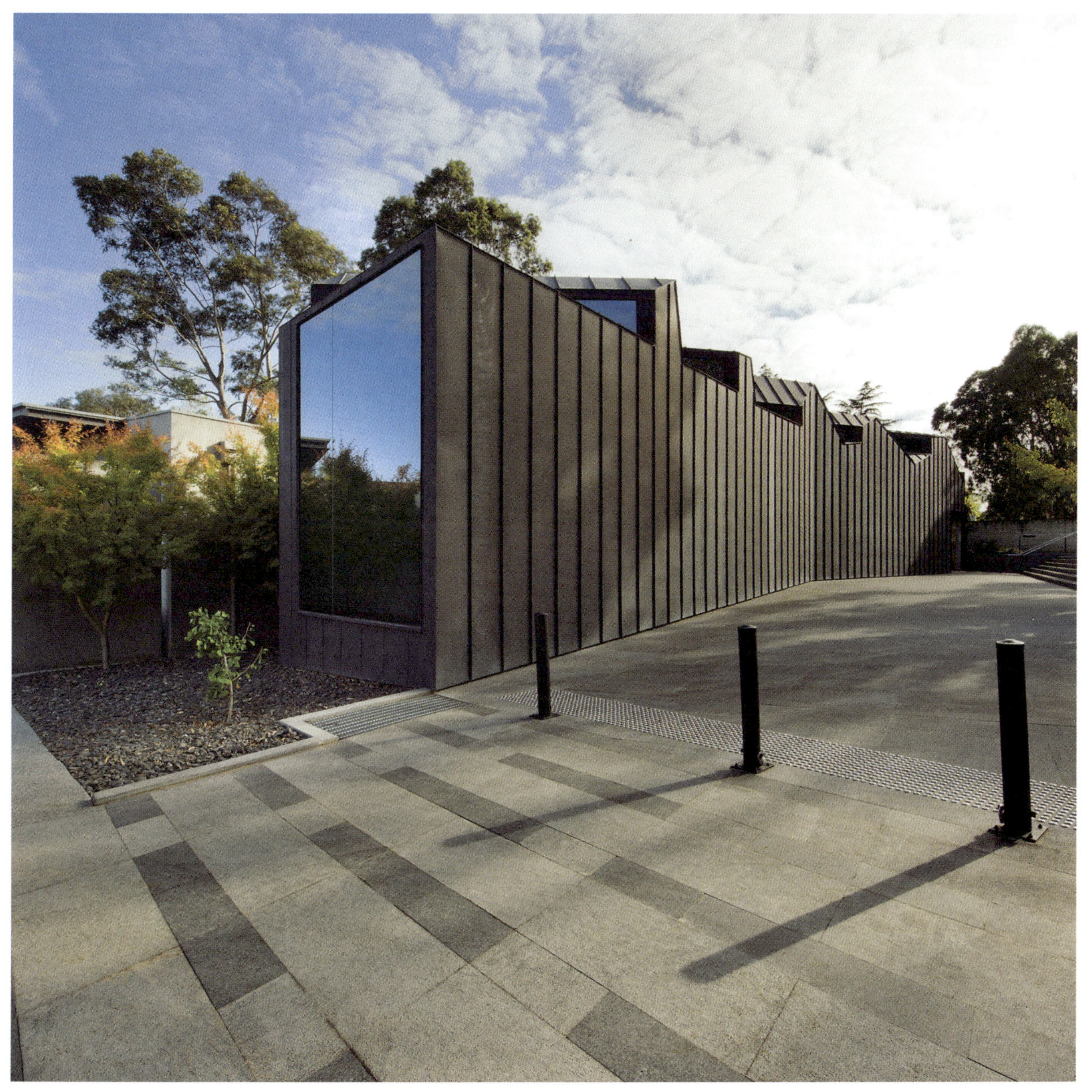

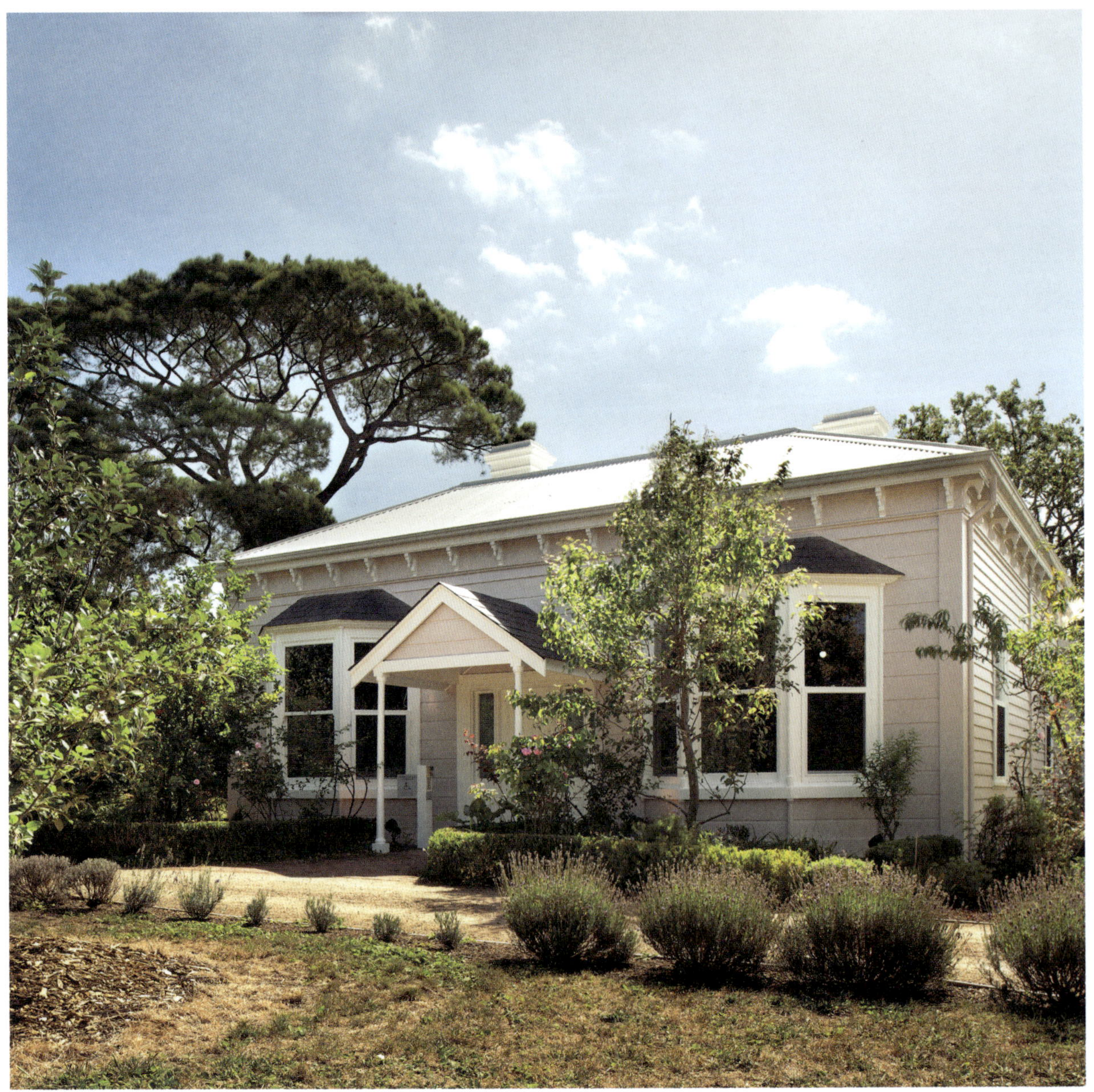

VISITOR INFORMATION

**Admission Fees:** Adult/Senior/Concession: $16/$14/$12; children under 12 are free. Access to the Garden & Sculpture Park is free

**Tours and other Events:** Heide offers a large variety of exciting tours and workshops.

**Access by car:** Leaving Central Melbourne on the Eastern Freeway/M3 (towards Doncaster/Ringwood) take the exit State Route 42/Bulleen Road/Thompsons Road. Stay left and follow the signs Templestowe/State Route 42/Bulleen. Turn left onto Bullen Road/State Route 52. Continue on State Route 52 by staying right. Heide can be found on the left side. Free parking is available on-site. Melway Ref. 32 E5.

**Access by public transport:** Take the Hurstbridge Line train from Flinders Street or Southern Cross Railway Station to Heidelberg Railway Station and Bus. Change to bus 903 (Mordialloc Shopping Centre bound) and disembark at the Bridge Street/Manningham Road stop. Walk to Heide through Banksia Park, via pedestrian path next to the *Helmet* sculpture.

**Extra Tips:** A visit to Heide can be easily combined with a trip to the TarraWarra Museum of Art (refer to page 72) or an appointment at the Lyon Housemuseum (refer to page 42).

**Restaurant Tips:** Shannon Bennett's delightful Café Vue offers delicious French-inspired dishes in the grounds of Heide. In the spirit of the Reeds' lifestyle, both Heide kitchen gardens are still in use, supplying the café with fresh produce. Driving back towards the city, the funky coffee shops, organic bakeries and restaurants on Gertrude Street in Fitzroy make for a good fuel stop. Foodies will enjoy the high-quality menu with an interesting Aboriginal influence at the Mission Australia social enterprise restaurant Charcoal Lane (136 Gertrude Street). Fatto A Mano offers organic breads, cakes and other treats as take-away (228 Gertrude Street) and Arcadia (193 Gertrude Street) serves interesting café-style food and great coffees.

Page 66
Anthony Caro, *Sidestep*, 1971
Synthetic polymer paint on steel and Cor-ten steel, 129.5 x 292 x 147.5 cm
Courtesy the artist and Heide Museum of Modern Art

Page 69
Heide III
Courtesy Heide Museum of Modern Art
Photograph John Gollings

Page 70
Heide I
Courtesy Heide Museum of Modern Art
Photograph John Gollings

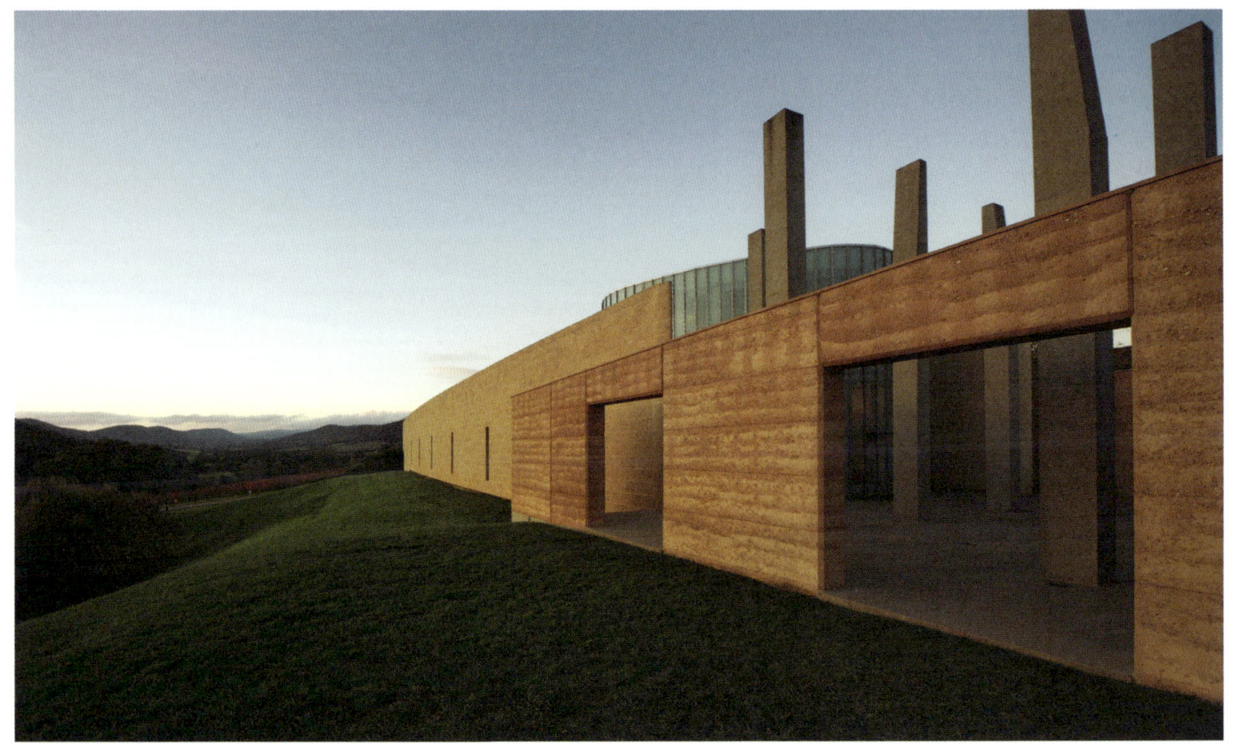

# TARRAWARRA MUSEUM OF ART

311 Healesville–Yarra Glen Road
Healesville, VIC 3777

OPENING HOURS
Tuesday–Sunday 11am–5pm
(open on public holidays ex. Christmas Day)
The museum is open 7 days a week during the summer season (Boxing Day–Australia Day)

Telephone: +61 (03) 5957 3100
museum@twma.com.au
twma.com.au

Since opening in 2003, TarraWarra Museum of Art has become recognised as the cultural jewel of the Yarra Valley, providing visitors with an enjoyable and inspiring experience that combines impressive architecture set in the rolling hills of a beautiful natural landscape with great modern and contemporary art.

Located just one hour north-east of Melbourne, the museum captures the vision of the museum's founders, philanthropists Eva Besen AO and Marc Besen AC, passionate collectors of Australian art from the 1950s to the present day, who have gifted both the building and its collection to the people of Australia. TarraWarra Museum of Art was established in October 2000. Operating as a not-for-profit institution, with the Besen Family Foundation as the museum's principal sponsor, it is the first significant privately funded public visual arts museum in the country to be set up under the Australian Government's philanthropic measures.

The Besens had long dreamt of sharing their inexhaustible admiration of Australian art with the people of Australia and beyond. When the museum opened in the Yarra Valley in December 2003, they donated a total of 142 artworks to form the beginnings of the collection. The collection features many renowned Australian artists who were instrumental in the development of modern art in this country. Major paintings of each decade of the last sixty years have shaped this significant collection. Highlights include works by Richard Bell, Sydney Ball, Arthur Boyd, John Brack, William Dobell, Russell Drysdale, Ian Fairweather, Rosalie Gascoigne, Brent Harris, Joy Hester, Joanna Lamb, Sidney Nolan, John Olsen, Jeffrey Smart, Edwin Tanner, Imants Tillers, Albert Tucker, Tony Tuckson, Danila Vassilieff, Brett Whiteley and Fred Williams. The museum continues to tell the story of Australian art as the museum's collection grows each year through new acquisitions and donations, mainly from the Besens and, on a smaller scale, from artists and other individuals. The collection currently holds over 400 artworks. Some of the most interesting contemporary entries have been site-specific commissions, which are a testament to the close connection to the Australian art community of Victoria Lynn, Director of TarraWarra Museum of Art. On average, the museum annually presents six to eight temporary themed exhibitions, covering a diverse range of stimulating and innovative Australian and – to a lesser degree – international art, in both group and single artists' shows. The thoughtful and very well curated exhibitions, which often draw on the museum's own collection as well as loans from other institutions or private collectors, provide the opportunity to experience a fresh context within which to view Australian art today. Two or three exhibitions are usually on display simultaneously in the three gallery rooms, which occupy about 700 square metres in total. Of particular interest for followers of contemporary Australian art is the TarraWarra Biennial, which takes place every even year parallel to the Melbourne Art Fair and the Melbourne Festival. Inaugurated in 2006, it is a well-received signature exhibition which identifies new developments in contemporary Australian art practice under an experimental curatorial platform.

Intended to emerge powerfully from the landscape, this ultra modern gallery displays the talents of Melbourne architect Allan Powell, the winner of the Besen's architectural competition of 2000. Almost like an earthworks sculpture, his design can be viewed as a monument to modernism. Situated on a hillside on TarraWarra Estate, which was originally created in 1986 on a 320-hectare dairy property, the building's sensually curved external walls of tan and clay-coloured limestone and rammed earth provide a perfect balance to the Yarra Valley landscape. Visitors can appreciate why Powell was awarded the winner of the Victorian Premier's Design Award for the museum in 2004. Other than the impressive columns in front of the edifice, the most stunning

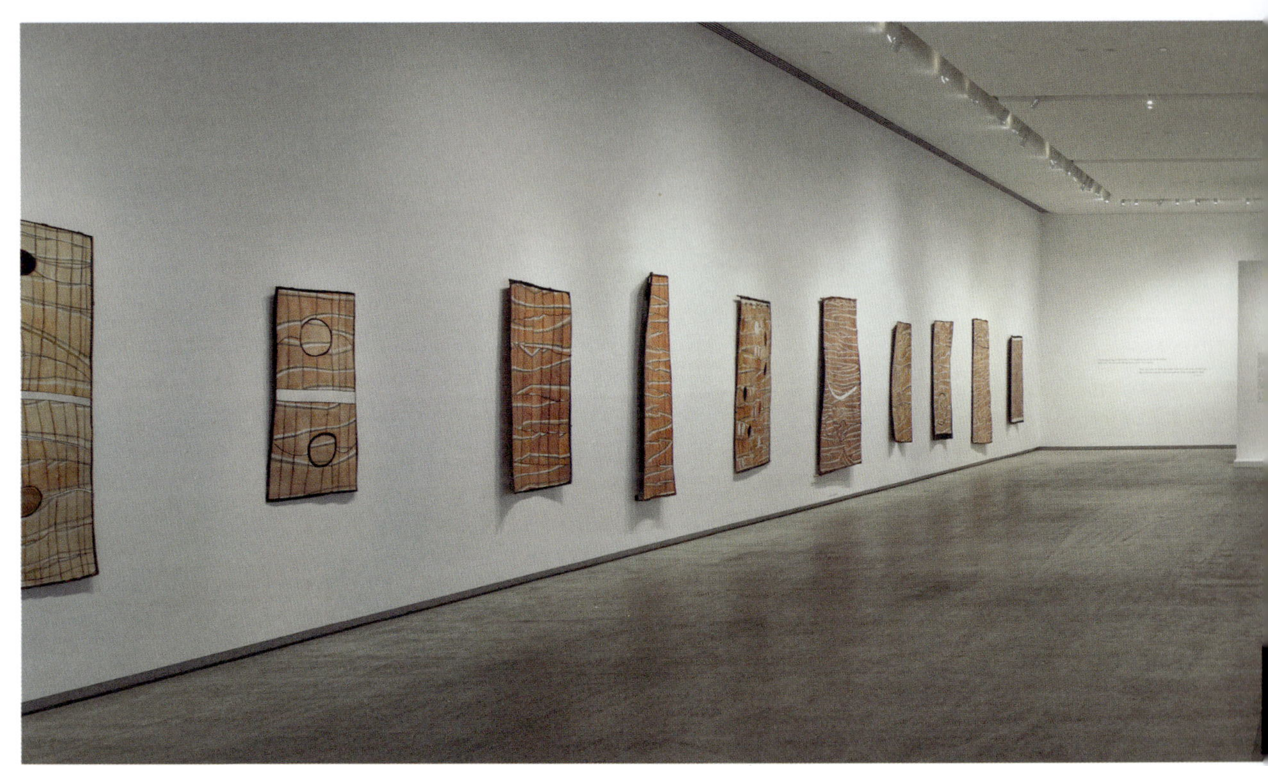

feature of the building are the tall narrow windows set in the walls which allow onlookers to take in the lush and cultivated landscape of water features, grapevines and weeping willows. TarraWarra Museum of Art curators often make clever use of the natural light that streams through these windows to enhance specific works.

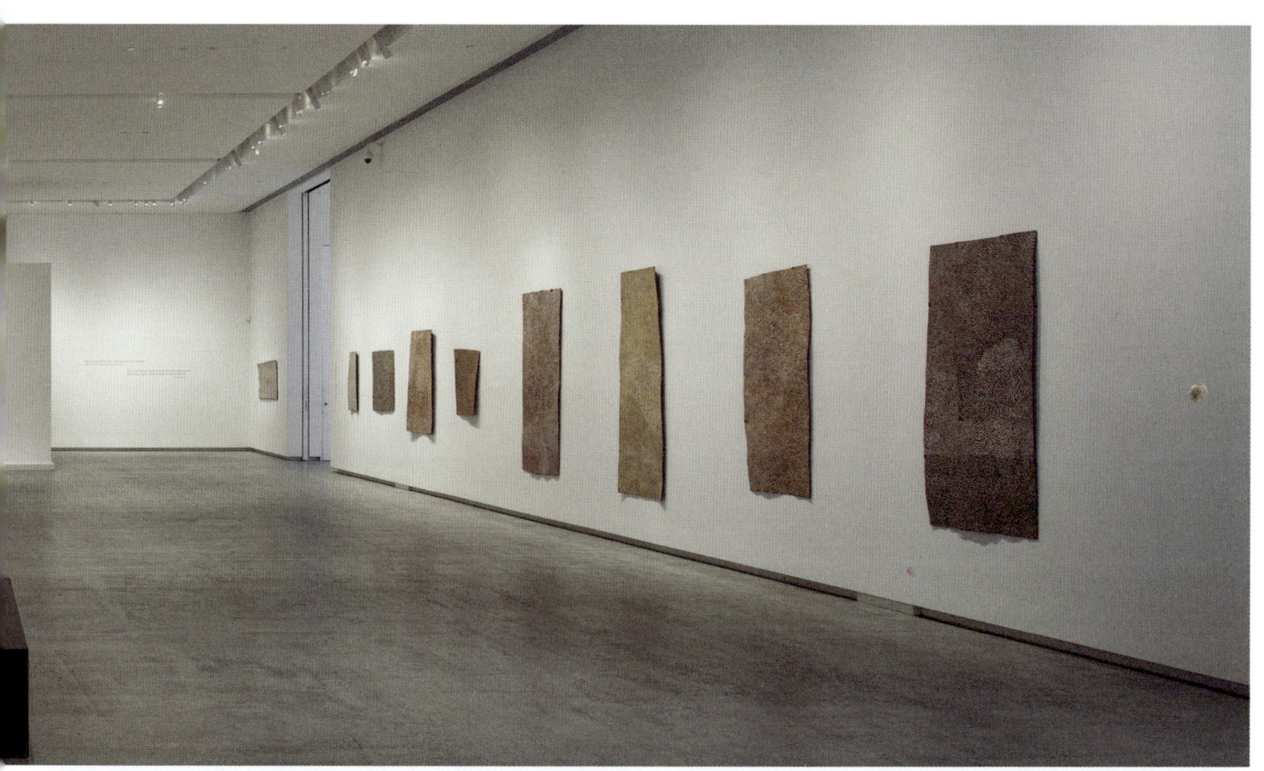

VISITOR INFORMATION

Children are always welcome and specially tailored children's activity sheets are available for each exhibition. The museum provides disabled car parking and easy access to all galleries.

**Admission Fees:** Adult/Senior/Concession: $7.50/$5/free (includes pensioners, students, children under 16 years). The entry prices are subject to change for each exhibition

**Tours and other Events:** TarraWarra Museum of Art organises stimulating public programs, workshops and lectures as well as the TarraWarra Festival, which features the stunning Australian Chamber Orchestra.

**Access by car:** The drive from Melbourne's CBD to TarraWarra takes about one hour without traffic. Take the Eastern Highway to the M3. Keep right to continue on the M3, follow signs for the Doncaster/Eastern Freeway, take the Ringwood Bypass exit towards Route 62/Ringwood, continue onto Ringwood Bypass/State Route 62, turn left onto Maroondah Hwy/State Route 34 (signs for Maroondah Hwy/Lilydale), turn left onto Victoria Road, which becomes Macintyre Lane and turn left onto the Melba Hwy/Yarra

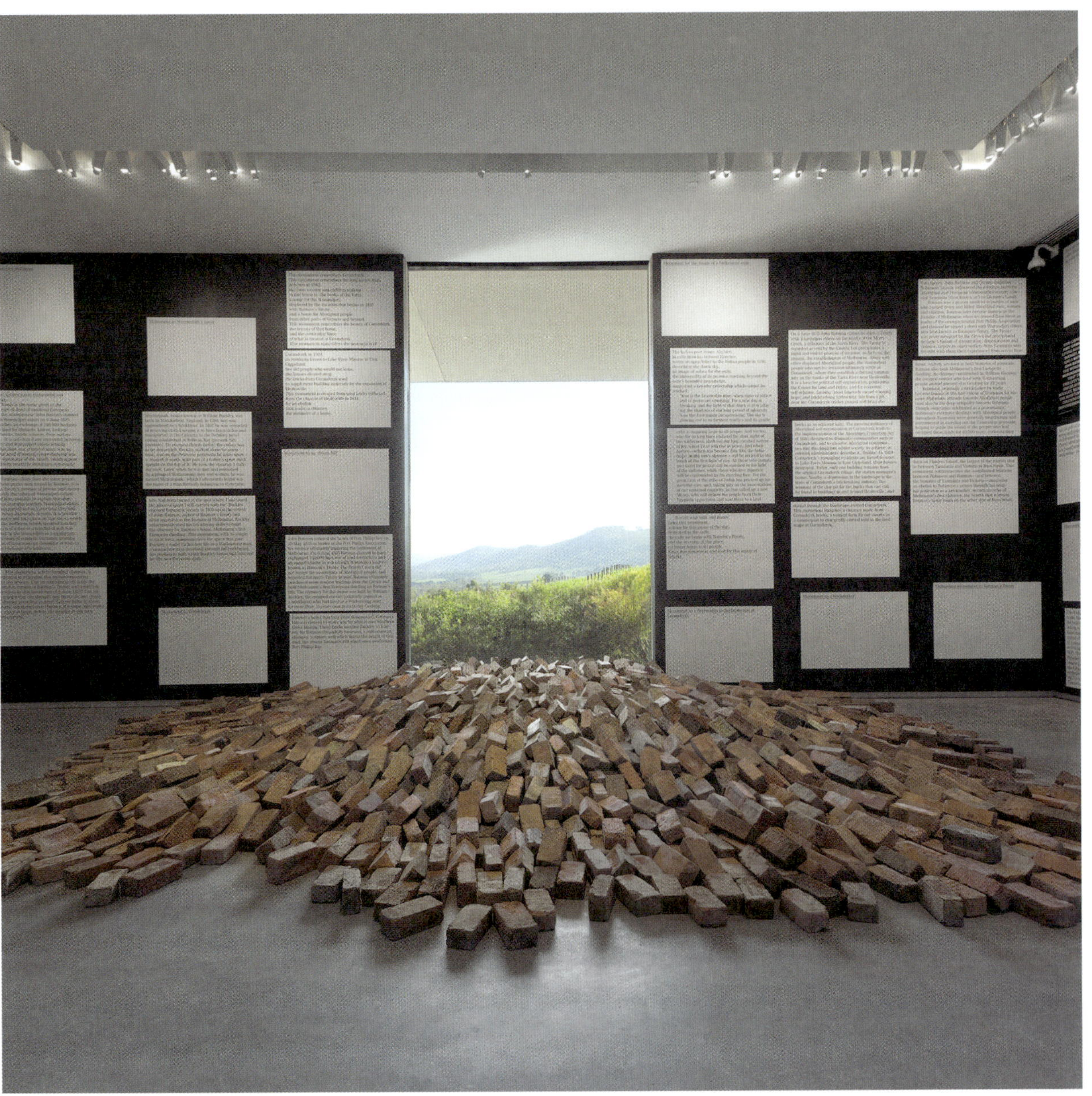

Glen Road/B300. At the roundabout, take the 2nd exit onto the Healesville–Yarra Glen Road/B300/C726 and again take the 2nd exit at the roundabout onto Healesville–Yarra Glen Road/C726 to find the driveway to TarraWarra on your right-hand side. Melway ref. 277 B2.

**Access by public transport:** Take the train from Flinders Street Railway Station to Lilydale Railway Station and then take Bus 685 towards Healesville via Yarra Glen. Ask the bus driver to drop you at the TarraWarra Museum of Art.

**Extra Tips:** Art also plays an important role at the nearby Yering Station winery. The Cellar Door and Matt's Bar upstairs are home to rotating exhibitions. An added dimension of art on the property occurs with the annual Yering Station Sculpture Exhibition and Awards, which take place each spring. Visitors are encouraged to explore the grounds and architecture in search of the creatively installed works (38 Melba Highway, Yarra Glen).

Visitors to Australia might want to plan for a stop at Healesville Sanctuary, which is world-renowned as the best place to see Australian wildlife in its natural habitat (Badger Creek Road, Healesville). A visit to TarraWarra can be easily combined with a trip to the Heide Museum of Art (refer to page 66).

**Restaurant Tips:** The Yarra Valley is renowned as a premier food and wine district with dozens of cellar doors and restaurants serving fresh local produce. Nearby attractive Healesville offers several excellent café and restaurant options. The Yarra Valley Harvest enterprise owns the prominent Healesville Hotel (256 Maroondah Highway), the Harvest Café next door, as well as the atmospheric delicatessen Kitchen & Butcher (258 Maroondah Highway). More adventurous gastronomes might want to head to the end of the village to visit Innocent Bystander, a pumping winery, coffee roasting house, restaurant, wine bar,artisan bakery and cheese room (336 Maroondah Highway).

Page 72
TarraWarra Museum of Art
Photograph Redfish Bluefish Photographic

Pages 74-5
'TarraWarra Biennial 2012: Sonic Spheres', installation view, TarraWarra Museum of Art, 2012
Courtesy the artists and Anna Schwartz Gallery
Photograph John Brash

Page 76
Tom Nicholson, *Towards a monument to Batman's Treaty*, 2008-13
101 A0 sheets pasted to the museum wall, 3456 used bricks collected by citizens in and around Healesville
Courtesy the artist and Milani Gallery
Photograph Christian Capurro

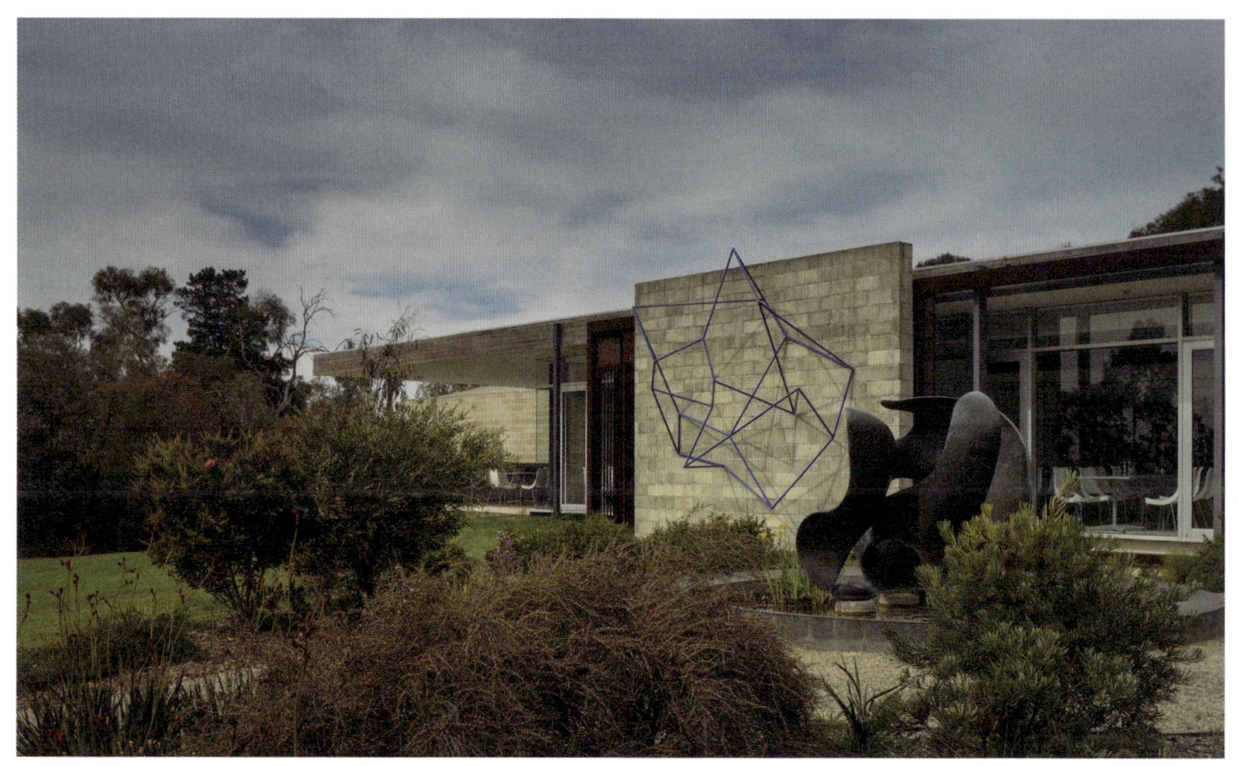

# MCCLELLAND SCULPTURE PARK + GALLERY

390 McClelland Drive
Langwarrin, VIC 3910

OPENING HOURS
Tuesday–Sunday 10am–5pm
(closed Mondays and some public holidays)

Telephone: +61 (03) 9789 1671
info@mcclellandgallery.com
mcclellandgallery.com

Australia's leading sculpture park is set in 16 hectares of coastal bushland in Langwarrin, 43 kilometres south of Melbourne, at the gateway to Victoria's beautiful Mornington Peninsula. McClelland is unique in Australia in many ways. Registered as a not-for-profit organisation, it is independently governed by the terms of a will and mainly funded through private donations.

The location that is now McClelland Sculpture Park + Gallery was originally known as Studio Park and is the site of Harry McClelland's 'country' painting studio. The simple stone building from the 1940s is still to be found in the grounds today but is open to the public only for special educational events. Harry McClelland (1887–1954) is from the generation of Australian artists now known collectively as 'The Gum Tree School'. Harry and his sister Annie May (Nan) moved to Long Island, Frankston with their mother Elizabeth McClelland in 1912. By the 1920s, they had established themselves as the centre of a bohemian group of creative personalities drawn from all strata of Victoria's social life. In 1969, Nan bequeathed the property and her estate in honour of her brother's memory and this led to the establishment of the McClelland Gallery in 1971.

The development of the gallery and park has been strongly associated with the outstanding artistic patronage of Dame Elisabeth Murdoch AC DBE (1909–2012) whose residence was the nearby Cruden Farm. In 1989, the creation of the Elisabeth Murdoch Sculpture Foundation acted as a catalyst for the acquisition and commission of sculptures and the establishment of a serious outdoor collection. Dame Elisabeth summed up her philosophy of life in an inscription at the start of the 1 kilometre long Elisabeth Murdoch Walk: 'Giving to the community is one of the most important, rewarding things people can do'. She remained a regular visitor and could be frequently seen lunching in the café even during her later years.

Ranging from Roman statues to quirky interactive contemporary artworks, over 100 sculptures by major Australian and a few international sculptors are permanently displayed in the original 8-hectare area of the property. The earliest sculptures in the outdoor collection, which are located on the back wall of the gallery building, are by artist William Charles Scurry (1862–1930). The works *Untitled (three allegorical figures)* from 1887 were originally commissioned for the lobby of the Federal Coffee Palace in Melbourne and were subsequently gifted to McClelland in 1996. A core focus of the outdoor sculpture collection is the representation of the Centre 5 group of artists who established themselves in Melbourne in 1959 to promote contemporary sculpture. Influenced by their knowledge of international art they looked outwards towards abstraction rather than maintaining figurative styles and nationalistic Australian subjects. The group included the sculptors Vincas Jomantas, Julius Kane, Inge King, Clifford Last, Lenton Parr, Norma Redpath and Teisutis Zikaras. Of particular interest here is the significant collection of works by Parr (1924–2003), one of Australia's pre-eminent sculptors working with welded steel.

Alongside acquisitions of the Centre 5 group, McClelland's outdoor collection extends through the representation of various significant periods of Australian sculpture from the 1960s onwards and includes sculptures by Bruce Armstrong, John Kelly, Ken Reinhard, David Wilson, Peter D Cole, Geoffrey Ricardo, Anton McMurray and Richard Goodwin. The biennial McClelland Sculpture Survey & Awards exhibition, initiated in 2003, has become the most important biennial outdoor sculpture exhibition in Australia. It nowadays takes place on the 8 hectares of bushland bought in 2007 and presents up to thirty-five Australian and overseas artists, highlighting the diversity and innovation of contemporary sculpture. Winners of the $100,000 award include Australian artists Lisa Roet, Rick Amor, Louise Paramor, Greg Johns and

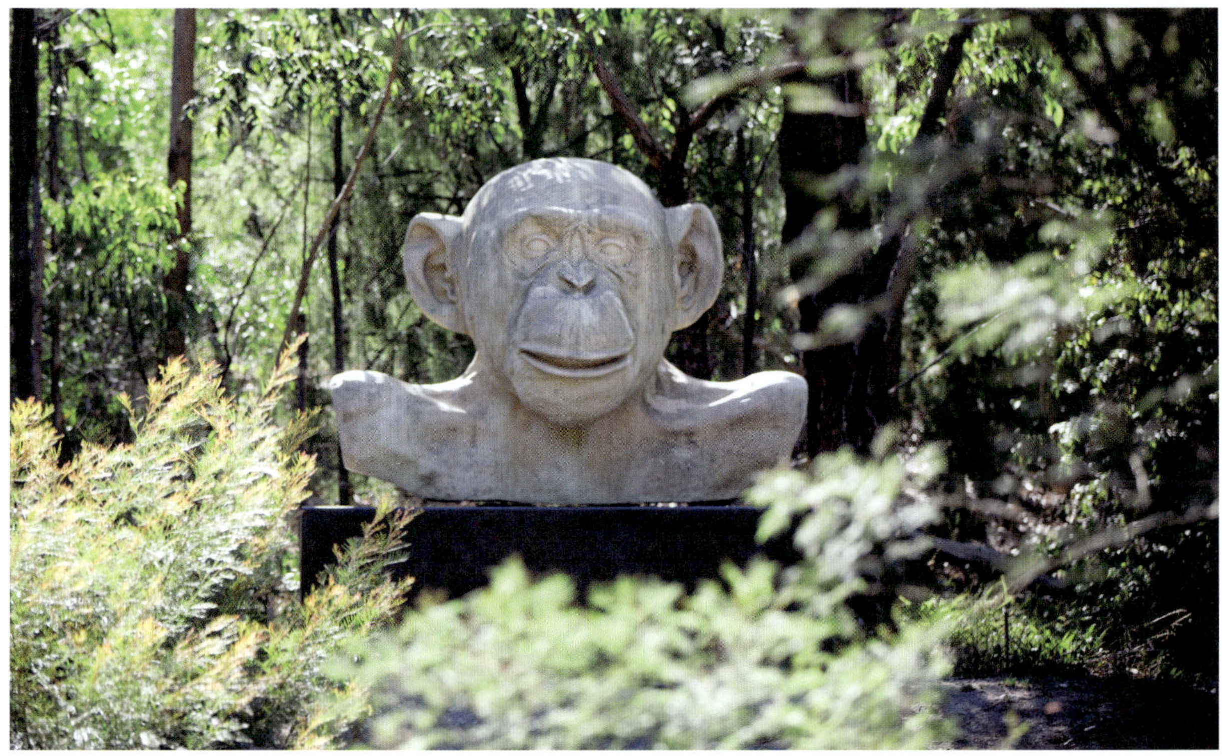

Matthew Harding. There are several additional non-acquisitive prizes, which are awarded as part of the Survey exhibition.

When the McClelland Gallery opened in 1971, its collection consisted of 138 works of art, seventy-one through the bequest of The McClelland Estate, which included thirty-three paintings and drawings by Harry McClelland as well as the 1930 Archibald Prize winning *Portrait of Harry McClelland* by William Beckwith McInnes, with the remaining works gifted by artists and collectors. McClelland's collection now consists of over 2200 works of art, encompassing historical, modern and contemporary sculpture, paintings, photography, works on paper and decorative arts dating from the nineteenth century to the present day. Highlights include paintings by Rupert Bunny, Emanuel Phillips Fox, Hilda Rix Nicholas, Max Meldrum and his followers, and a large collection of works on paper by George Bell and his school. The large majority of works entered the collection through private bequests and donations. Recent acquisitions of major contemporary statements in Australian sculpture include Patricia Piccinini's *Doubting Thomas* and the monumental *Wild man* by Ron Mueck.

The original modernist building from 1971 was altered and extended by Williams Boag Architects in 1999 to facilitate three indoor exhibition spaces. The McClelland Gallery features up to six temporary exhibitions annually of works on paper, photography, paintings and sculptures. One or two of those are usually travelling shows. Curated and travelling exhibitions are exhibited primarily in the Elisabeth Murdoch Gallery (300 square metres) and French Gallery (130 square metres). The McClelland Room is used for smaller exhibitions, which either complement the current exhibitions, or which pertain to the history of the Sculpture Park and Gallery. The team at McClelland constantly manages to impress visitors with high-calibre and well-curated exhibitions despite the space limitations of these galleries, which makes frequent visits worthwhile.

The McClelland Sculpture Park + Gallery and its programs are generously supported by the Elisabeth Murdoch Sculpture Foundation in partnership with The Balnaves Foundation.

## VISITOR INFORMATION

It is advisable to pick up a sculpture map at the information desk in the entrance area of the building. Visitors should allocate at least two hours for their tour around the park and gallery. The park is a great place for kids. Less mobile visitors might want to consider booking ahead for the electric golf buggy, which seats five and includes an experienced tour guide.

**Admission Fees:** Entry by donation

**Tours and other Events:** McClelland offers a range of guided tours, including free tours on Wednesdays and Thursdays at 11am or 2pm (bookings essential) as well as tours of the collection highlights and Survey Trail twilight tours which incur a small fee. McClelland also facilitates innovative educational and public programs, including an Art and Nature program, children's workshops, and artists' lectures.

**Access by car:** McClelland Sculpture Park+Gallery is a 45-minute drive from Melbourne's CBD along the Eastlink/M3 and Peninsula Link Freeway/M11. Turn off at either the Skye Road or Cranbourne–Frankston exits to get to 390 McClelland Drive.

Starting in Frankston, drive east on Fletcher Road, turn left onto Beach Street, turn half left onto Cranbourne Road/State Route 4 and once again turn left onto McClelland Drive. The Sculpture Park is on the right-hand side. Free parking is available on-site. Melway ref. 103 E3.

**Access by public transport:** There are frequent trains from Southern Cross Railway Station or Flinders Street Station to Frankston Railway Station. In Frankston, take Bus 789 towards Langwarrin or 790 towards Cranbourne West from platform 9. Get off at the corner of McClelland Drive and

Cranbourne/Frankston Road. From here, it is a 15-minute walk north up along McClelland Drive. One can avoid the walk by opting for the following, less frequent option: Take Bus 789 as above, get off at Karingal Shopping Centre, take bus 777 to McClelland Sculpture Park. A taxi ride from the Frankston Railway Station will cost around $15.

**Extra Tips:** Attentive drivers can already enjoy stunning sculptures en route to McClelland. As part of the biennial Southern Way McClelland Commissions, every two years until 2037 one new sculpture will be commissioned to alternate between sites at Skye Road and Cranbourne Road, along the new Peninsula Link Freeway. After a four-year cycle of display on the Peninsula Link Freeway these commissions will form part of McClelland's permanent sculpture collection. The inaugural Southern Way McClelland Commissions were awarded to Australian sculptor Dean Colls and New Zealand artist Phil Price. Price's large-scale, wind-activated kinetic sculpture, *The tree of life* was replaced by Gregor Kregar's *Reflective lullaby* in April 2015. It is equally impossible to overlook the work *Panorama station*, which is permanently located on the Peninsula Link at the EastLink interchange. This work, by Louise Paramor, was awarded by the Peninsula Link Sculpture Commission.

A visit to McClelland can be easily combined with a trip to Montalto Vineyard (refer to page 82). On the way, one might want to consider a brief visit to the small but enchanting Mornington Peninsula Regional Gallery, which presents a changing program of contemporary and historical exhibitions (Civic Reserve, Dunns Road, Mornington).

Garden enthusiasts will feel inspired by the beauty and diversity of more than 170,000 individual native plants at the award-winning Royal Botanical Garden Cranbourne (corner Ballarto Road and Botanic Drive (off the South Gippsland Freeway), Cranbourne).

**Restaurant Tips:** The upmarket McClelland Gallery Café offers seasonal menus during the park's opening hours; bookings highly recommended. The park includes many inviting picnic areas (no open fires or barbeques allowed).

Page 78
McClelland Sculpture Park + Gallery
Photograph John Gollings

Page 80
Lisa Roet *White ape*, 2005
Fibreglass and Cor-ten steel, 310 x 300 x 150 cm
Photograph Mark Chew

Right
Terrance Plowright, *Tubular resonance*, 2012
Stainless steel and sound, 430 x 252 x 231 cm
Photograph John Gollings

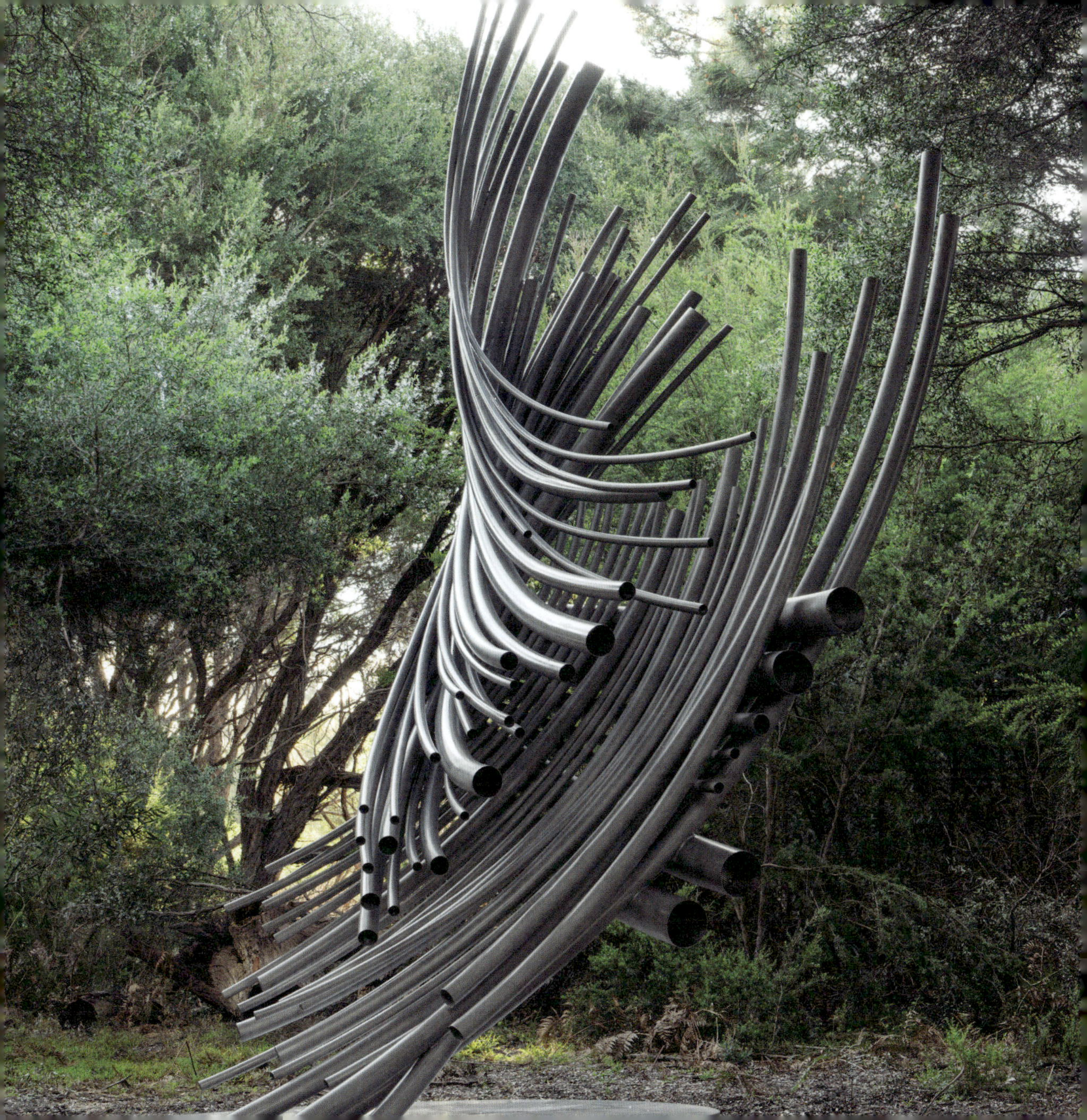

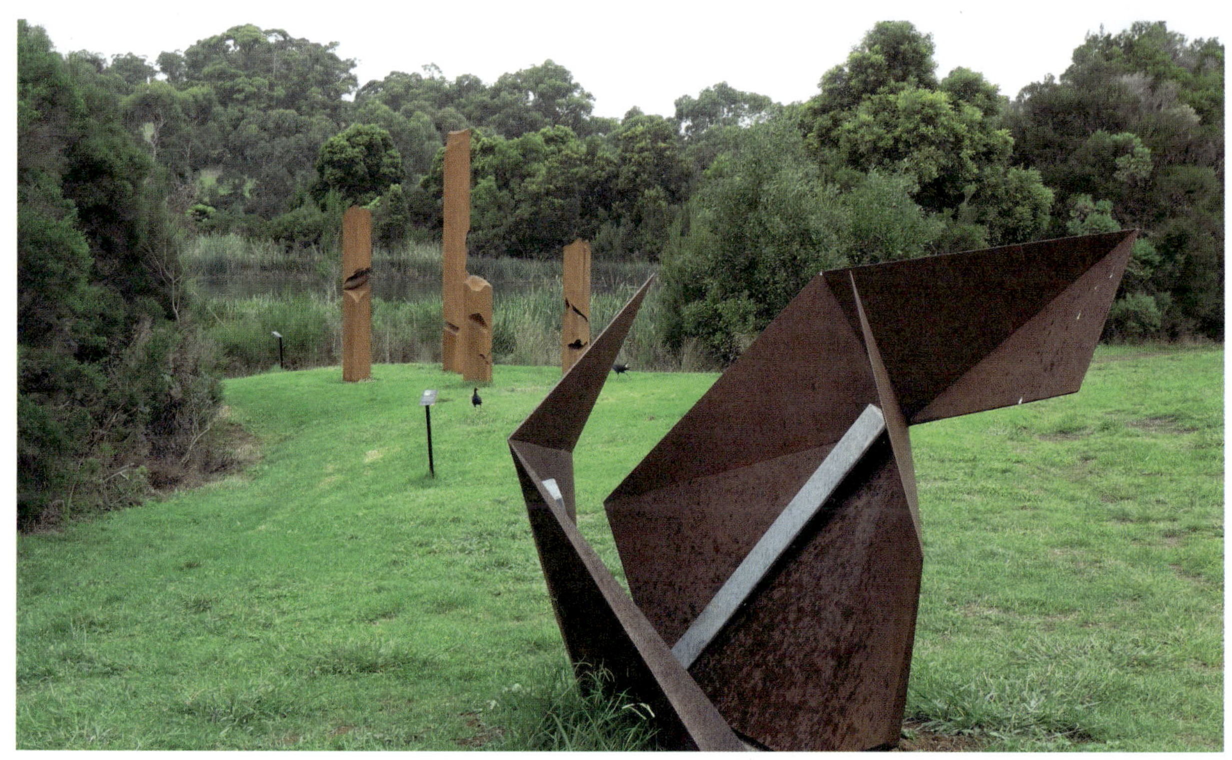

# MONTALTO VINEYARD + OLIVE GROVE

33 Shoreham Road
Red Hill South, VIC 3937

OPENING HOURS
Daily 11am–5pm

Telephone: +61 (03) 5989 8412
info@montalto.com.au
montalto.com.au/sculpture

Montalto is the quintessential wine, food and art travel experience on Victoria's attractive Mornington Peninsula. The family-owned business is the successful result of a family retirement project. During his years as a food industry executive, John Mitchell lived in the United Kingdom and spent many holidays in the south of France where he and his family were captivated by the sight of vineyards growing on hills that sloped towards the sea. Seeing similarities in the landscape of the family's property at Merricks, John decided to plant a few vines after he retired. Hobby soon turned to passion and when the right opportunity arose, in 1997, he purchased the first 10 hectares and in the following year the adjoining 10 hectares of the beautiful Red Hill South site. The idea for the Montalto Vineyard & Olive Grove crystallised and the Mitchells instructed Williams and Boag Architects to design a contemporary building as a recessive element in the rural landscape. The resulting complex, which was opened in 2002, is a well-integrated low-scale form made from natural materials, which overlooks the vineyard previously established on the land, as well as the thoughtfully planted vegetable garden.

The Montalto sculpture collection on the property is the product of John and Wendy Mitchell's desire to combine their passion for the arts with their love of nature. Having swapped ideas with artist friend Andrew Rogers, they created the first Montalto Sculpture Prize show in 2003. Acquiring a new work each year through the prize, plus some carefully chosen additional pieces, has provided Montalto with an interesting permanent collection of twenty-five contemporary sculptures. The collection holds works by Australian artists such as Sebastian Di Mauro, Marcus Tatton, Andrew Rogers, Jon Dixon, John Kelly, Phillip Doggett-Williams, Michael Needham and David Waters as well as by well-known New Zealand sculptor Hannah Kidd. The diverse sculptures are sensitively sited throughout the Montalto grounds. Monumental works are situated in open spaces; more intimate pieces need to be discovered among the natural wetlands, gardens and vines. From mid-February through to the end of April, this permanent collection is joined by at least another twenty-five works which form the annual Montalto Sculpture Prize. This $30,000 acquisitive award is open to all artists working in any medium. All artworks of this annual temporary show, other than the winning sculpture, are for sale.

VISITOR INFORMATION

Checking in at the cellar door prior to the walk is advisable. The trail is about 1 kilometre and suitable for most ages and abilities. The grounds are undulating, and reasonably steep in sections; there are benches dotted along the walk. Walking shoes, and gumboots through the wet winter period, are recommended. The trail is manageable with off-road children's strollers. Unfortunately, the trail is not suitable for wheelchairs, however with advanced notice Montalto can arrange transport to various sections of the trail.

**Admission Fees:** No entry fee

**Access by car:** Leave Melbourne east on the M1, take the exit onto Eastlink/M3 towards Frankston, take the exit onto the Mornington Peninsula Freeway/M11, take the C787 exit towards Red Hill/Flinders, turn left onto the Nepean Highway/B110/C787, at the roundabout, take the 1st exit onto White Hill Road/C787/C788, turn left onto Arthurs Seat Road, turn right onto Red Hill Road and you will see Montalto signposted on the left hand-side after 4.3 km. Melway ref. 256 B2.

**Extra Tips:** Wine connoisseurs might want to visit the Mornington Peninsula during the Winter Wine Weekend, which gives visitors the fabulous opportunity to sample the best wines from the region at the Red Hill Reserve and Showgrounds and at over 50 Cellar Doors (Arthurs Seat Road, Red Hill).

A visit to Montalto can be easily combined with a trip to McClelland Sculpture Park + Gallery (refer to page 78) or an appointment at Elgee Park (refer to page 88).

**Restaurant Tips:** Guests can enjoy fantastic wines and regional French and modern Australian food at the chef's hat rated Montalto Restaurant, casual dining at the European-inspired alfresco Piazza Café (on weekends and public holidays only) and upmarket catered picnics at selected locations on the Montalto estate during the summer months (booking is essential). The renowned Montalto wine varieties and olive products can be tasted at the Cellar Door. The cosy Pier Provedore serves delightful homemade café food (38 Cook Street, Flinders; open 8.30am–5pm, Tuesdays and Wednesdays closed). Chocoholics might want to visit the nearby Mornington Peninsula Chocolates, a small manufacturer of award winning chocolates (45 Cook Street, Flinders; closed Tuesdays and Wednesdays). Cheese addicts might prefer a visit to the Main Ridge Dairy, a renowned farmhouse cheese factory and goat dairy (295 Main Creek Road, Main Ridge; open Thursday–Sunday).

Page 84 and right
All images courtesy Montalto Vineyard & Olive Grove

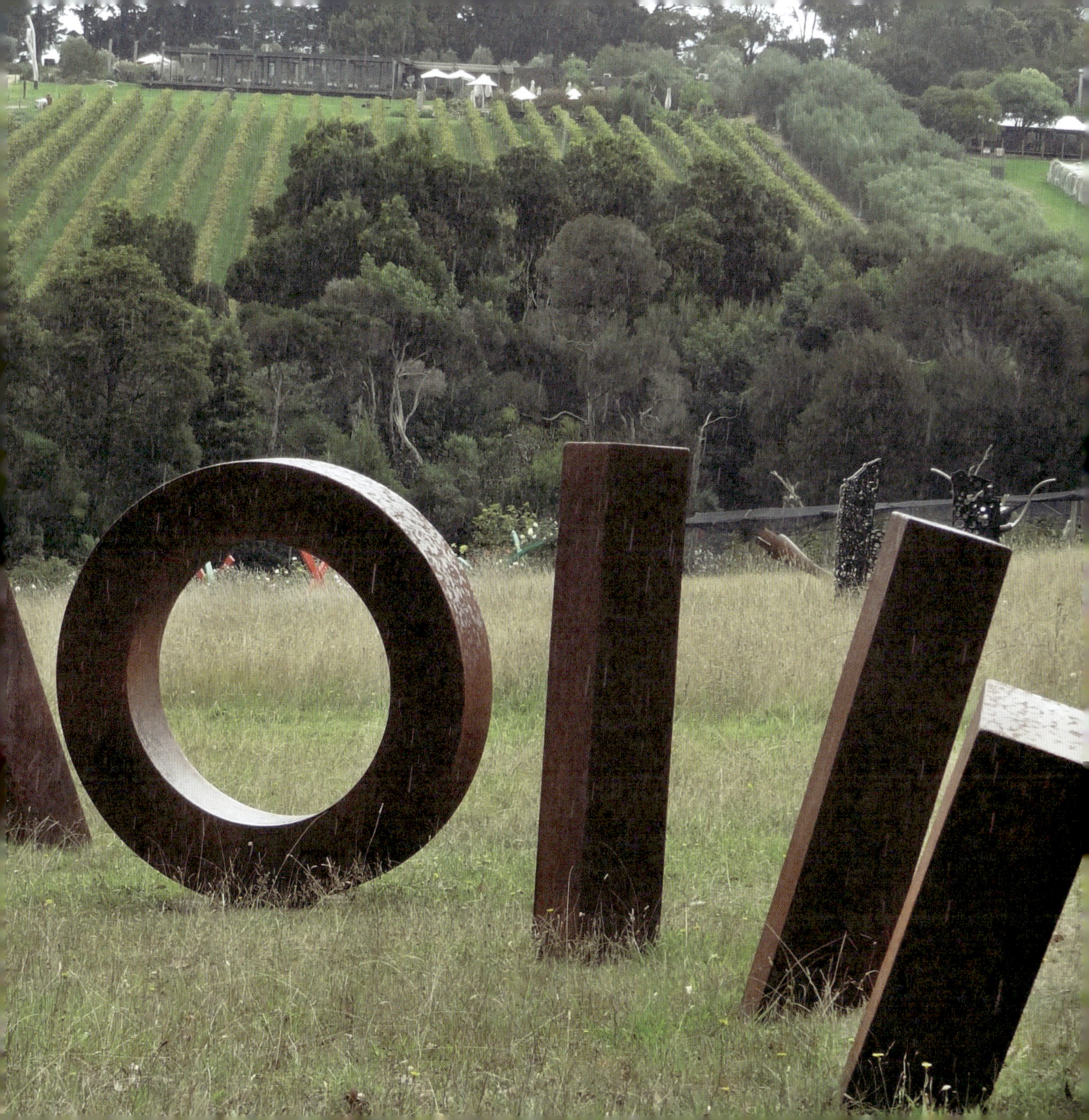

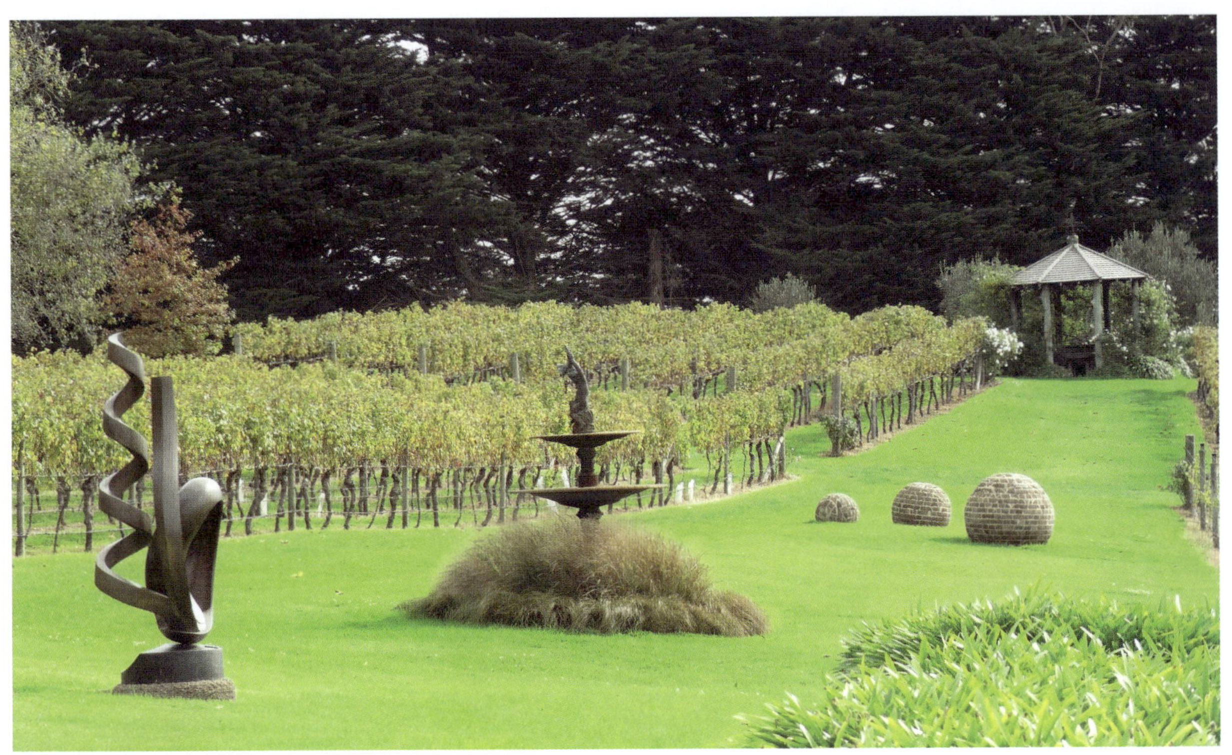

# ELGEE PARK

24 Junction Road
Merricks North, VIC 3926
Please note, the entrance to the property is via Wallaces Road, Dromana, off the Nepean Highway

OPENING HOURS
By appointment only
Art groups are preferred

Telephone: +61 (03) 5989 7338
elgee@pac.com.au
elgeeparkwines.com.au

Elgee Park is the oldest vineyard on the Mornington Peninsula and also the home of the earliest major private sculpture collection in Australia. Art benefactor Baillieu (Bails) Myer AC and his wife Sarah Myer have seen the fulfilment of their vision, initiated in 1972 when they planted their first vines and some years later installed their first sculptures. The picturesque vineyard was formerly part of a cattle paddock that surrounded the house and garden, but was soon extended to 5 hectares and incorporated into the garden.

Myer's first venture into collecting started in the 1980s when he purchased Australian paintings with Georges Mora of the Tolarno Gallery as his adviser. After 1992, when the Myer Collection was donated to the Museum of Modern Art at Heide (nowadays called Heide Museum of Modern Art) Myer, together with his nephew Carrillo Gantner AO, turned his attention to contemporary Aboriginal art. After donating virtually all these works to public collections by 2002, Australian sculpture became his main focus as a collector. Myer's interest in sculpture had begun when a sculpture by Stanley Hammond originally commissioned in 1960 for a Myer shopping complex at Chadstone was erected at Elgee Park in 1986. Titled *Commerce*, it can still be found next to the winery building. Works by David Wilson, Lenton Parr, Geoffrey Bartlett and Inge King followed soon after. The collection now consists of over eighty-five works, ranging from sculptures that were bought at blue-chip galleries in Australia to an artwork found at the local Red Hill market. With very few exceptions, Myer acquires the sculptures from living artists, whether through commissions or exhibition purchases. The friendships he develops with artists and the processes of commissioning and positioning the works often bring as much joy to the Myer family as the sculptures themselves. About fifty sculptures are situated in diverse positions throughout the gardens, paddocks and hilltops and around dams and buildings on the 322–hectare property. In 2015 artist Simon Normand installed the Elgee Park Labyrinth dedicated to the Boonwurrung people of the Mornington Peninsula and the men of the region who fought in the First World War.

Sculptural works surround visitors as soon as they park the car. The newly sawn surfaces of Roman Liebach's weathered timber sculpture *Silent chorus* immediately invite touch. Myer first saw this impressive installation when it was displayed at the McClelland Sculpture Survey & Awards exhibition in 2003. Close by is a range of works by Geoff Harvey, Greg Johns, Inge King and Simon Normand, among others. From the winery buildings the collection spreads alongside the vineyards, around the gardens, down to the dam and along the Junction Road exit route. The house garden delights with more intricate works, such as a small stone carving by Valda Cuming or Ashika Marek Ostapkowicz's subtle fountain. Next to the garden one can find a small, powerful sculpture by Clement Meadmore, the playful installation *Brick balls* by David Howell, and an abstract work by Andrew Rogers. Turning towards the small lake, works by Ron Robertson-Swann and Robert Hague, together with other sculptures, materialise. Two gates lead into the fenced area around the dam. A bench designed by Grant Featherston, which was originally made for the Sidney Myer Music Bowl in 1957, invites visitors to enjoy the exotic mix of local bush, planted natives, European willows, water-irises and climbing roses. A footbridge leads to a small wooden island, which is the home of the welded steel sculpture *Dream of India* by David Wilson. In the distance, on the other side of the lake, the gorgeous wooden artwork *Spires* by Christabel Wigley grabs attention. Instead of walking back up to the main house, visitors might consider taking the path eastwards in the direction of the Junction Highway exit to view David Long's monumental stone structure *Revolution* on the crest of the hill. Walking along the track back to the winery and the car, this fascinating sculpture trail concludes with *Castlemaine slate* by renowned New Zealand artist Chris Booth.

VISITOR INFORMATION

A visit to Elgee Park is possible by appointment only. Art groups are preferred.

**Admission Fees:** No entry fee

**Access by car:** Leave Melbourne east on the M1, take the exit onto Eastlink/M3 towards Frankston, take the exit onto the Mornington Peninsula Freeway/M11, take the C787 exit towards Red Hill/Flinders, turn left onto the Nepean Highway/B110/C787 and watch out for the Elgee Park Winery sign on the left-hand side. Turn left again onto the unsealed Wallaces Road. The entrance is 3.5 km up on the right-hand side. Please park in front of the first building.

**Extra Tips:** Less than 18 km away, the Gandel family plans to develop the Point Leo Estate Restaurant, Cellar Door & Sculpture Park, which is set within vineyards and boasts amazing views to the seascapes of Western Port Bay. The park will display over forty major contemporary sculptures by prominent Australian artists such as Inge King, Greg Johns, Lenton Parr and Geoffrey Bartlett (Frankston–Flinders Road, Merricks).

A visit to Elgee Park can easily be combined with a trip to Montalto Vineyard & Olive Grove (refer to page 84) and to McClelland Sculpture Park + Gallery (refer to page 78).

**Restaurant Tips:** Located in a beautiful heritage building, the atmospheric Merricks General Wine Store serves delicious country food. It also functions as the Cellar Door for Elgee Park, Baillieu & Quealy wines (3460 Frankston–Flinders Road, Merricks; daily 8.30am–5pm). The nearby Port Phillip Estate was honoured with several architectural awards for its striking, ultra-modern building. The upmarket Dining Room and the Cellar Door Bistro are renowned for their food and wine (263 Red Hill Road, Red Hill). Foxeys Hangout's cellar door offers informal lunches in a casual and rambunctious atmosphere (795 White Hill Road, Red Hill).

Page 88 and right
All images courtesy Elgee Park

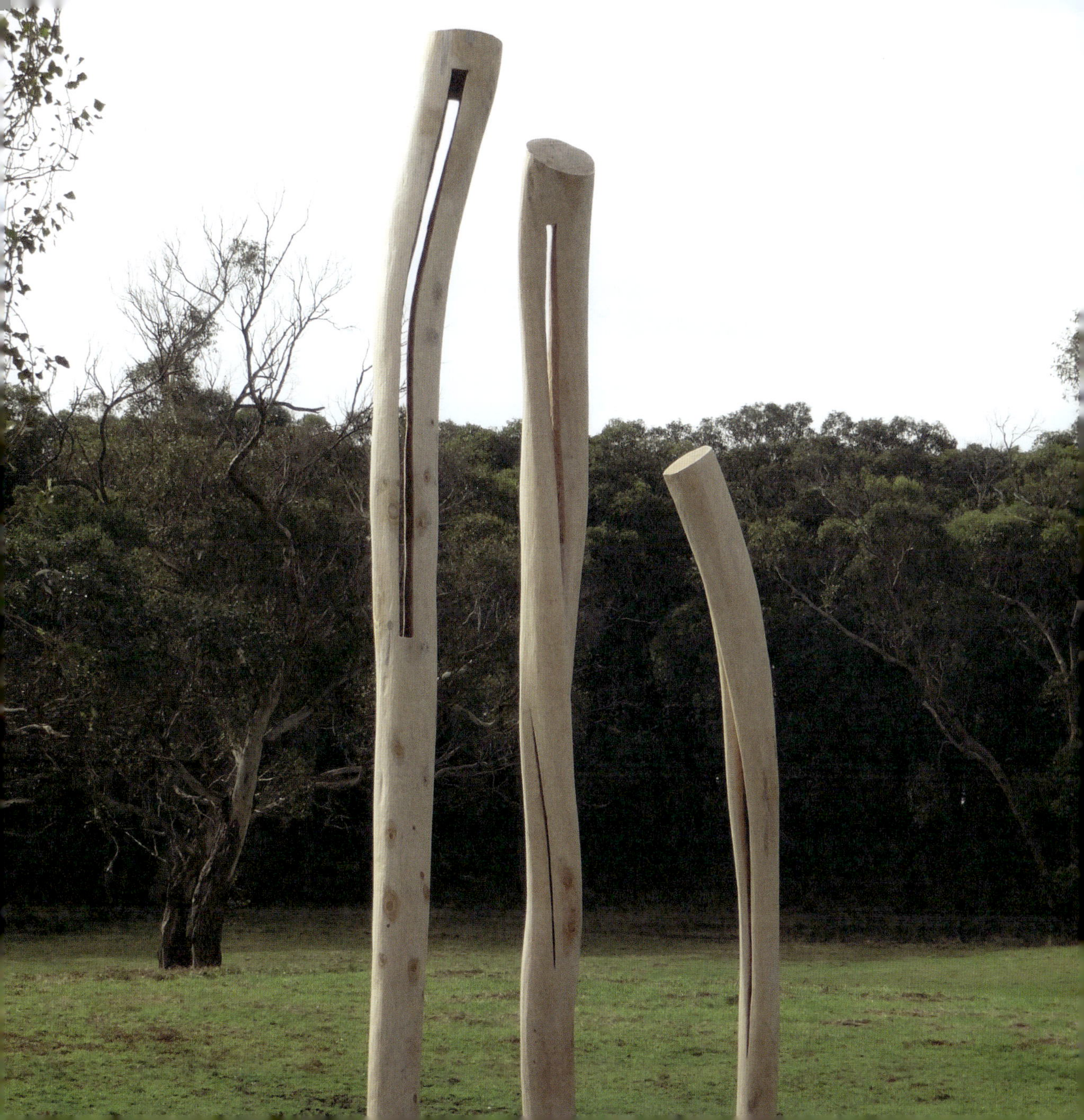

# SOUTH AUSTRALIA

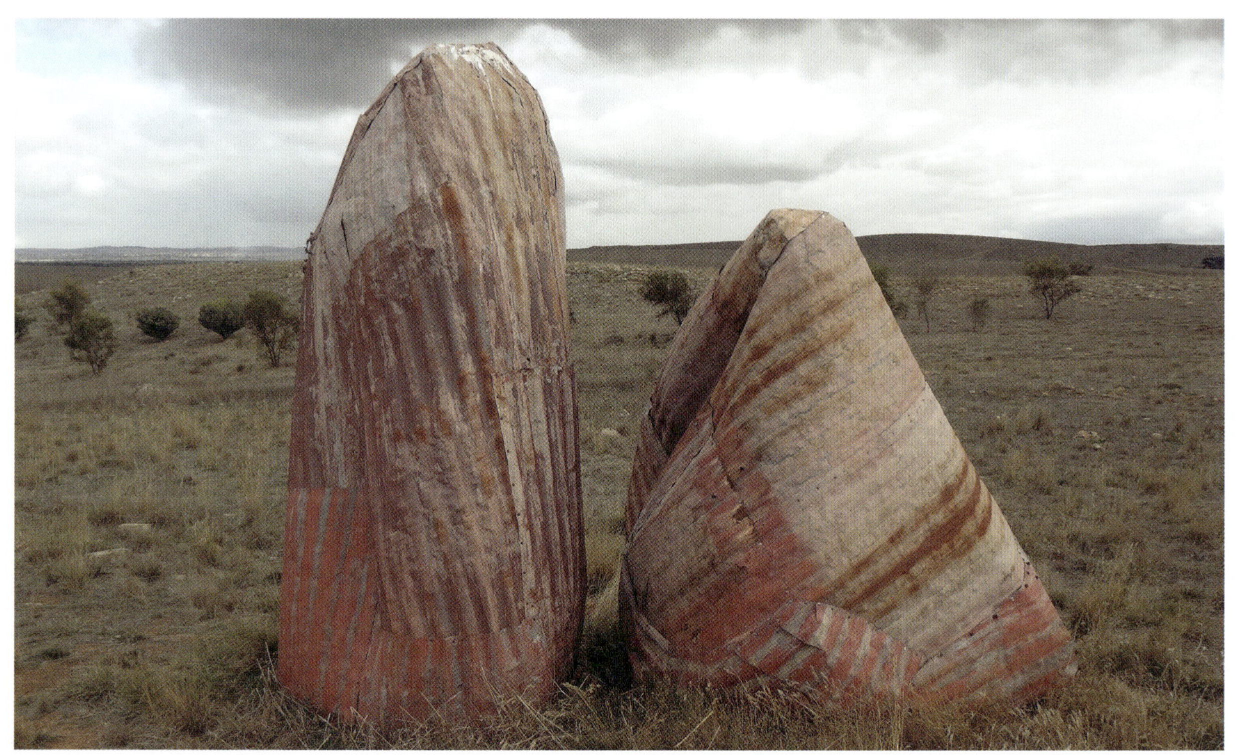

# PALMER SCULPTURE LANDSCAPE

372 Davenport Road
Palmer, SA 5237
(3.5 km from the Palmer Hotel, Main Road, Palmer, SA 5237,
+61 (08) 8569 4054)

OPENING HOURS
Daily 11am–5pm

Telephone: +61 (08) 8278 3273
gjoh4899@bigpond.net.au
gregjohnssculpture.com
palmersculpturebiennial.org

The renowned Adelaide sculptor Greg Johns bought an abandoned former sheep-grazing property at Palmer in 2001. It is situated in the rain-shadow country of the Adelaide Hills, about 70 kilometres east of South Australia's capital. Since then, Johns and a few like-minded individuals have been revegetating 163 hectares of this bare-boned environment while also carefully selecting and placing sculptures that engage with what is an archetypal Australian landscape. This extraordinary property reflects the steadily evolving linkages between art and environmental sustainability.

Johns's main intention at Palmer is to create a 'sculpture landscape' rather than an artificially constructed 'sculpture park' by animating the landscape with works that are quintessentially Australian. His work addresses the interconnectedness of all life by including elements of contemporary physics, mythology and the spirit. The thirty sculptures he has placed at Palmer since 2002 clearly demonstrate this approach. Johns's work is not 'environmental sculpture' as such; it is born from a deeper symbolic reading of place, resulting in forms that have a guardian feel about them. Looking at the peaceful, grazing kangaroos in this exciting 'natural theatre of art', visitors cannot avoid being touched by his endeavour.

Unrestricted by man-made obstacles, visitors are invited to view Johns's carefully placed sculptures from afar: what first appears as a dot on the horizon often turns out to be a massive Cor-ten steel sculpture when seen up close. Any sense of proportion and time seems to get lost in this otherworldly landscape, which offers amazing views from the top of the escarpment to the distant Murray River. It is hard to imagine that this land once was covered by casuarina trees, stripped away by early nineteenth-century European settlers to power the local gold and copper mines.

An 'understory' of work by eight other artists also exists on the property. These works are mostly environmental in nature and, unlike Johns's mainly large-scale sculpture, tend to be more at ground level. Deb Sleeman's *Mortal wound*, a rusting corrugated iron sculpture of two boulders, was created at Palmer and purchased by Johns in 2006. One can also find sculptures by David Kerr, Evette Sunset, Gavin Malone, Mal Waas, Ted Jonsson, Matthew Harding and André Lloyd Lawrence.

Since 2004, Greg Johns has made Palmer available on a biennial basis for an exhibition of sculpture by other artists who wish to relate to the Australian landscape. Nine artists, among them Max Lyle and the recently deceased Bert Flugelman, exhibited in the inaugural exhibition. By 2014, the numbers had grown to twenty-three Australian and international artists. Each exhibition runs for two weeks. As part of the event, there is also the Palmer Sculpture Prize. In contrast to its more famous and commercially oriented counterparts, the exhibiting artists at Palmer vote for the winner. The prize comes in the form of a small sculpture by Greg Johns, a cash prize and an Artist's Residency in another Australian state.

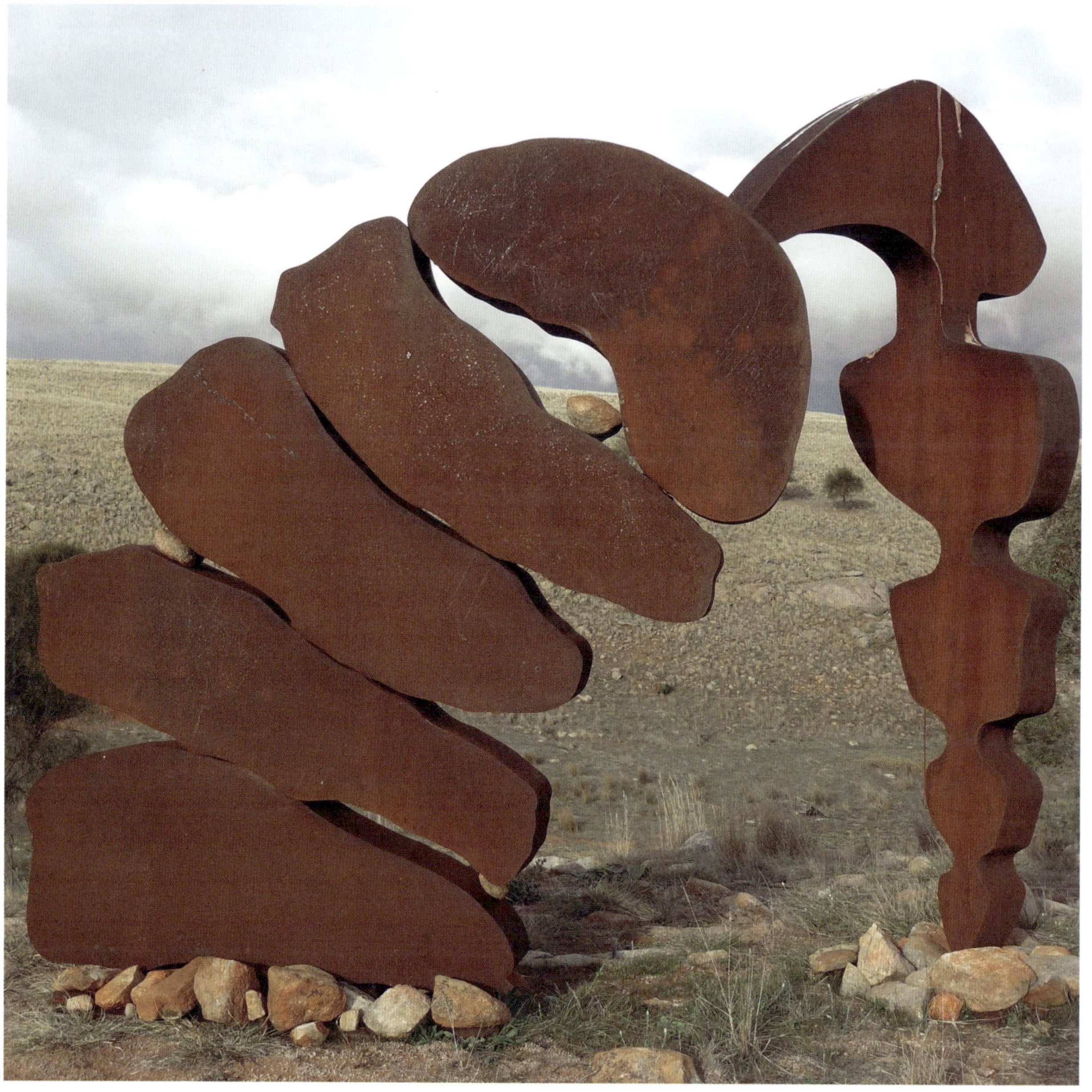

## VISITOR INFORMATION

Visitors are asked to check in and out at the Palmer Hotel (Main Road, Palmer, SA 5237, + 61 (08) 8569 4054), located 3.5 km from Palmer Sculpture Landscape. No cars to be taken onto the property. Appropriate walking shoes, headwear and clothing must be worn. It is highly recommended to take bottled drinking water and a mobile phone on site. There are no walking trails on the property and the trek over stony ground is difficult at times. Please refrain from leaving any rubbish behind. Smoking is strictly prohibited.

**Admission Fees:** There is no charge for entry but donations (to be left at the Palmer Hotel) are welcome for the environmental care of the property

**Access by car:** Take the first road on the left when entering Palmer, opposite the Palmer Hotel. Travel 3.5 km along the road; the property is on the right-hand side. The entrance is next to a grass tree. Please park outside of the gate.

**Extra Tips:** A visit to one of South Australia's historic and artistic treasures, The Cedars, the estate of Hans Heysen, is well worth seeing. The private family collection reveals Hans Heysen's versatility in subject and medium as well as his daughter Nora Heysen's artistic talent (Heysen Road, Hahndorf). During April 2016, visitors will, for the third time, have the opportunity to observe sculptors at work in the parkland of The Cedars. Communities in the Adelaide Hills and the Fleurieu Peninsula have commissioned eight Australian and international artists at each Adelaide Hills International Sculpture Symposium to create sculptures for their respective district. By the second part of 2016, twenty-four sculptures will form a permanent Sculpture Trail throughout the region.

**Restaurant Tips:** The 'German' village of Hahndorf can be overcrowded and borders on being kitsch in places, but features a large variety of restaurants and cafés, which are ideal to break the journey from Adelaide to Palmer. At Chocolate @ No. 5 the hot chocolate is frequently rated as the best in South Australia (5 Main Street, Hahndorf).

Page 96
Deb Sleeman, *Mortal wound*, 2006
Discarded corrugated iron tank, wire

Left
Greg Johns, *Merging-emerging figure*, 2011
Cor-ten steel, 240 x 240 x 120 cm

All images courtesy Palmer Sculpture Landscape

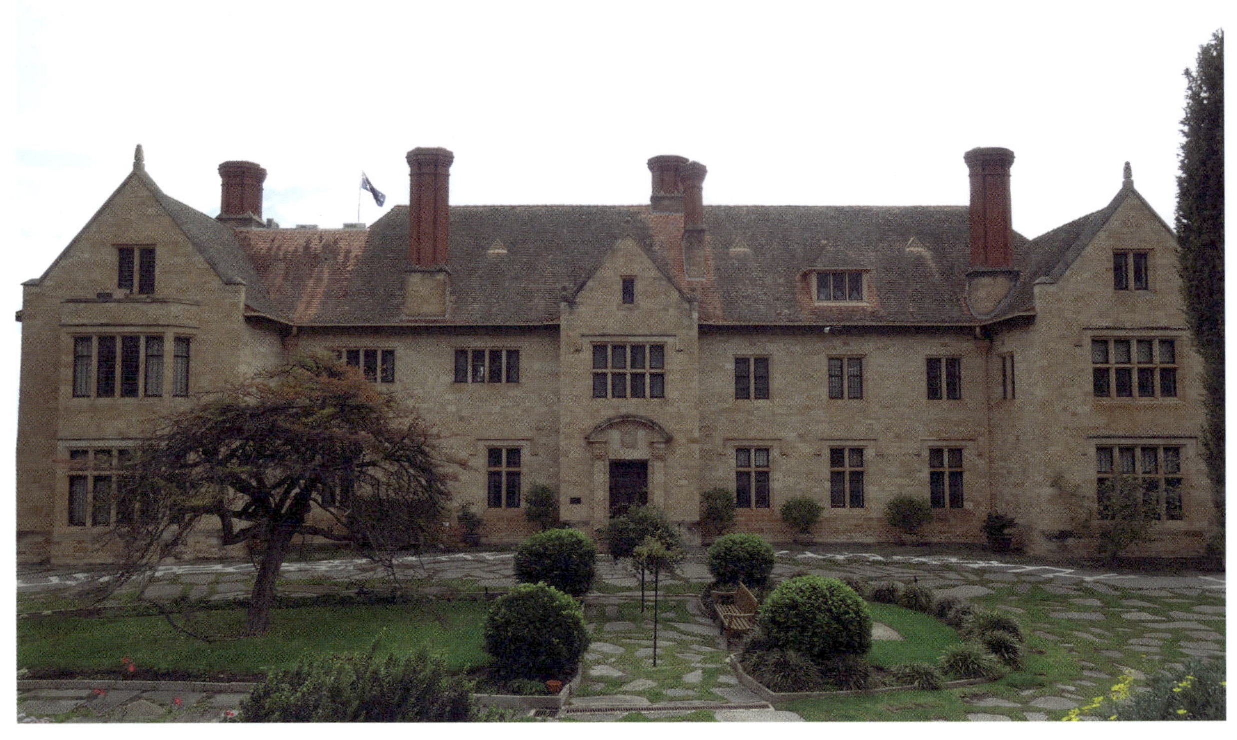

# CARRICK HILL

46 Carrick Hill Drive
Springfield, SA 5062

OPENING HOURS
Wednesday–Sunday and most public holidays 10am–4.30pm
Closed during July
Parts of the estate are occasionally closed for private functions

Telephone: +61 (08) 8433 1700
curator.carrick@sa.gov.au
carrickhill.sa.gov.au

This heritage-listed Elizabethan mansion set in 40 hectares of undiminished grounds, with its Australian, British and French collections displayed in intimate domestic settings, offers a unique insight into South Australia's mid-twentieth-century cultural elite.

The Carrick Hill estate, now run by the Carrick Hill Trust, was established with the marriage, in 1935, of members of two of Adelaide's most prominent families: Edward (Bill) Hayward, a son of the wealthy merchant family that, for more than one hundred years, owned Adelaide-based John Martin & Co. Ltd, colloquially known as Johnnies, and his bride, Ursula Barr Smith, daughter of an even wealthier family of pastoralists who owned many fine houses in the area. Ursula's father gave the couple the land on which Carrick Hill now stands as a wedding present. During their year-long honeymoon, the couple acquired many of the centuries-old panelled doors, staircases and windows from the demolition sale of Beaudesert, a Tudor mansion in Staffordshire, England. A family friend, Adelaide architect James Irwin, designed the house around these fittings and, while the overall appearance is of a seventeenth-century English manor, it incorporates the latest technology of the 1930s. Oak panelling and pewter light fittings happily blend with heated towel rails, ensuite bathrooms and intercom systems.

Carrick Hill was under construction from 1937 to 1939, during which time Ursula designed the garden in a similarly English style. With the outbreak of the Second World War, Sir Edward had to leave his wife soon after moving into Carrick Hill to serve with the Australian Army in the Middle East and the Pacific. After the war, the Haywards continued filling the house with a wealth of paintings, sculptures, antiques and drawings spanning nearly 500 years of artistic achievement. This highly personalised collection is an interesting mix of Georgian and Victorian pieces, mostly inherited from Ursula's family; Tudor and Jacobean furniture, collected to match the house; and contemporary, often quite avant-garde Australian, British, and French paintings and sculptures. Many of the artists represented in the collection, such as William Dobell, Russell Drysdale, Jacob Epstein, Ivor Hele, Nora Heysen, John Dowie and Adrian Feint, were close friends of the Haywards.

Carrick Hill was just one of the Haywards' four homes. They also owned a country property at Delamere, a beach house at Port Willunga, and a townhouse in Mayfair, London. The Haywards were known both for their lavish entertaining and for their hard work. Ursula primarily saw herself as an artist in her own right. Since she drew particular pleasure from painting flowers, she marshalled significant resources to construct an artistic ambience for herself at Carrick Hill, hence the extensive flower gardens. In the early 1950s, she was appointed to the board of the Art Gallery of South Australia, the first female trustee in the entire country. Bill joined the family firm in 1932 and was for decades an admired and successful director of John Martin & Co. In 1970, the then Sir Edward and Lady Hayward generously decided to bequeath Carrick Hill to the public. Lady Hayward died that same year and, in 1972, Sir Edward remarried. After his death in 1983 Carrick Hill became the property of the Government of South Australia. Queen Elizabeth II officially opened it to the public in 1986.

The Carrick Hill Collection is very personal and idiosyncratic. It consists of 3000 books, 1000 objects, including around 200 artworks, over 30 sculptures, 150 items of furniture (Carrick Hill has the finest collection of antique oak furniture in Australia) as well as other objects including ceramics, glassware, silverware, William Morris arts-and-crafts movement, textiles and furnishings, in addition to the Haywards' personal collection of watches, medals and garments. The Carrick Hill collection of Australian paintings and drawings is, interestingly enough, lesser known than the more cohesive collection of British paintings of the first half of the twentieth century and the highly visible collections of French works of the late nineteenth and early twentieth centuries. The Haywards collected historical Australian works (such as those by Emanuel Phillips Fox, Arthur Streeton and George Lambert) as well as what were, in their time, works by contemporary artists such as Nora Heysen, Ivor Hele and Horace Trenerry. They also collected works by the fathers of modern Australian art, Russell Drysdale and William Dobell. In addition, a number of Australian works have been given to the collection since it was bequeathed to the public.

The British collection holds paintings by Alfred Munnings, Matthew Smith and Victor Pasmore, as well as, most importantly, eight superb Stanley Spencer paintings depicting landscapes and gardens. Augustus John, Paul Nash and Walter Sickert are equally represented in the British collection. Of particular interest are several sculptures and floral drawings and paintings by renowned British artist Jacob Epstein. His striking life-size bronze sculpture *Mother and child* is situated in the great hall. The oldest piece in Carrick Hill's French collection is a carved oak panel dating from about 1600, and the latest are bright paintings of Provence in 1962. In between are works by major masters from the nineteenth and twentieth centuries. One of Carrick Hill's masterpieces is a watercolour study of roses by Pierre-Joseph Redouté. Other famous paintings that are still part of the French collection are by Edouard Vuillard and Eugène Boudin, together with a study by Henri Matisse and one artwork on tapa by Paul Gauguin, *The big tree*.

Twice a year Carrick Hill holds themed art exhibitions over a period of two to three months in the rooms upstairs. As part of a Collection Connection series, these exhibitions are designed to focus on and celebrate the legacy of Carrick Hill's art and heritage collections. Recent exhibitions showcased works by artists such as Jeffrey Smart and Adrian Feint, as well as by living realist artist Robert Hannaford.

Carrick Hill's well-maintained hillside garden, which was partially designed in the arts-and-crafts style, is as highly individual as its art collection. It commands panoramic views across the foothills out to the Gulf Saint Vincent. Based on the Haywards' interest in outdoor sculpture, the Carrick Hill Collection was expanded by the trust to include sculptures by contemporary Australian artists such as Arthur Boyd, Lenton Parr, Guy Boyd and Inge King, together with local sculptors such as Neil Cranney and Greg Johns.

VISITOR INFORMATION

**Admission Fees:** Adult/Concession/Family: $12/$8/$28
Entry to the garden and grounds is free
Picnicking is permitted

**Tours and other Events:** Free guided tours through the house are conducted daily by well-informed volunteers at 11.30am and 2.30pm. Carrick Hill provides a free leaflet which takes children on a storybook trail through the enchanting park and which also explains what is blooming in the garden. Refer to website for special events at Carrick Hill.

**Access by car:** Leave the centre of Adelaide south on the Princes Highway, continue straight onto Fullarton Road and turn left onto Carrick Hill Drive. The driveway to the car park of Carrick Hill is on the left-hand side. The house is a short walk away from the car park area.

**Access by public transport:** Take Bus 171 from Currie Street Stop E3 (north side) towards Mitcham to Stop 16A (Maitland Street). Walk a few metres back to turn right onto Carrick Hill Drive and then left onto Rectory Walk to find the pedestrian-only side entrance to Carrick Hill on the right-hand side.

**Extra Tips:** Housed in one of Adelaide's most stunning historical buildings, the Art Gallery of South Australia is home to one of Australia's largest art collections (North Terrace, Adelaide). The University of South Australia's Anne & Gordon Samstag Museum of Art presents interesting temporary art exhibitions and events in architecturally stimulating premises (Hawke Building, City West campus, University of South Australia, 55 North Terrace, Adelaide; closed on Sundays and Mondays, public holidays and during exhibition changeovers). The nearby Australian Experimental Art Foundation organises quirky shows in their gallery (Lion Arts Centre, North Terrace (west end)). JamFactory is one of Australia's leading organisations for promoting design and craftsmanship (19 Morphett Street; closed on weekends).

Both the Adelaide Biennial and the Adelaide Festival of Arts (usually held during the first two weeks of March) are highly acclaimed events on the Australian cultural calendar.

A visit to Carrick Hill can be easily combined with a trip to Palmer Sculpture Landscape and Hahndorf (refer to page 94).

**Restaurant Tips:** Carrick Hill Café, catered by the highly acclaimed 'the food business', offers cake, coffee and picnic boxes as well as an all-day dining menu until 4.30pm when the museum is open.

Page 98
Courtesy Carrick Hill

# TASMANIA

# HOBART

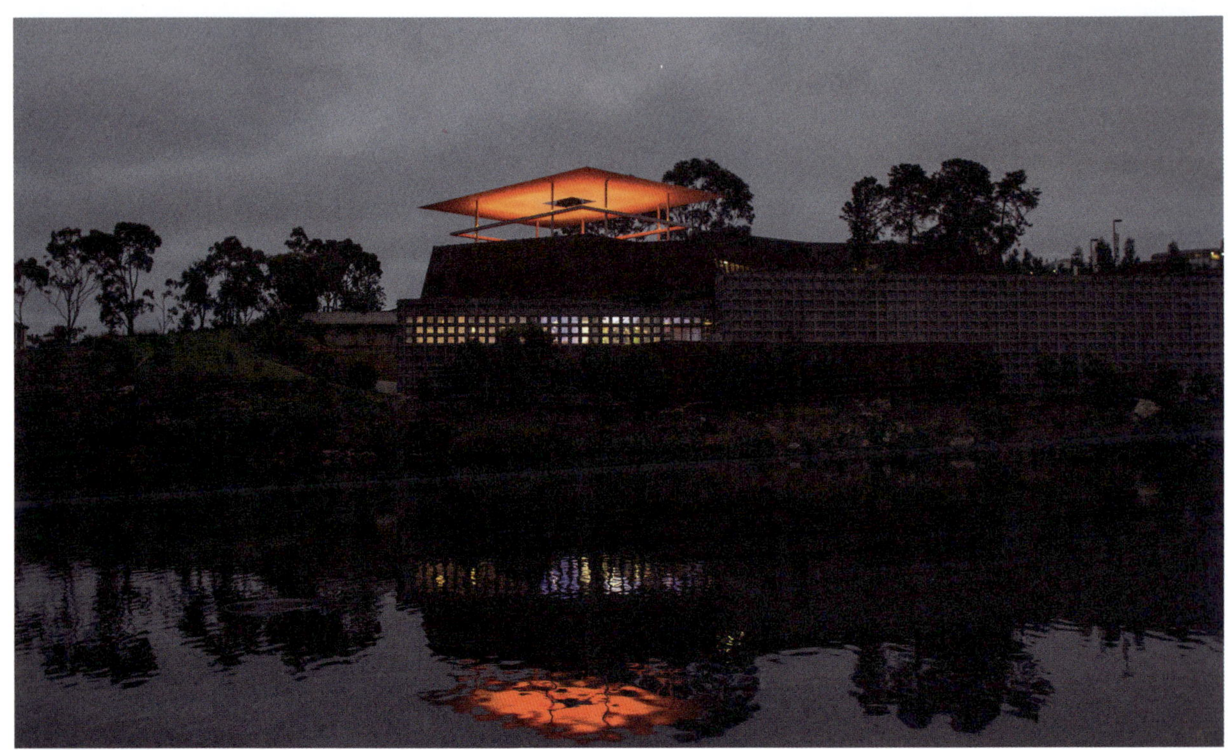

# MUSEUM OF OLD AND NEW ART (MONA)

655 Main Road, Berriedale
Hobart, TAS 7011

OPENING HOURS
Wednesday–Monday 10am–6pm (last entry 5.30pm) December–May; Wednesday–Monday 10am–5pm (last entry 4.30pm) May–December; open 7 days in January

Telephone: +61 (03) 6277 9900
info@mona.net.au
mona.net.au

To see Australia's most cutting-edge museum, visitors need to make their way to the island state of Tasmania. Mona, the largest private collection of art and antiquities in the Southern Hemisphere, is a must-see institution for open-minded architecture and art admirers alike. Opened in January 2011 by David Walsh to house his diverse collection, this *Gesamtkunstwerk* (total work of art) has changed the art and tourist scene in Hobart forever.

David Walsh (born in 1961) started collecting stamps and coins as a child. His infatuation with art and antiques began with visits to the Tasmanian Museum and Art Gallery instead of attending Sunday Mass. The first artwork Walsh acquired was a Yoruba palace door from Northern Nigeria by Areogun (1900–1954). He bought the door in South Africa in 1992 with profits from a blackjack spree. Having left a university science degree for wealth creation based on the mathematics of gambling, he started buying metates (corn-grinding stones) along with other ancient objects. His appetite for international contemporary and Australian modern art grew substantially in the late 1990s. Currently, the permanent collection contains around 1500 works, of which fewer than 700 are Australian.

The estate on Hobart's northern fringe was originally purchased by Italian immigrant, winemaker and art patron Claudio Alcorso in 1948. He named the site 'Moorilla', meaning 'rock by the water' in various Australian Aboriginal dialects. In 1958, he asked the great Australian modernist architect Roy Grounds to build two houses which today are heritage protected and serve to 'bookend' the museum complex: the Courtyard House (now the entrance, gift shop and café) and the Round House (now the underground library). When Moorilla ran into financial difficulties in 1995, Walsh and his consortium purchased the property and upgraded the Courtyard House to become the enchanting little Moorilla Museum of Antiquities, which opened its doors in 1999. Wanting to accommodate his rapidly growing art collection, Walsh closed the museum in 2006 and engaged Melbourne architect Nonda Katsalidis to design a 'deliberately underwhelming' building wherein the art on display would be discovered by the visitor rather than 'shown off'. Walsh wanted a subterranean and adaptable 'non-museum', hence the tennis court almost obscuring the museum entrance. In addition, there are several roof gardens and extended walkways alongside minimalist concrete and Cor-ten (weathered, fine-grain) steel panels.

Over a five-year construction period, more than 35,000 cubic metres of material, primarily Triassic sandstone, was removed from the site to make way for three subterranean levels. The impressive sandstone walls inside remain 'living' and partially flow with water during rain, the atmosphere kept sweet by a state-of-the-art air-conditioning system. Today, a spiral staircase and a glass lift take visitors beneath the Courtyard House entrance and through the 17-metre high rock face. Stepping out of the lift, visitors are greeted by a well-stocked cocktail bar before they venture into the dark and often seemingly uncoordinated space. The design of the interior encourages visitors to discover the museum incrementally and lose themselves on the dimly lit, cave-like exhibition floors.

The total gallery space comprises 6000 square metres, of which 1300 square metres is reserved for temporary exhibitions, held approximately twice a year, often in cooperation with other Australian or international art institutions. About 15 per cent of the entire collection is always on display as part of the 'unthemed', largely permanent exhibition called 'Monanism'. Visitors can expect to see Egyptian, Roman, Greek, African and pre-Columbian artefacts and curiosities alongside more contemporary works. The Australian art scene is represented by, among others, Vernon Ah Kee (who exhibited at the city pavilion of Australia at the

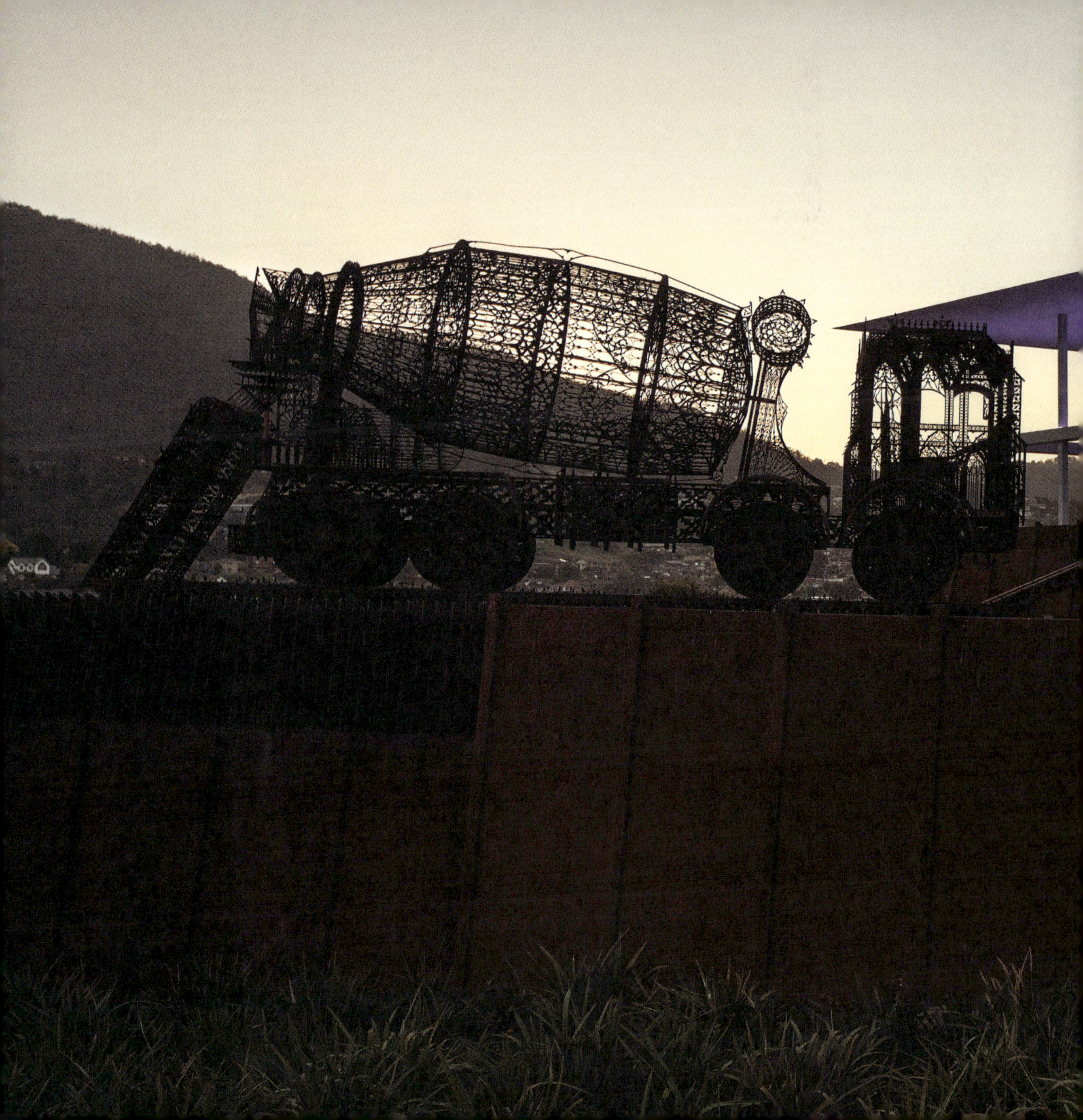

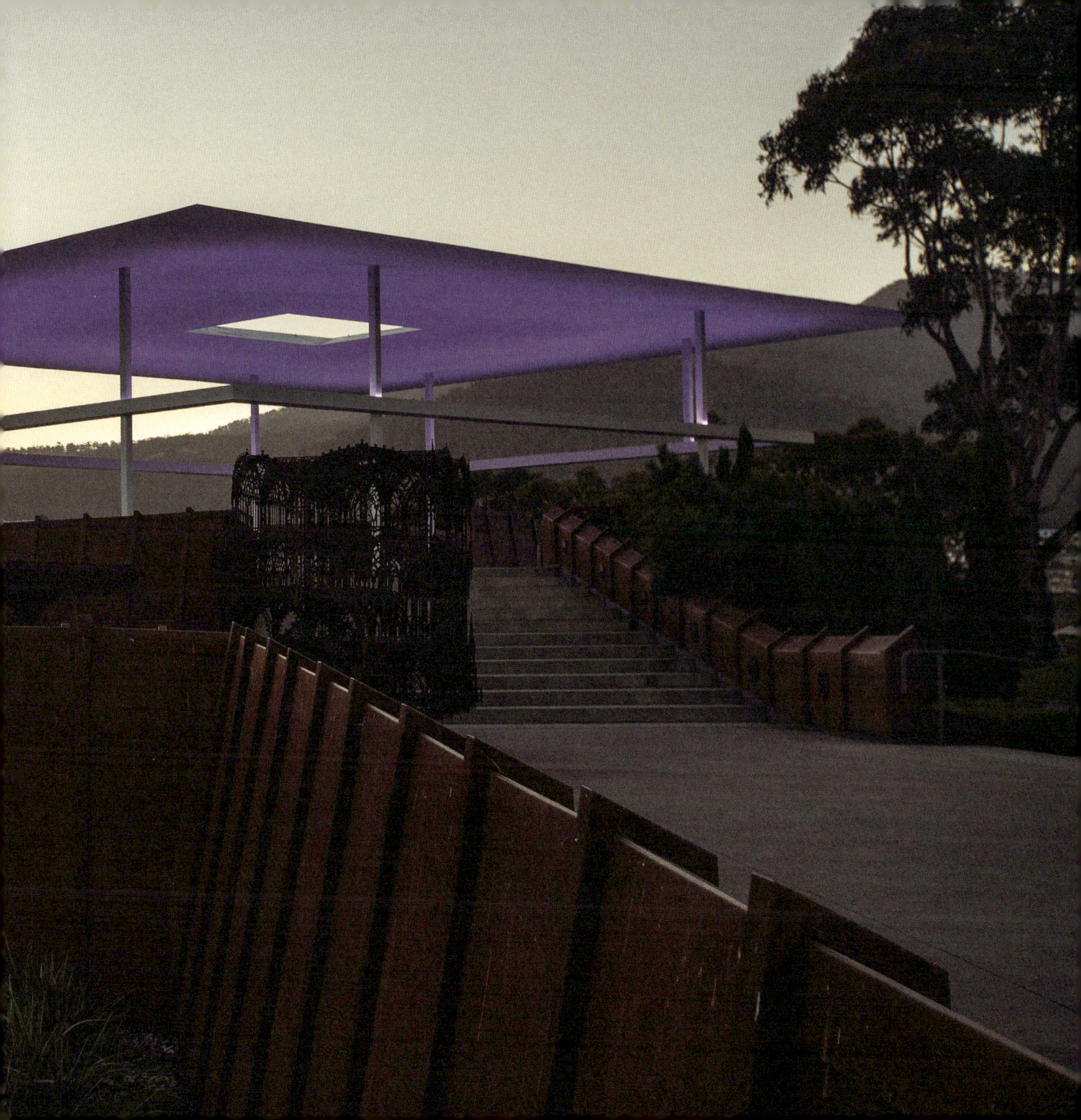

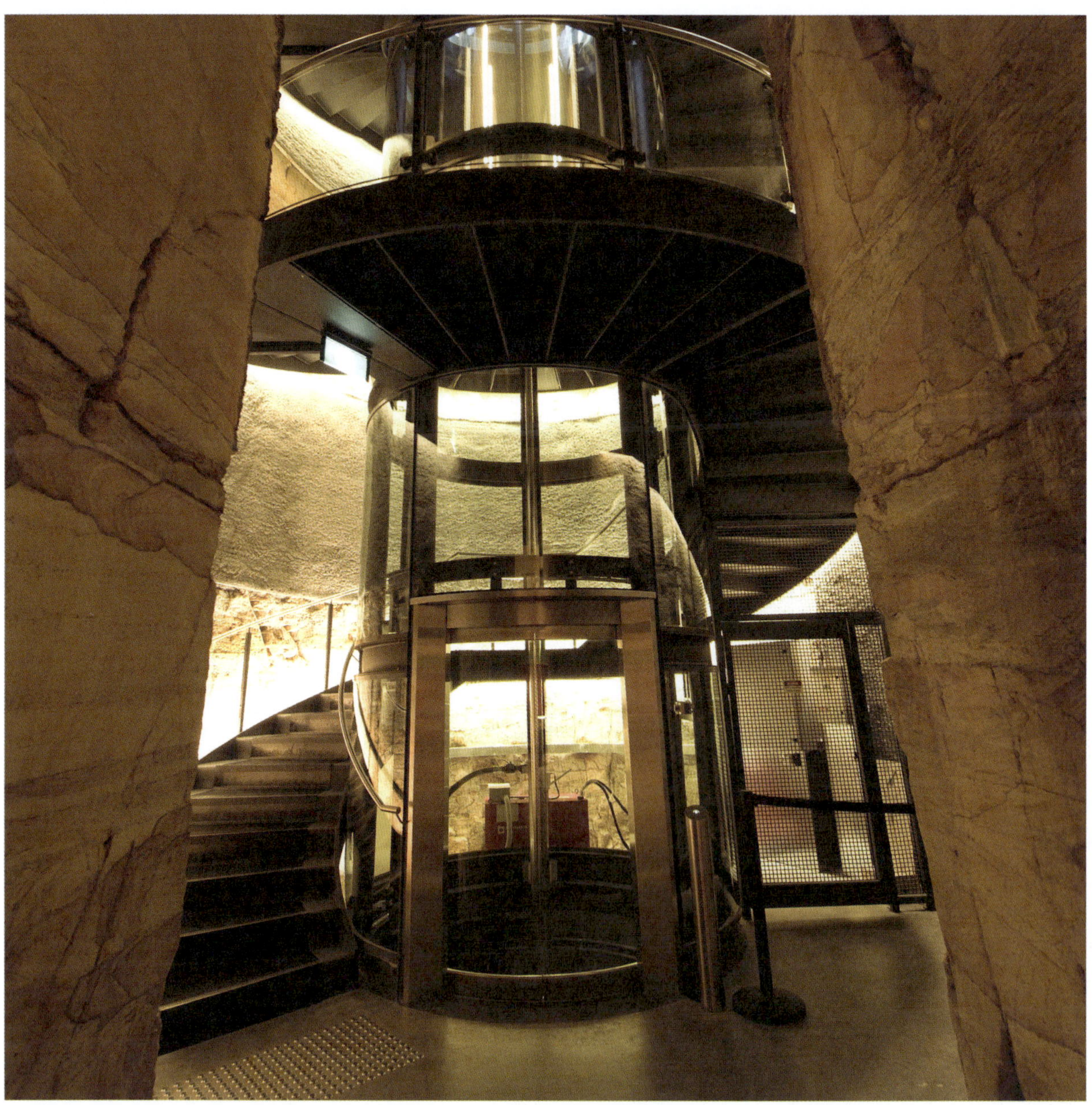

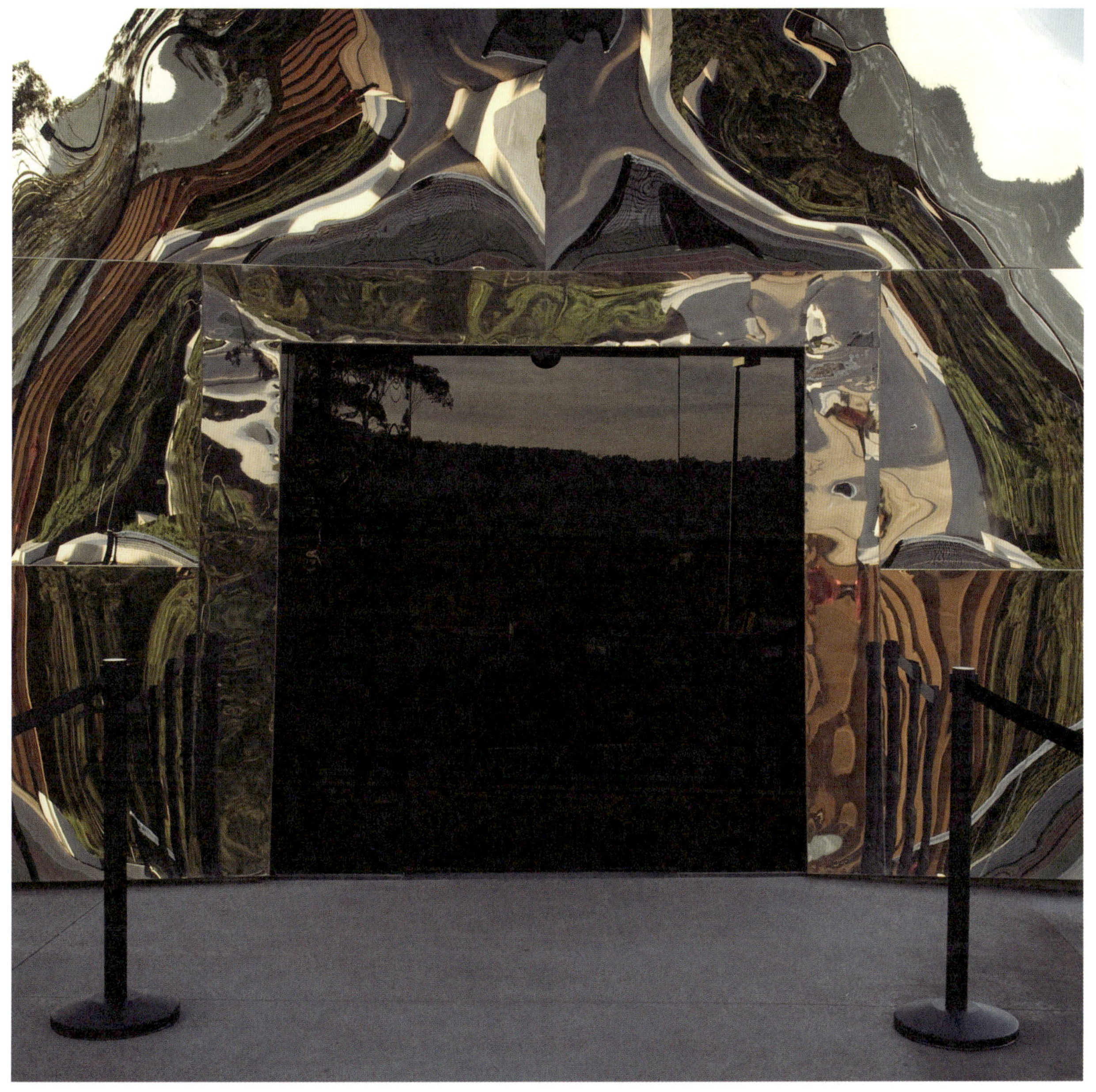

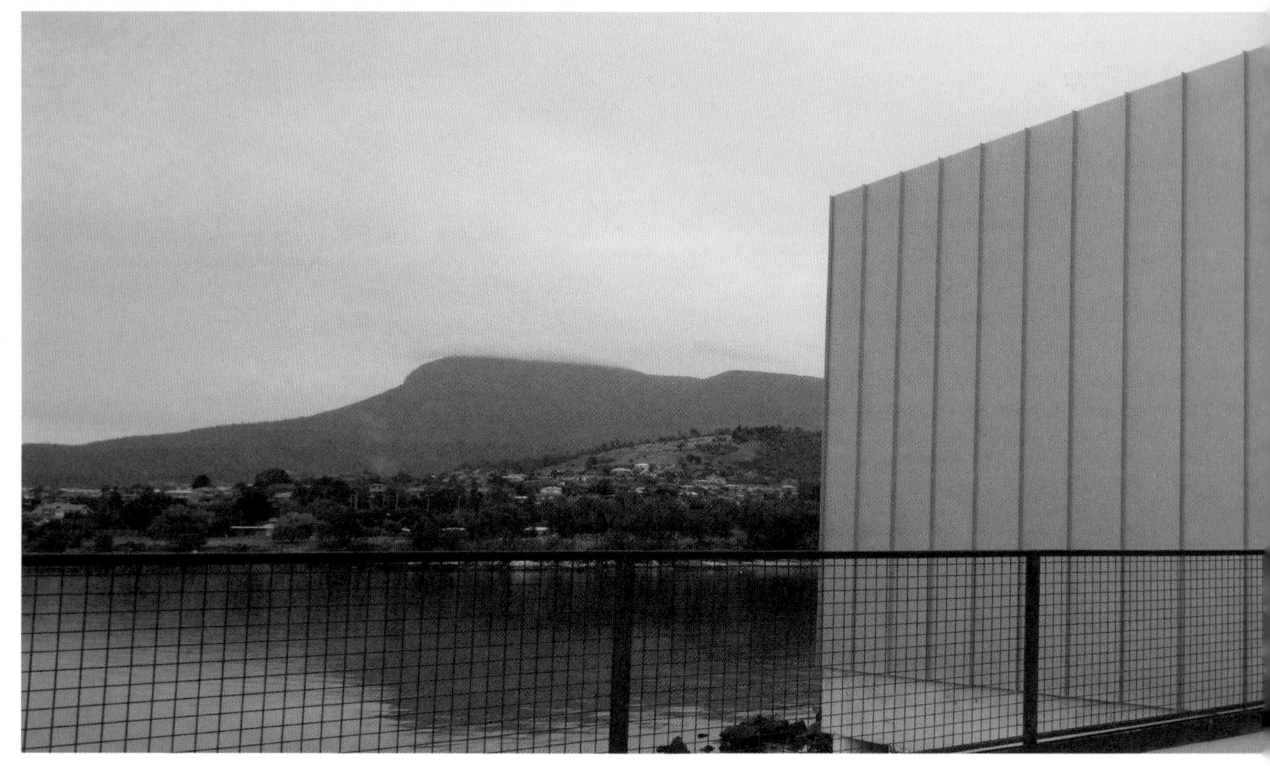

Venice Biennale in 2009) and Fiona Hall (who is Australia's 2015 representative at the Venice Biennale). There is an impressive installation by Brigita Ozolins as well as works by major Australian artists Arthur Boyd, Sidney Nolan (whose gigantic *Snake* from 1970–72 is the 'heart' around which the museum is built) and Brett Whiteley. Europe is, for example, represented by Damien Hirst, Marina Abramović, Pipilotti Rist and Wim Delvoye, responsible for the museum's most 'hated' artwork *Cloaca professional*. In addition, there are works by Anselm Kiefer (*Sternenfall/Shevirath ha kelim* occupies an entire pavilion on the lowest floor), Jannis Kounellis, Julius Popp and Erwin Wurm. The list of American artists in the collection includes Paul McCarthy, Rafael Lozano-Hemmer and Jenny Holzer. (In 2014–15 Matthew Barney presented his symphonic-film-opera-exhibition project, 'River of Fundament', at Mona).

Art aficionados can, for a 'life-and-after-death membership fee' of $75,000, elect to have their ashes stored at the museum's cocktail lounge, next to the cremated mortal remains of David Walsh's father. Those up for a laugh inside a lavatory are urged to visit the third toilet on the right on the same floor, just behind the Void Bar. Here, the Austrian artists collective Gelitin have cleverly arranged mirrors so that users of this stainless steel facility, named *Locus focus*, can inspect their own anus. If watching a video is more to your liking, visit the toilet diagonally opposite.

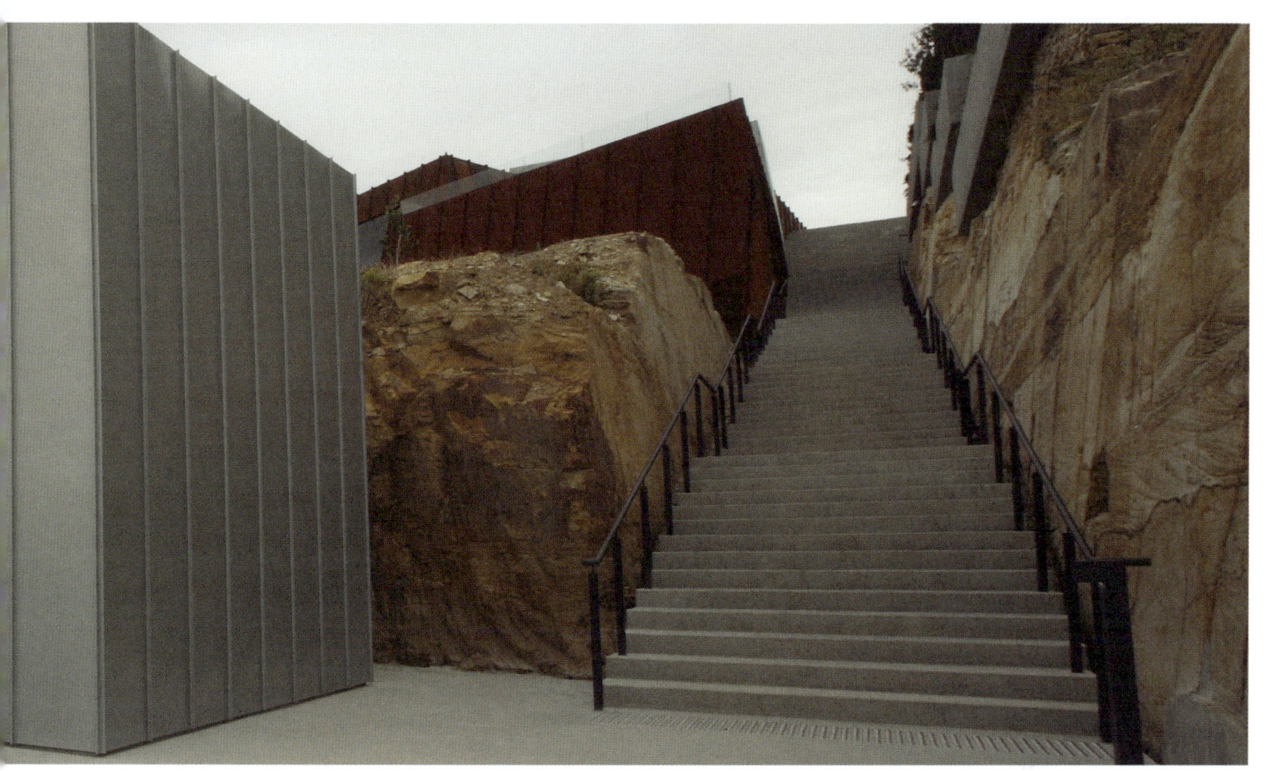

Having been designed around specific art pieces, Mona would also be one of few museums in the world to have a water-covered gallery floor. A visit to the Mummy of Pausiris, in the reflecting Death Gallery on the top exhibition floor (close to the glass lift), is a memorable experience; as is a video installation by Christian Boltanski, who represented France at the Venice Biennale in 2011 (located in the silver shed en route to the ferry). This artwork became internationally known due to a somewhat macabre twist. The installation involves four video cameras permanently filming Boltanski's studio in suburban Paris. Instead of paying up front, Walsh hands over a regular fee until the artist dies, rendering the price of the work dependent on Boltanski's (or Walsh's) lifespan. Another art site infrequently visited is Walsh's own twenty-first-century version of a 'Wunderkammer' (cabinet of curiosities), found behind the open-air stage alongside the pathway in front of the accommodation pavilions.

Walsh and his team are continually striving to stimulate visitors by pushing boundaries on various levels. Renowned American artist James Turrell's *Amarna*, installed in 2015 and the most recent of his (almost ninety) Skyscapes around the world, is now part of the museum's rooftop. Aficionados might want to look out for the installation of Turrell's *Perceptual cell* and 'Ganzfeld' series, which also recently entered the Mona collection.
A self-proclaimed atheist, Walsh favours art that is driven by

polemics as much as aesthetics. He relishes conceptual art that scoffs at any perception of elite art. By creating what he calls a 'subversive adult Disneyland' and a 'secular temple', he certainly succeeds in being a restless, intelligent agent provocateur.

VISITOR INFORMATION

Instead of having labels next to the artworks, Mona supplies visitors with an innovative electronic device called the Mona 'O' which provides information and even encourages visitors to rate each individual artwork 'love' or 'hate'. David Walsh and Elizabeth Pearce, a friend and collaborator who challenges artists and their ideas about art, give their personal response to some of the works under the icon 'Gonzo'. Jane Clark's ironically titled 'Art Wank' gives a more objective, conventional observation on the artworks. 'Ideas' throw in additional thoughts and 'Media' usually offers interviews with some artists, or music. Visitors can type in their email address and save their tour and by doing so, the entire 'O' library becomes available online from the following day onwards.

**Admission Fees:** Adults/Concession/Under 18 and Tasmanians: $20/$15/free
Higher prices apply for special exhibitions

**Tours and other Events:** Visitors who stay in Hobart in mid-January will be spoiled with a great contemporary music festival curated by Brian Ritchie. MONA FOMA offers a fantastic line-up of international stars for very modest ticket prices (mofo.net.au). Equally interesting is Dark Mofo, the winter festival that can be enjoyed in June (darkmofo.net.au). David Walsh and his team frequently invent new exciting happenings.

**Access by car:** From Hobart's waterfront and city centre, head north on Brooker Avenue (follow the signs to National Highway 1). Stay on NH 1 for about 10 km up to the exit Main Road/Berriedale (follow the signs to Mona). The unassuming entrance to the vineyard is a grey concrete gate on the right side, just across from a liquor store. Follow the path all the way up the hill. The car park is to the left of the building complex at the top.

**Access by public transport:** The MR-I fast catamaran departs from the stunning Brooke Street terminal in Hobart several times a day. Please check the website for timetable and bookings. The Mona Roma Express bus departs from the same terminal at 9.30am, noon and 1pm and leaves Mona at 11.30am, 12.30pm and 2.30pm with additional services during winter ($20 return). The Airport Express Bus has services that link up with the boat to Mona (one way $20, return $30). Bookings for all transport services are possible by phone + 61 (03) 6223 6064. One can also hire a bike at the Mona Brooke Street terminal (Hobart), or at Mona ($20 per person).

Public Metro Bus 42 departs at 242 Elizabeth Street (towards Austins Ferry) and Metro Bus X1 (towards Cove Hill Fair) departs the bus terminal on Elizabeth Street at Stop F.
Both services reach 658 Main Road in about 45 minutes (call 13 22 01 for timetables – buying a Day Rover bus ticket is advisable). Leaving the bus, follow Main Road for about 5 minutes and enter a grey gate on the right side. Mona is at the end of the path that leads up the hill on the right.

**Extra Tips:** A library with 5000 books on ancient and modern art can be found on the premises in the Round House. Guests can stay at eight superbly appointed pavilions on the grounds, each overlooking the Derwent River and featuring artworks from the Mona collection.

A visit to Mona is easily combined with a trip to Detached (refer to page 116).

One kilometre south of Mona, pedestrians and cyclists can enjoy the evolving Glenorchy Art & Sculpture Park (GASP) project. The picturesque 3 km boardwalk, connecting Montrose Bay and Wilkinsons Point, features two contemporary open pavilions. The walkway has been the home of temporary artworks and will be the site for several installations in the future.

About 3 hours north of Hobart, design devotees can indulge in stunning surroundings at the luxurious Saffire Freycinet Lodge (access for guests only). A walk at the magnificent Friendly Beach and the views towards Wineglass Bay make for an unforgettable experience. Contemporary Art Tasmania presents and organises exhibitions and events of contemporary culture (27 Tasma Street, North Hobart). The free street magazine *Warp* gives a good overview of the current art events in Tasmania.

Visitors who are heading north to the second largest city of Tasmania, Launceston, might want to consider staying at the Hatherley Birrell Collection, divine inner-city boutique accommodation which displays museum-quality art pieces in their diverse properties.

**Restaurant Tips:** The Museum Café, the Void Bar, the Wine Bar and the Source Restaurant are to be found on the premises. Moorilla wine and Moo Brew beer can be sampled at the Cellar Door for $10 inside the Ether Building.

Driving (or by taking the public bus) through North Hobart, treating oneself to sensational cakes and homemade ice-cream at Sweet Envy is a highly recommended experience (341 Elizabeth Street).

Pages 108
James Turrell, *Armarna*, 2015, from the 'Skyspace' series
Installation view, museum rooftop plaza
Steel frame, fibreglass foam sandwich roof construction, fibreglass, reinforced concrete seating, 70 x 2830 x 2115 cm
Courtesy Mona, © James Turrell
Photograph Mona/Rémi Chauvin

Pages 110-1
James Turrell, *Armarna*, 2015
Wim Delvoye, *Flatbed Truck, Trailer and Cement Truck*, 2007
Laser-cut Cor-ten steel
Courtesy Mona, Hobart
Photograph Mona/Rémi Chauvin

Page 110
Cylindrical lift and spiral staircase
Underground view at the base of the circular elevator and spiral staircase
Courtesy Mona, Hobart
Photograph Matt Newton

Page 111
Mirrored Wall on Courtyard House
Courtesy Mona, Hobart
Photogprah Matt Newton

Page 112-3
Boltanski Pavilion
Secure air-conditioned bunker of concrete, timber and zinc cladding, containing The Life of C.B.
Courtesy Mona, Hobart
Photograph Mona/Leigh Carmichael

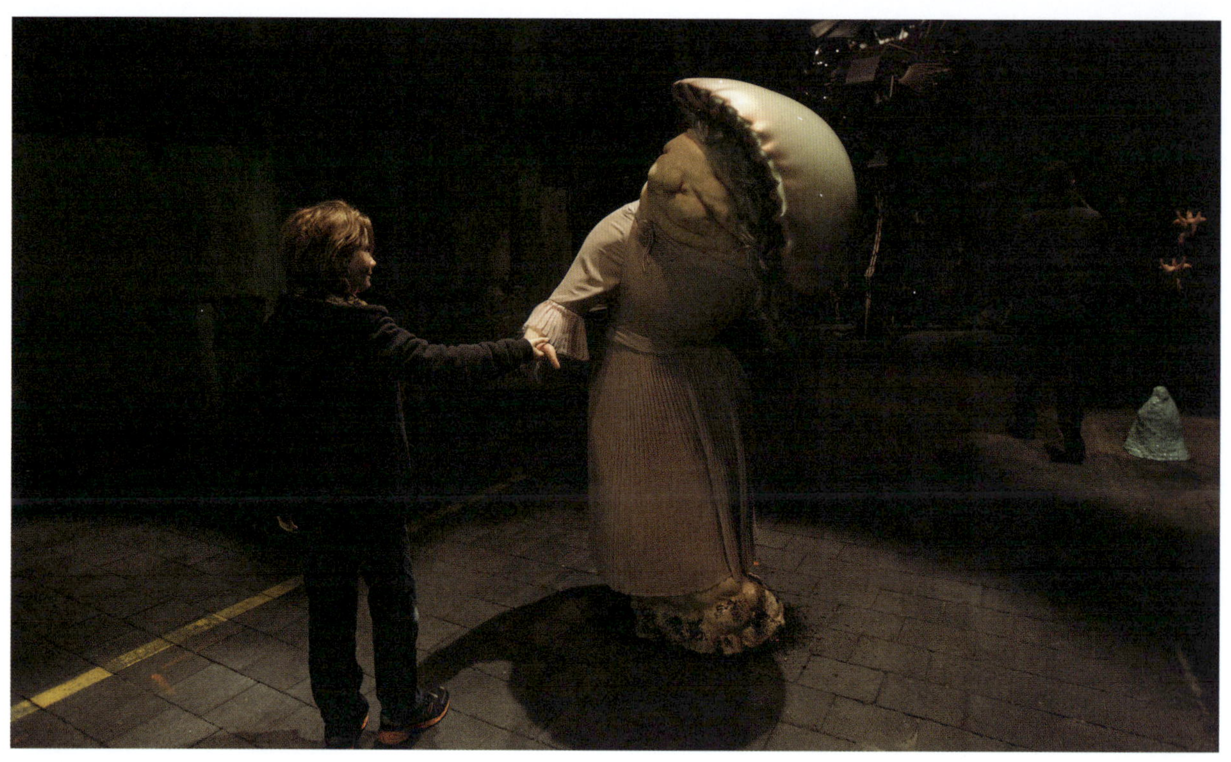

# DETACHED

Old Mercury Building (enter via Argyle Street Tunnel)
91–93 Macquarie Street
Hobart, TAS 7000

OPENING HOURS
Please refer to the website

Telephone: +61 (03) 6234 4111
info@detached.com.au
detached.com.au

Established in 2008 by Penny Clive, Detached Cultural Organisation is a privately funded, not-for-profit organisation focusing on national and international contemporary art and operating across multiple arts, science and education platforms worldwide.

From 2008 to 2014, Detached was located in a state-of-the-art project space constructed within the shell of a heritage-listed church in Hobart's Campbell Street. The intimate exhibition space saw fascinating temporary exhibitions by renowned artists, who are also represented in the permanent collection, including Mike Parr, Anne Ferran, Patricia Piccinini, Brook Andrew, Sonia Leber and David Chesworth, Shaun Gladwell, Chiharu Shiota and Yin Xiuzhen. In 2015, Detached moved to the old Mercury Newspaper offices in Hobart's CBD, redeveloping the site into an important cultural hub which now houses permanent and temporary exhibition galleries as well as several event spaces. Detached facilitates exhibitions drawn from its permanent contemporary art collection in addition to temporary exhibitions, all of which are accompanied by in-depth public and education programs making use of Detached's significant cultural partnerships.

In addition to funding its own cultural program and assisting many cultural institutions, Detached generously contributes to the Tasmanian Museum and Art Gallery's annual exhibition and AccessArt programs.

VISITOR INFORMATION

**Admission Fees:** Free of charge

**Extra Tips:** The Tasmanian Museum and Art Gallery (TMAG) is a combined museum, art gallery and herbarium (Dunn Place; closed on Monday). The Salamanca Arts Centre houses many arts organisations, art and music events, exhibitions and commercial galleries (65–77 Salamanca Place). The Salamanca Market is one of the best outdoor markets in Australia (every Saturday 8:30am–3pm; Salamanca Place). The Plimsoll Gallery at the Tasmanian School of Art showcases local, national and international contemporary art and design (Hunter Street). Next door the Henry Jones Art Hotel, Australia's first of its kind, is a must-see for every art admirer. This former jam factory has been transformed into an enthralling first class hotel showcasing the work of Tasmania's visual artists. Guests and visitors are invited to learn more about the history of this idiosyncratic luxurious place whilst wandering through the art-filled corridors. Tours take place most Fridays at 4pm ($15 for non-guests, booking is essential; 25 Hunter Street).

**Restaurant Tips:** Great pastries, artisan bread and coffees are on offer at Daci & Daci (11 Murray Street). A cup of coffee and interesting Asian-inspired meals can be enjoyed at Shoebox Café (211 Elizabeth Street). First-class coffee and food are also served at the quirky Machine Laundry Café (12 Salamanca Square). Boutique Tasmanian beer on taps, a wine and cider selection alongside a small tapas menu can be enjoyed in a rustic local atmosphere at nearby Preachers (5 Knopwood Street). One of the best upmarket Tasmanian fish and chips meals can be found at the waterfront restaurant Fish Frenzy (Elizabeth Street Pier).

Left and pages 118-9
All images courtesy Patricia Piccinini, Peter Hennessey and Detached

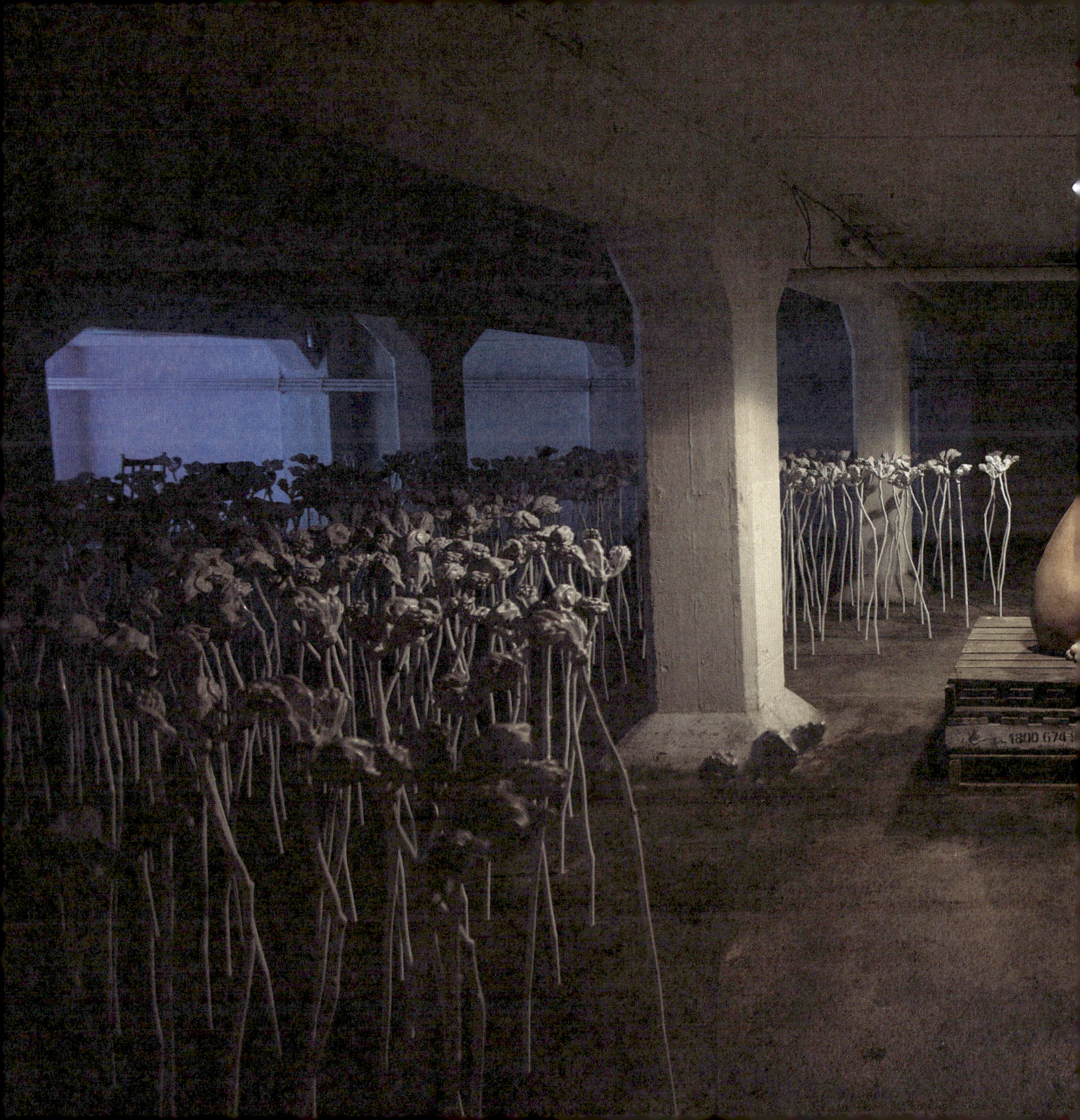
1800 674

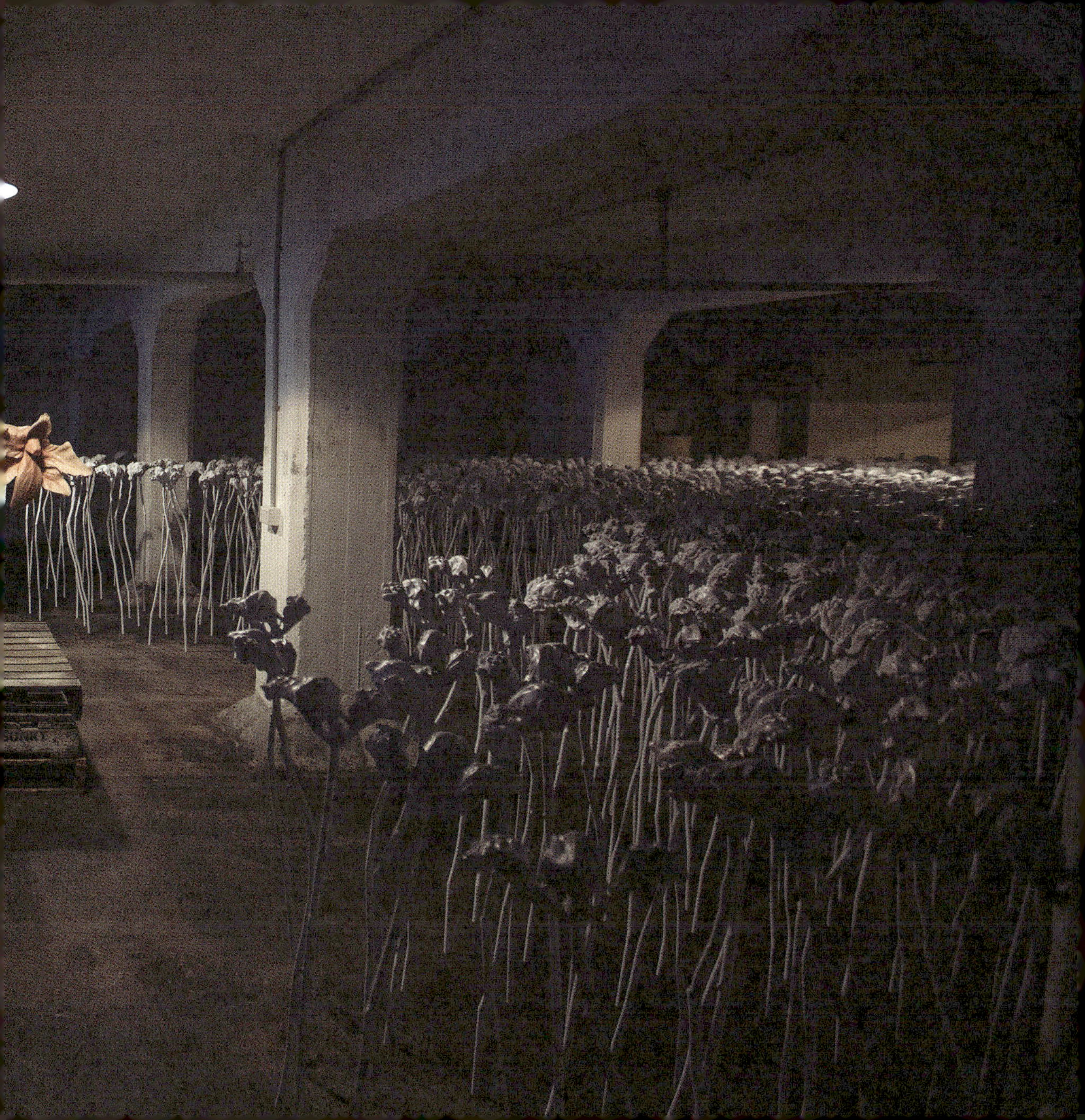

# WESTERN AUSTRALIA

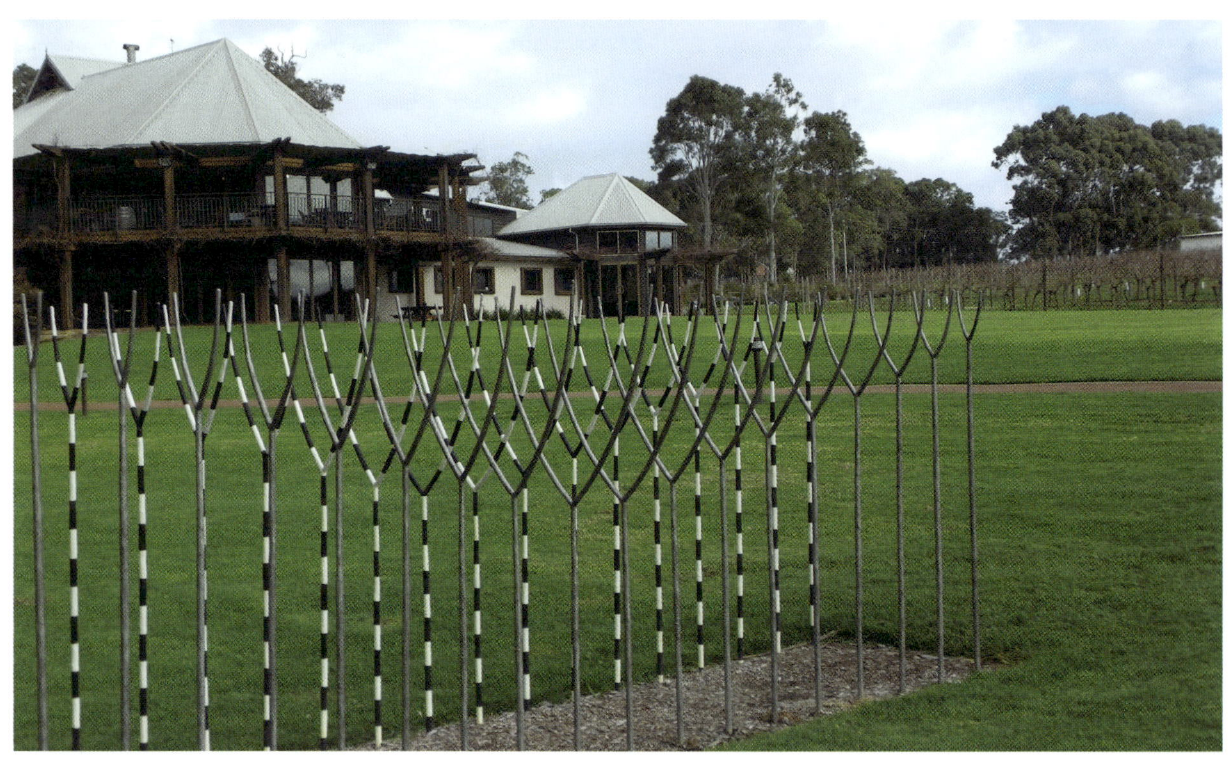

# JANET HOLMES À COURT COLLECTION

Vasse Felix
Corner Tom Cullity Drive & Caves Road
Cowaramup, WA 6284

OPENING HOURS
Daily 10am–5pm, closed on certain public holidays

Telephone: +61 (08) 9756 5000
hacgallery@heytesbury.com.au
holmesacourtgallery.com.au
vassefelix.com.au

The scenic Margaret River Region is a mecca for wine connoisseurs and foodies, and, happily, visitors to this area also have the opportunity to see a selection of artworks from one of the country's largest private art collections.

Previously known as the Holmes à Court Collection, the collection was started in 1966 by the late millionaire industrialist Robert Holmes à Court and his wife Janet Holmes à Court. It grew from the family's interest in Australian and Indigenous art and has steadily developed over time into an internationally renowned collection. From the very beginning, the Holmes à Courts not only acquired what they liked, but also had a vision of future exhibitions in mind. Artists and their works were always collected in terms of the connections and relationships that could be formed between them. A core collection strategy has always been to follow certain artists groups over many years. Contrary to what public museums are obliged to do, the Holmes à Courts never had an interest in pursuing the chronological or historical recording of Australian art history. Instead, they frequently bought community collections and exhibitions in their entirety to assure their survival as a group of artworks. This was, for example, the case in 2005, when Janet Holmes à Court acquired the Yäkumirri exhibition of bark paintings in Darwin to prevent the break-up of this powerful group show by Yolngu artists from North-East Arnhem Land.

It is, and has always been, Janet Holmes à Court's mission to ignite a greater understanding of contemporary Aboriginal art. In some cases, she and her late husband's input transformed entire Aboriginal communities, as was the case with the remote community of Utopia in Central Australia. Being already interested in a batik project of the early 1980s which came out of Utopia, they became aware of the unique collective and individual strengths from which Emily Kame Kngwarreye emerged as a major artist. Subsequently, the Holmes à Courts supported the community, and not only bought works by Emily Kame Kngwarreye and her family members, but also collected three bodies of work from Utopia in their entirety. They acquired one collection of works on silk by eighty-eight artists, one on canvas by eighty women artists, as well as one collection of ninety watercolours. In addition, the collection holds artworks by well-known Aboriginal artists such as Rover Thomas, Paddy Jaminji and Peter Skipper. The collection nowadays consists of over 4000 registered artworks in total, of which about 40 per cent are by Indigenous artists. The remainder includes major works by some of Australia's leading artists, such as Western Australian artists Robert Juniper, Howard Taylor and Brian McKay, as well as by renowned Australian artists Fred Williams, John Olsen, Russell Drysdale, Sidney Nolan and Brett Whiteley. The collection originally also included works by well-known international artists, however those were sold in the 1980s.

Robert Holmes à Court built his fortune by acquiring over 200 companies, including TVW Channel 7 in Perth, and the largest media group in the United Kingdom, while Janet pursued her various interests and commenced what became the significant art collection. After the death of Robert Holmes à Court in 1990, Janet Holmes à Court became the Chairman of one of Australia's largest private companies, Heytesbury Pty Ltd. She retained ownership of the Heytesbury Group until being bought out in 2008 by her son Paul Holmes à Court. Part of the buyout included her becoming sole owner of the renamed Janet Holmes à Court Collection. She opened the Holmes à Court Gallery in East Perth in 2000, which relocated to its present site in October 2010. A renowned patron and board member of a wide range of cultural and arts organisations in Australia, Janet Holmes à Court holds honorary doctorates from three Australian universities and has received numerous

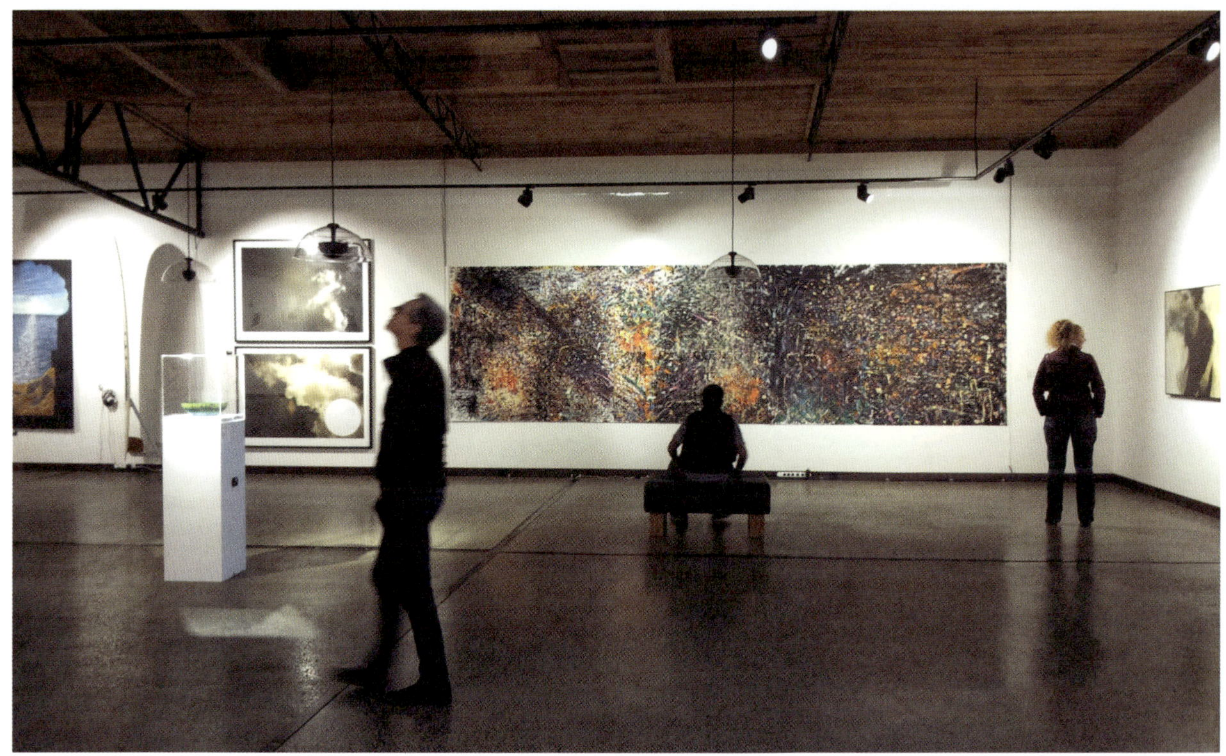

awards recognising her contribution to the community and to business, the most prestigious being Companion of the Order of Australia.

The family's 'old' Vasse Felix Winery now comprises an art gallery and performing arts facility. The 300-square-metre space retains the winery ambience with its exposed steel trusses and original catwalks, reminding visitors of the early Vasse Felix vintages made there. The gallery hosts three exhibitions annually. The large majority of the shows are collection based, but occasionally include artworks by other artists on loan or for sale. The art experience extends to the Vasse Felix grounds, where glorious gardens of local flora have been embellished with a sculpture walk. Visitors can enjoy seven permanently installed artworks by well-known artists such as Michael Le Grand, Mitsuo Takeuchi and Keizo Ushio.

VISITOR INFORMATION

**Admission Fees:** Free of charge

**Tours and other Events:** The Janet Holmes à Court Collection and Vasse Felix offer a variety of floor talks, live performances (among others by the brilliant ACO) and additional special events.

**Access by car:** The drive from Perth will take about 3 hours 30 minutes. Leave Perth south on the Kwinana Freeway/ State Route 2, which will turn into the Forrest Highway. Continue heading south on Forrest Hwy/National Route 1 until you arrive at Bunbury. At the roundabout, take the 1st exit onto Bunbury Bypass/Roberson Drive/National Route 1. Drive slightly left towards Bussell Hwy/State Route 10. At the roundabout, take the 1st exit onto Busselton Bypass. At the next roundabout take the 2nd exit and stay on Busselton Bypass. At the following roundabout, take the 1st exit onto Bussell Hwy/State Route 10. Turn right onto Harmans Mill Road (one after Metricup Road); follow Harmans Mill Road until just past the Margaret River Chocolate Factory. Turn left onto Tom Cullity Drive. Follow this until you cross a small bridge and you will see Vasse Felix on the right.

**Extra Tips:** Superb restaurants, quaint shops, art galleries, great beaches as well as interesting cave formations make the Margaret River region a highlight of any trip to Western Australia.

The Leeuwin Estate is well known for its big open-air concerts as well as its strong links with the artistic community. Having specifically commissioned over 100 artworks to be reproduced as part of the Leeuwin Estate label series, The Leeuwin Estate collection now comprises over a hundred artworks from artists such as John Olsen, Arthur Boyd, Sidney Nolan, Lloyd Rees, Albert Tucker, Fred Williams and Imants Tillers. Many of the original paintings and sculptures can be admired free of charge at the Leeuwin Estate Art Gallery (Stevens Road, Margaret River).

A visit to the Janet Holmes à Court Collection at Vasse Felix could be combined with a trip to the Gomboc Gallery and Sculpture Park (refer to page 126).

**Restaurant Tips:** Vasse Felix's renowned Cellar Door is open daily from 10am to 5pm. The highly acclaimed Vasse Felix Restaurant, which is considered to be one of the finest restaurants in the region, is open for lunch between noon and 3pm (reservations (08) 9756 5050). The nearby Margaret River Chocolate Company is famous throughout Western Australia. The Chocolate Café focuses on sumptuous sweet treats and also serves light lunches. The café, the factory and the tasting centre are open daily (corner Harman's Mill Road and Tom Cullity Dr, Metricup). The friendly Café at Clairault offers a range of gourmet boards and irresistible desserts to complement their renowned wines (3277 Caves Road, Wilyabrup). Foodies might want to visit the praised Restaurant at Wills Domain. The winery also showcases works by emerging and established artists in their Art Gallery (corner Abbey Farm and Brash Roads, Yallingup).

Page 122
Kevin Draper, *Sequence*, 2007
Mild steel and paint, dimensions variable
Courtesy Janet Holmes à Court Collection
Photograph Megan Schlipalius

Left
'Art of Sound', installation view, 2013, Holmes à Court Gallery
Courtesy Janet Holmes à Court Collection
Photograph Megan Schlipalius

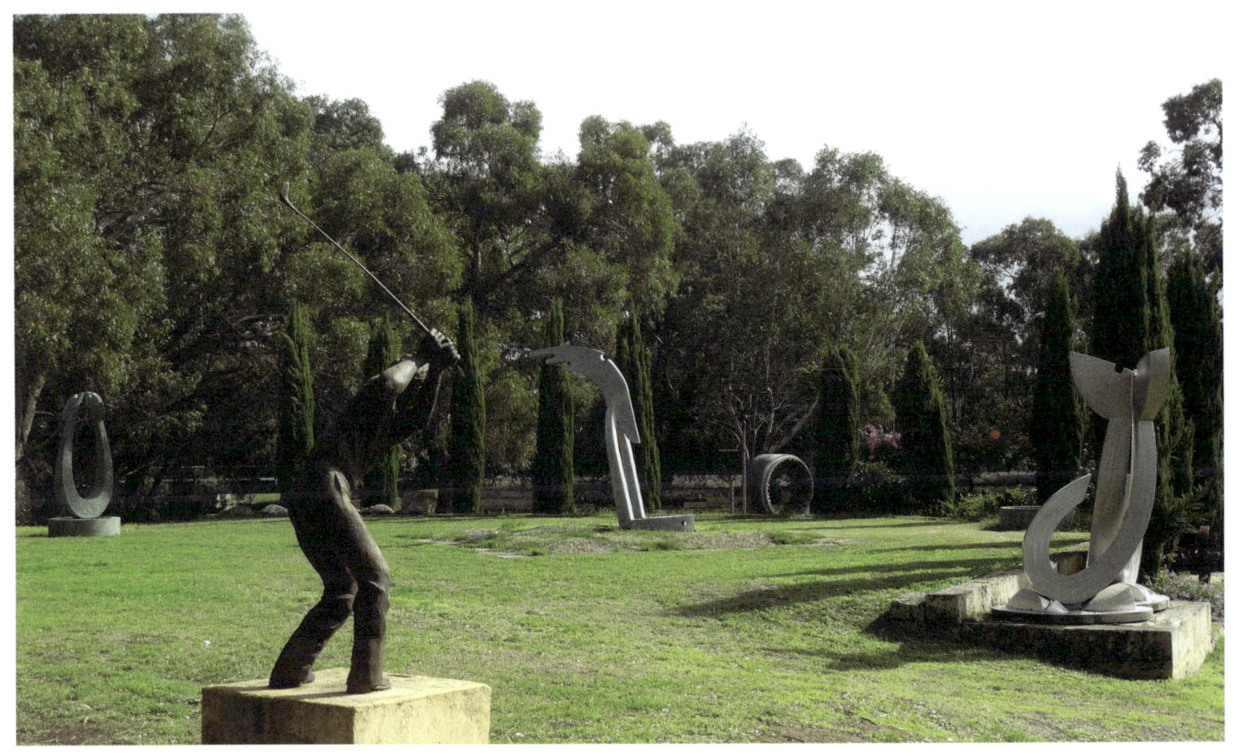

# GOMBOC GALLERY AND SCULPTURE PARK

50 James Road
Middle Swan, WA 6056

OPENING HOURS
Wednesday–Sunday 10am–5pm;
during January by appointment only

Telephone: +61 (08) 9274 3996
rm@gomboc-gallery.com.au
gomboc-gallery.com.au

The only privately owned sculpture exhibition space and one of the oldest galleries in Western Australia is situated in the wine-growing district of the Swan Valley. Established in 1982 by R.M. (Ron) and Terrie Gomboc, the Gomboc Gallery and Sculpture Park complex is an active and creative hub for sculptors and admirers of art.

Entering the spacious 4.5-hectare grounds, visitors are immediately welcomed by a number of large sculptures, some by Ron Gomboc himself, and others by emerging artists as well as by other well-known sculptors from Australia and around the world, such as Jean-Pierre Rives, Maris Raudzins, Mitsuo Takeuchi and Yoshio Nitta. Over sixty sculptures of different materials are exhibited throughout the property at any given time, about one-third created by Gomboc. The remaining two-thirds are largely sculptures that have been produced for earlier Sculpture Survey shows, for the Sculpture by the Sea Cottesloe exhibition, or by artists in residence who have been fortunate enough to be invited by the Gombocs to work on the grounds. These works are all for sale, with the entire proceeds reinvested into the Sculpture Park.

Gomboc was born in 1947 in Ljubljana, Slovenia. At the age of thirteen, he emigrated to Australia with his parents. During the 1970s he studied art and sculpture at Midland Technical College and Perth Technical College. Having started his own studio practice, he realised that Western Australia offered sculptors few prospects for exhibiting. After many consultations with fellow artists, Gomboc decided to initiate the first Sculpture Survey on his property in 1984. Since then, he and his wife organise the now well-known exhibition on an annual basis. Each June, around fifty students of the Edith Cowan University, Curtin University, Polytechnic West–Midland Campus, and Central Institute of Technology are invited to display their works alongside sculptures by distinguished Australian and international artists such as Ron Robertson-Swann, Koichi Ogino, Sang-Wook Oh, Peter Lundberg, Michael Le Grand and Phil Spelman.

Being passionate about international cultural exchange possibilities, Ron and Terrie Gomboc have funded numerous opportunities for Western Australian artists to exhibit in Asia. They have personally hosted residencies for invited artists from all over the world to work in Gomboc's workshop and foundry. Since its inauguration in 2005, the Gombocs have also helped support the initiatives of interstate and international artists associated with Sculpture by the Sea Cottesloe. Ron Gomboc himself has participated in every Cottesloe event. His hospitality during these events has led to invitations to exhibit overseas and participate in several reciprocal cultural exchanges. Among the most meaningful works in the last years was a three-piece sculptural monument, commissioned by the Ledger family to mark the anniversary of their son Heath's untimely death. It was installed at Heathcote Park, Applecross. Gomboc's largest commission to date is the 12-metre tall steel sculpture *Northern spirits*, which was commissioned by the Fortescue Metals Group. Installed in South Hedland, this sculpture serves as a monument to all those who have lost their lives in the mining industry. Ron's most widely known artwork is the 22ct gold-plated cast bronze Australian Academy of Cinema and Television Arts (AACTA) Awards statuette. Having been commissioned in 2011 by the Australian Film Institute, he designed and made a statuette depicting a human silhouette based on the shape of the Southern Cross.

Ron and Terrie Gomboc's interest in art also extends to other disciplines. Their two-storey Art Gallery provides five large exhibition spaces where established and emerging artists of all disciplines are represented. A new major exhibition is mounted each month, featuring the works of an individual artist or group. Among the artworks for sale are indoor sculptures by Geoffrey Bartlett, Campbell Robertson-Swann,

Xia Yang, Greg Johns, Stefanie Von Quost, Keizo Ushio and Peter Weiner, as well as paintings by artists such as Margaret Woodward, Craig Gough and Bob Colcutt.

Pages 126 and 129
All images courtesy Gomboc Gallery and Sculpture Park

VISITOR INFORMATION

**Admission Fees:** Free of charge

**Access by car:** Leave Perth on State Route 5, take the Great Eastern Highway/Route 94 ramp to Route 1/Midland, stay on Route 94, turn left onto Roe Hwy/National Hwy 94/ State Route 3 (signs for National Hwy 95/Midland), turn right onto Toodyay Road/State Route 50 and turn left onto James Road. The entrance to the Sculpture Park is on the right-hand side. The drive will take about 30 minutes from the CBD and 20 minutes from Perth Airport.

**Access by public transport:** Leave Perth Station catching the Midland Line train to Midland Station. Catch Bus 315 at Midland Station Stand 1 to 'Toodyay Road before Lewis Jones corners'. Walk back along Toodyay Road and turn right onto James Road. The trip takes about 70 minutes (refer to train and bus schedule).

**Extra Tips:** Every March, 'Sculpture by the Sea' sees over seventy local, interstate and international artists transform Perth's most popular beach, Cottesloe Beach, into a sculpture park. Being one of the world's largest free to the public events, the 'Sculpture by the Sea' exhibitions attract hundreds of thousands of visitors.

Visitors who like to take a step back in time might want to venture out into the desert to explore the New Norcia Benedictine Community. Established on its present site by Abbot Bernard Rooney in 1978, the New Norcia Museum & Art Gallery was formerly St Joseph's Aboriginal Girls' Orphanage. The museum traces the history of the monastery and houses paintings by Spanish and Italian masters as well as the largest moveable collection of post-Renaissance religious art in Australia. A number of the works are prize-winners from the Mandorla Prize for Religious Art. A tour through the monastic town and a stay at the Monastery Guesthouse complete an unusual and interesting cultural experience (Great Northern Highway, New Norcia).

A visit to the Gomboc Gallery and Sculpture Park could be combined with a trip to the Janet Holmes à Court Collection (refer to page 122). There are also interesting exhibitions of Australian and international art staged at the Art Gallery of Western Australia (Perth Cultural Centre, Roe Street; closed Tuesdays), the nearby Perth Institute of Contemporary Arts (51 James Street; closed Mondays) and the Lawrence Wilson Art Gallery at the University of Western Australia (35 Stirling Highway (corner Fairway), Crawley; closed Mondays and during exhibition changes).

**Restaurant Tips:** The semi-rural Swan Valley region features several galleries, breweries, wineries and restaurants. Houghton's Café at Houghton Wines, one of Australia's oldest operating wineries, serves great lunches overlooking lovely gardens (148 Dale Road, Middle Swan). The upmarket restaurant at the modern Sittella Winery is known for serving excellent lunches (100 Barrett Street, Herne Hill). The exclusive restaurant at the RiverBank Estate serves Modern Australian cuisine during the day (126 Hamersley Road, Caversham). The Margaret River Chocolate Company Swan Valley's Chocolate Café is a pleasant place for an indulgent treat or light lunch (5123 West Swan Road, West Swan).

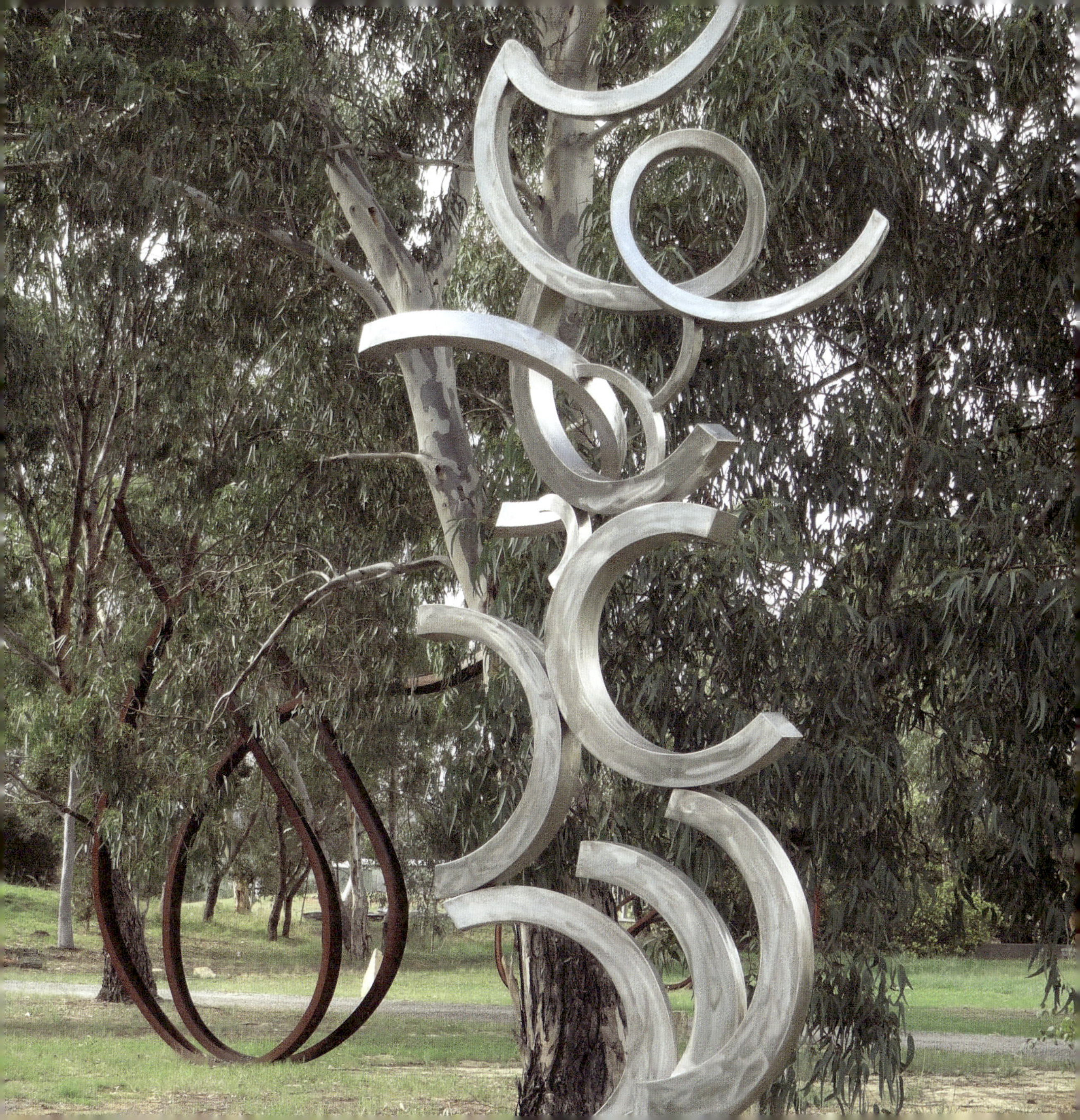

# NEW ZEALAND

# NORTH ISLAND

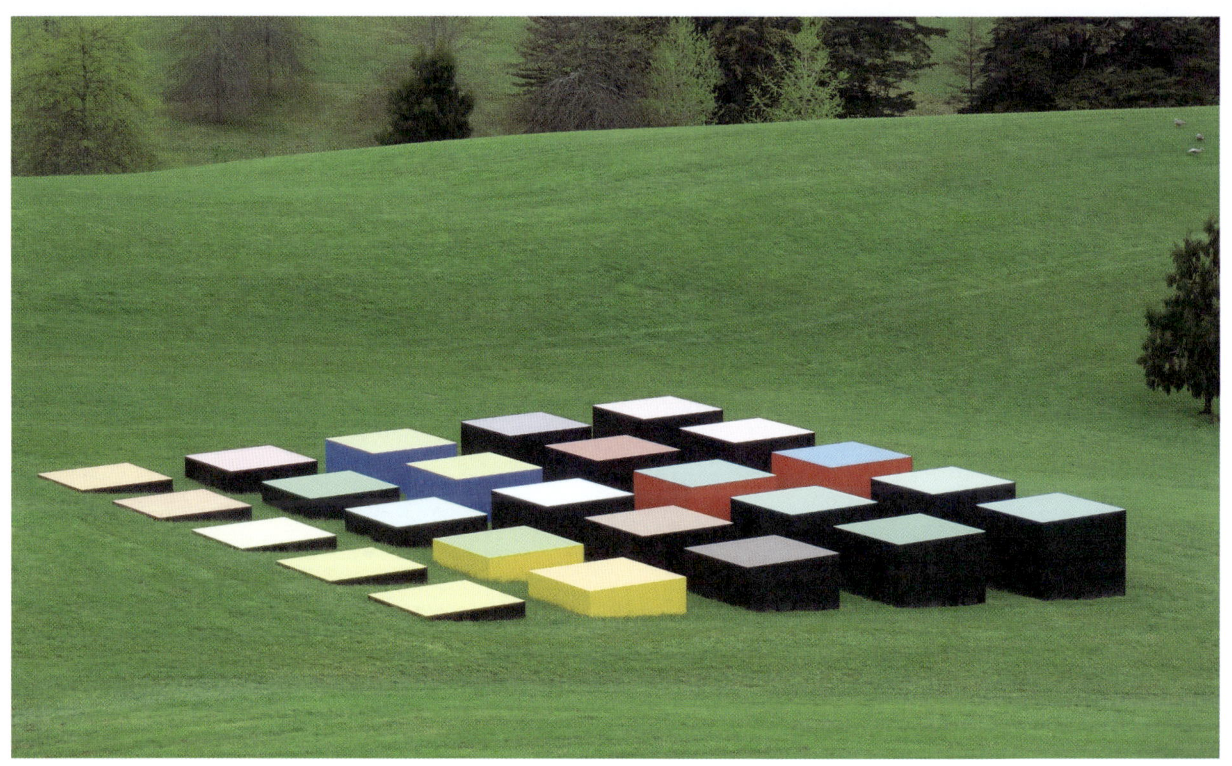

# GIBBS FARM

2421 Kaipara Coast Highway
Makarau

OPENING HOURS
Open to the public once a month by prior appointment only
Please visit the website for details

info@gibbsfarm.org.nz
gibbsfarm.org.nz

Until recently, only a few devotees knew that one of the world's best sculpture parks is tucked away in the Kaipara Harbour area, just one hour north-west of Auckland. Comparable to Storm King Art Centre, NY, Gibbs Farm features stunning site-specific works from key New Zealand and international artists on a scale rarely seen.

Alan Gibbs and his then wife Jenny started collecting art in the 1960s. By the mid-1990s, when they parted company, they had amassed an outstanding collection by significant New Zealand artists, including Gordon Walters, Colin McCahon, Milan Mrkusich, Gretchen Albrecht, Stephen Bambury and Max Gimblett, as well as by famous international artists. After starting with an interest in abstract expressionism, Gibbs developed a taste for minimal art. Having bought the 405-hectare property in 1991, a new era of art collecting began for him. With the assistance of his son-in-law, architect Noel Lane, he has made a commitment to commissioning major artworks. Gibbs enjoys solving engineering challenges and he and his team frequently become closely involved in all aspects of the artists' creative process. This drive for excellence paired with the picturesque but challenging landscape of the property has produced many exceptional installations.

Nowadays, Gibbs's sculpture collection includes twenty-eight key, and in many cases the largest, works by Andy Goldsworthy, Anish Kapoor, Bill Culbert, Chris Booth, Daniel Buren, Eric Orr, George Rickey, Graham Bennett, Kenneth Snelson, Len Lye, Leon van den Eijkel, Marijke de Goey, Neil Dawson, Peter Nicholls, Peter Roche, Ralph Hotere, Richard Serra, Richard Thompson, Russell Moses, Sol LeWitt, Eric Orr, Tony Oursler, Zhan Wang, Jeff Thomson, Maya Lin and Bernar Venet. Collected at the rate of about one installation a year, many take several years to develop and all, bar three of the sculptures, are unique and site-specific.

Encompassing approximately 30,000 square metres, Maya Lin's enormous land sculpture *A fold in the field* from 2013 is the largest artwork that has been commissioned for the Gibbs Farm so far. It is the first earthwork depicting folds in the ground by the American artist and architect, who designed the famous Vietnam Veterans Memorial in Washington, DC in 1982. Among the most impressive sculptures is Indian-born British sculptor Anish Kapoor's *Dismemberment, site 1* from 2009, which relates closely to the artist's earlier temporary installations at the BALTIC and the Tate Modern's Turbine Hall. Anish Kapoor and Alan Gibbs have placed the eight-storey high work nestled in a cleft cut into a high ridgeline. Composed of a vast blood-red PVC membrane stretched between the two giant steel ellipses, it provides for an intense sensual and exhilarating experience. Equally striking is Richard Serra's *Te tuhirangi contour* from 1999/2001. The 252-metre long and 6-metre high steel wall has the delicate quality of a dark ribbon curling across the evergreen pastures. Each of the fifty-six steel plates, which together weigh 11 tonnes, lean out by 11 degrees from the vertical, so the materiality of mass and form is intensely felt. The story behind the sculpture adds to its dramatic impact. The project nearly foundered twice in the five years it took to achieve. First, there was an impasse resulting from opposing views of the material to be used. Then there was a logistical disaster which nearly sank the ship on which the work was transported from Germany. Some of the plates were damaged because the captain ignored the carefully calculated stacking instructions. A discoloured band along the base of the sculpture where sheep have rubbed against the warm steel adds an organic touch to the work. Among the recent additions to the park is Bernar Venet's impressive Cor-ten steel sculpture *88.5° ARCx8*. Eight arcs, each 27 metres in height, seem to spring vertically from a hill-top. Standing underneath the 100-tonne heavy sculpture is an unforgettable experience.

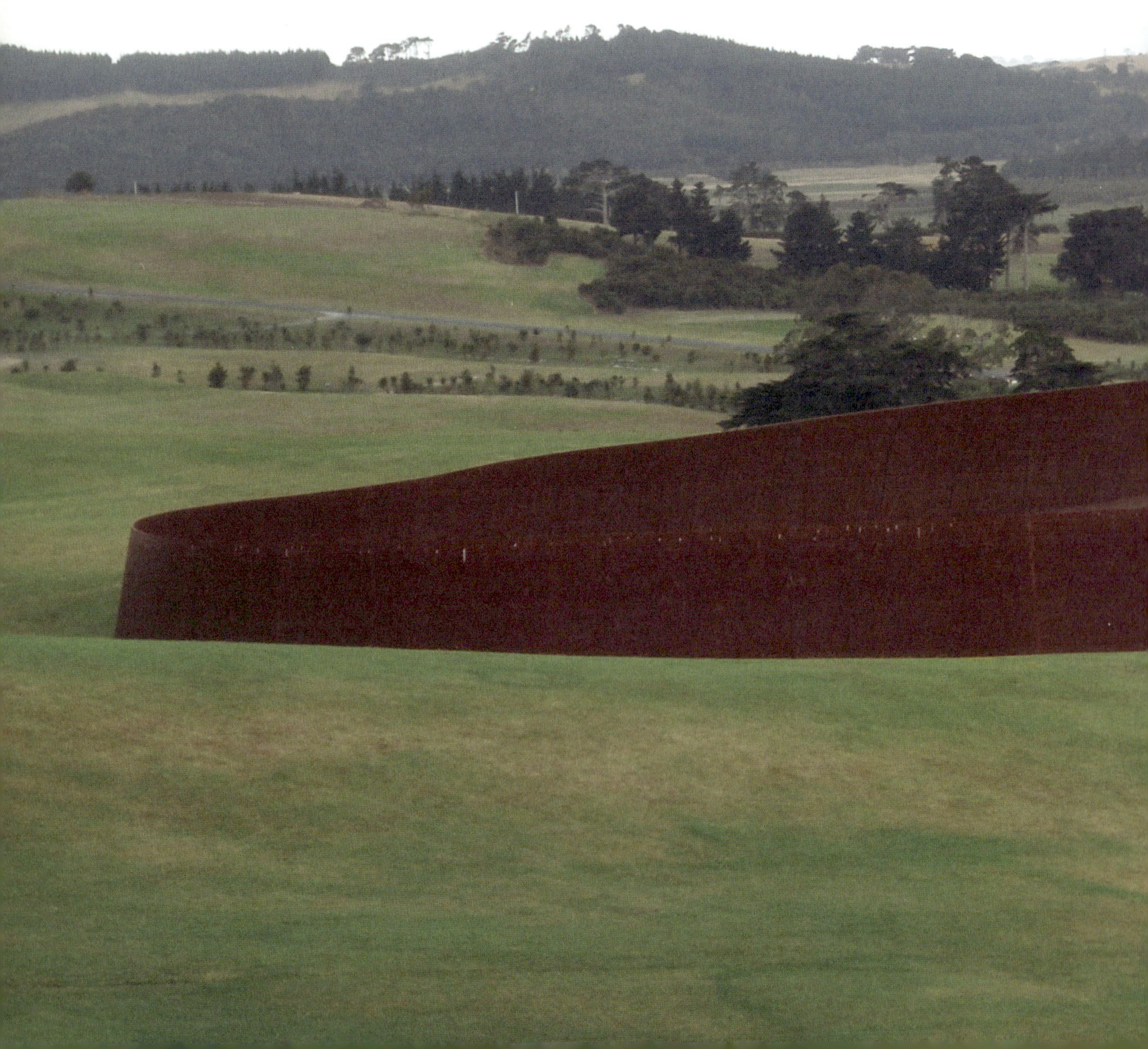

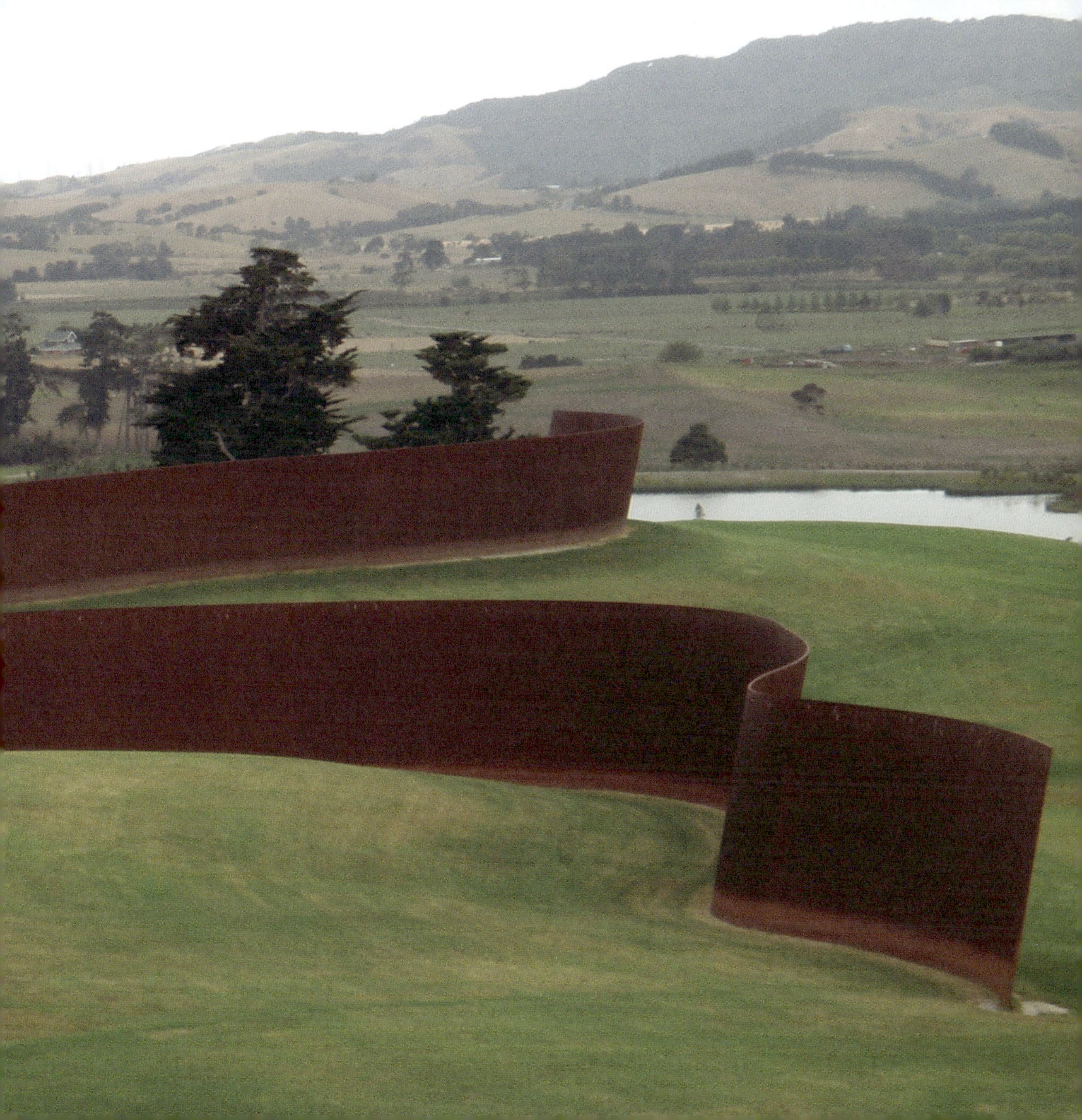

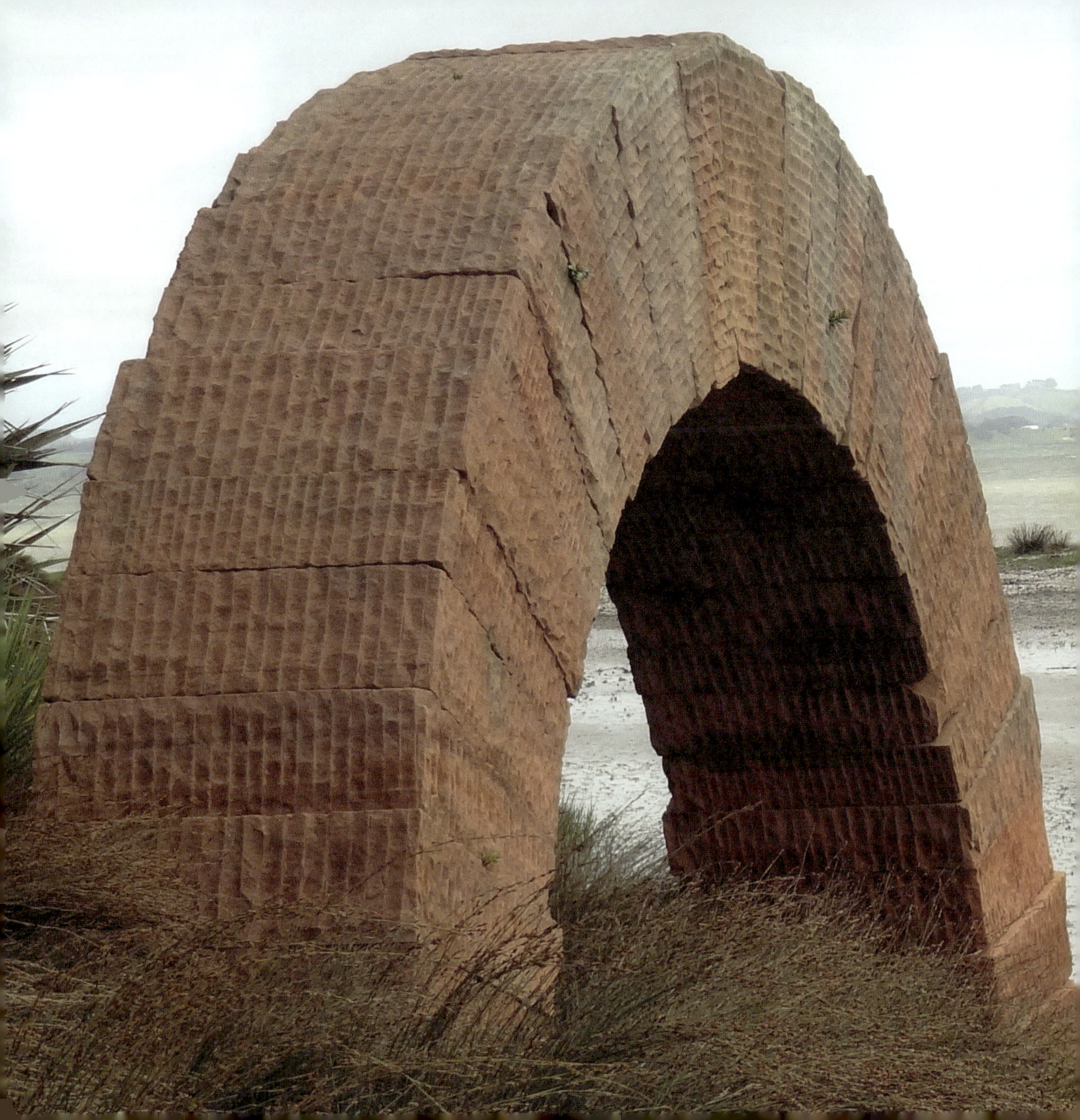

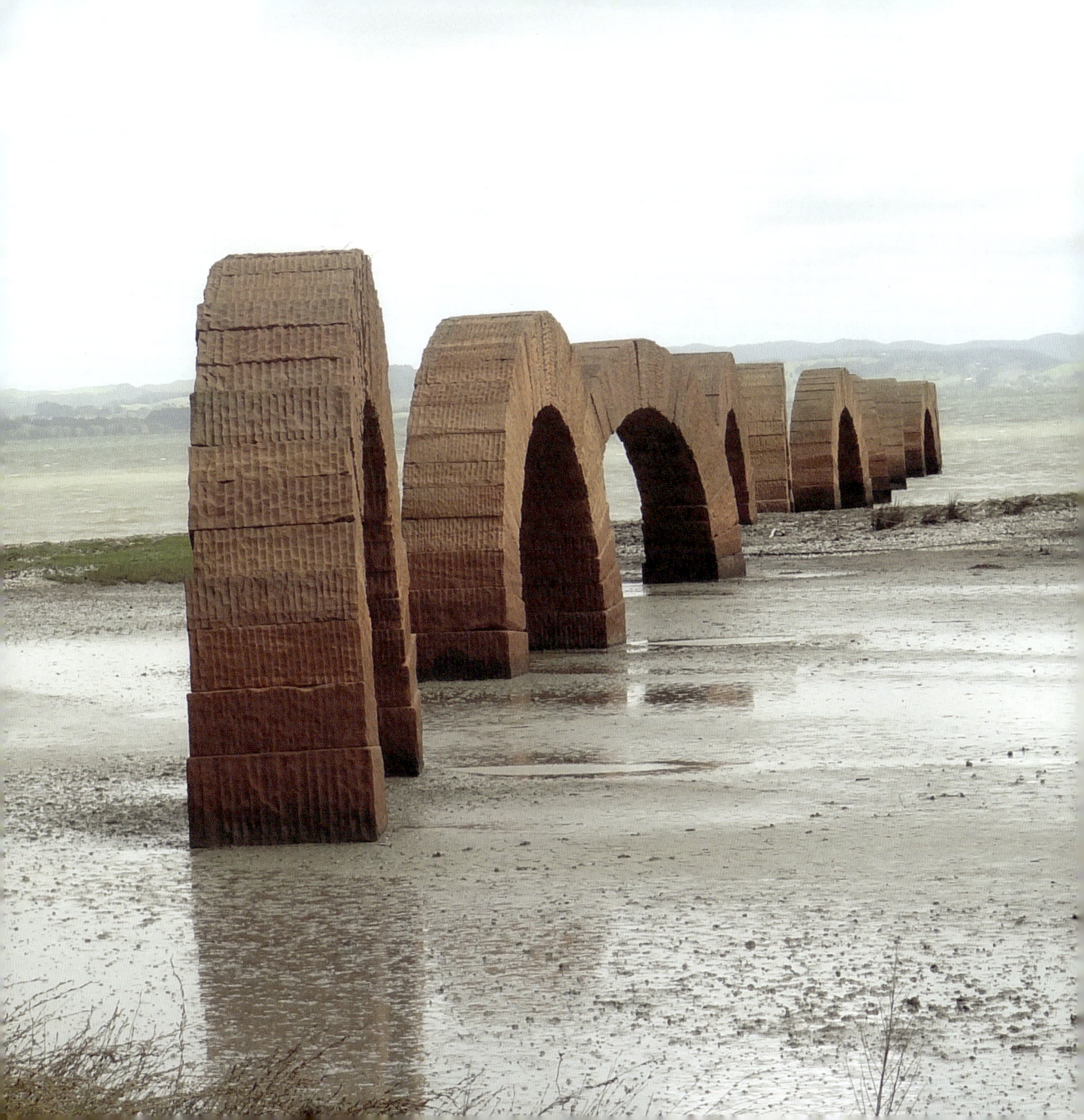

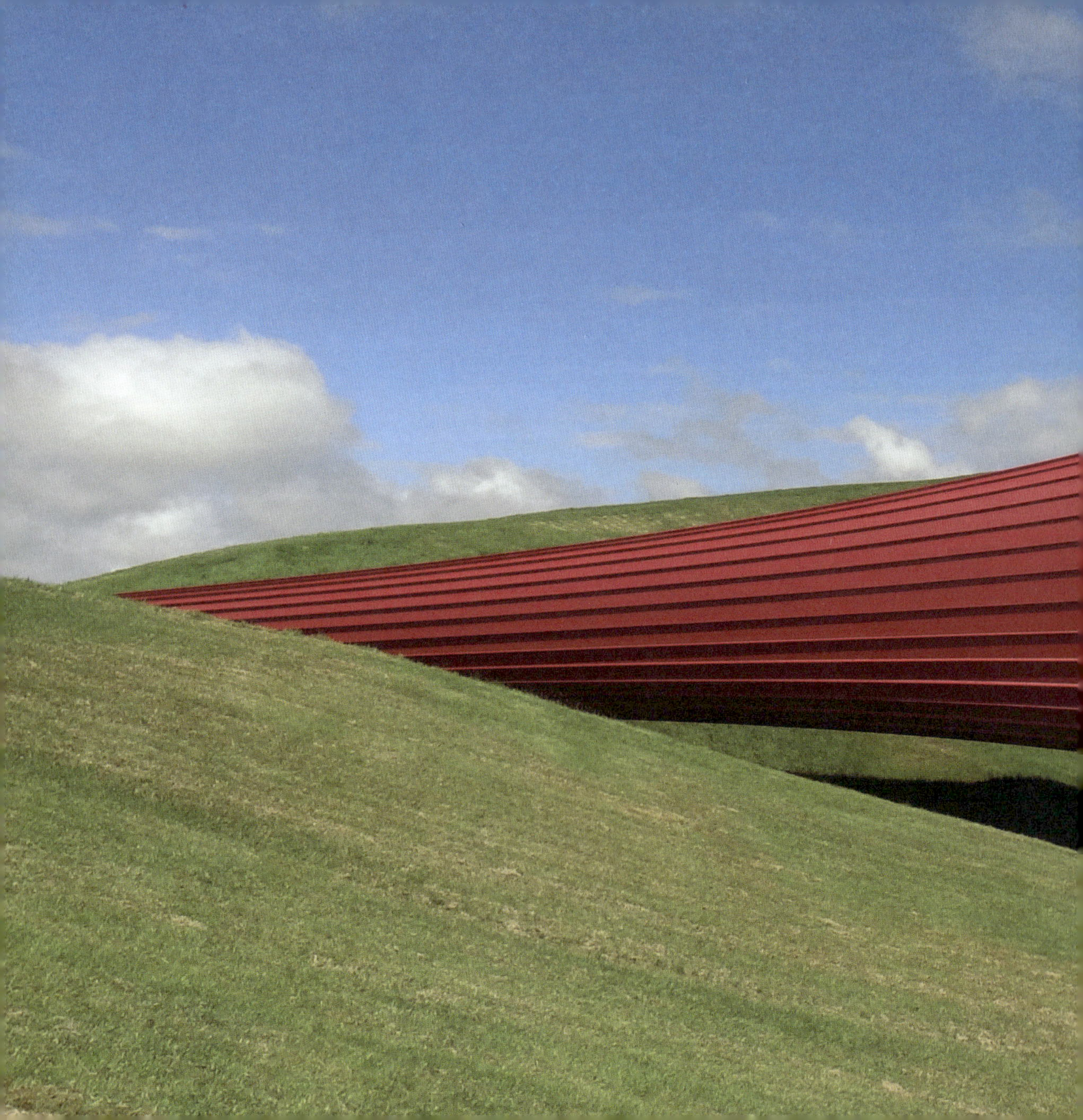

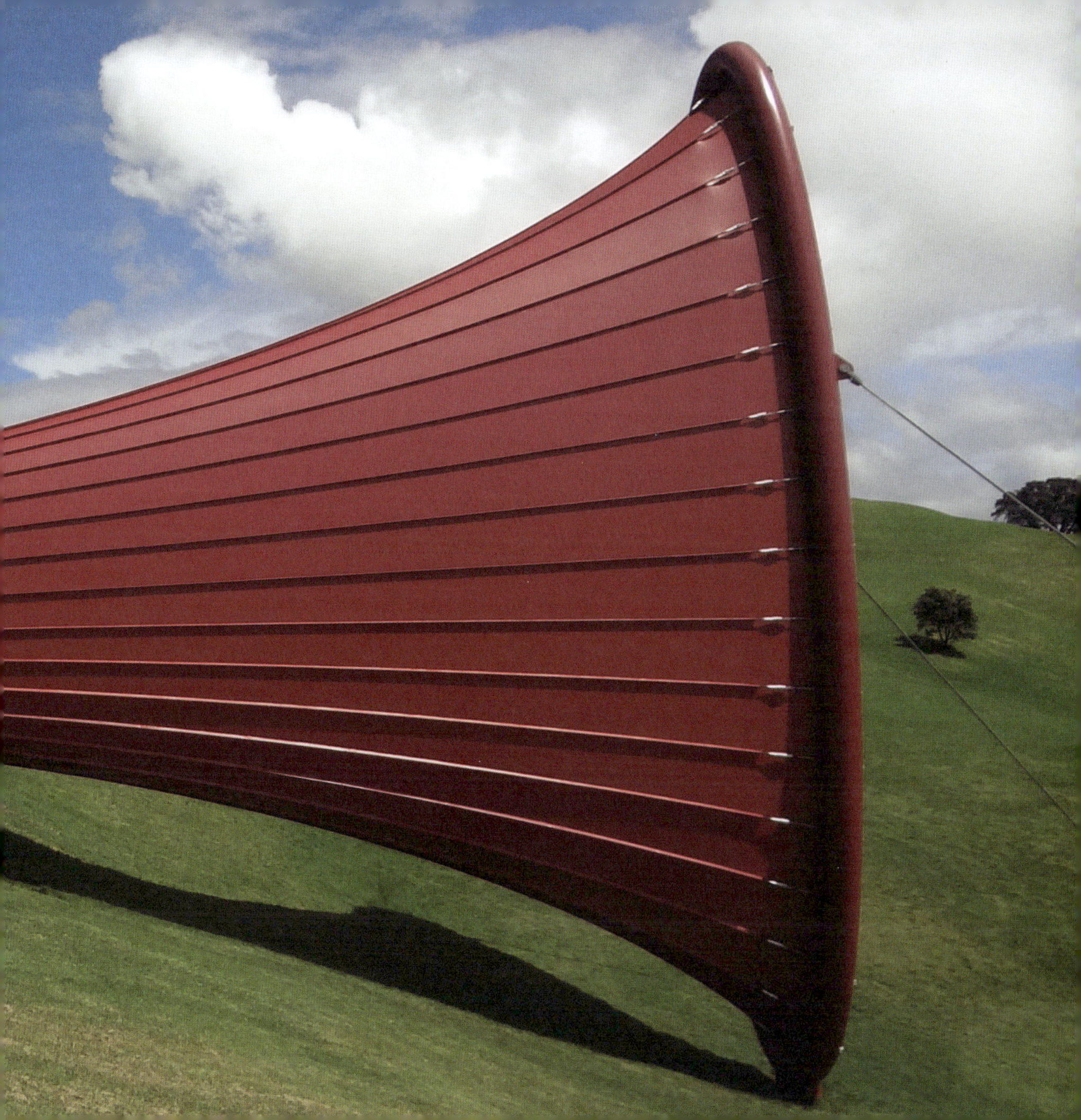

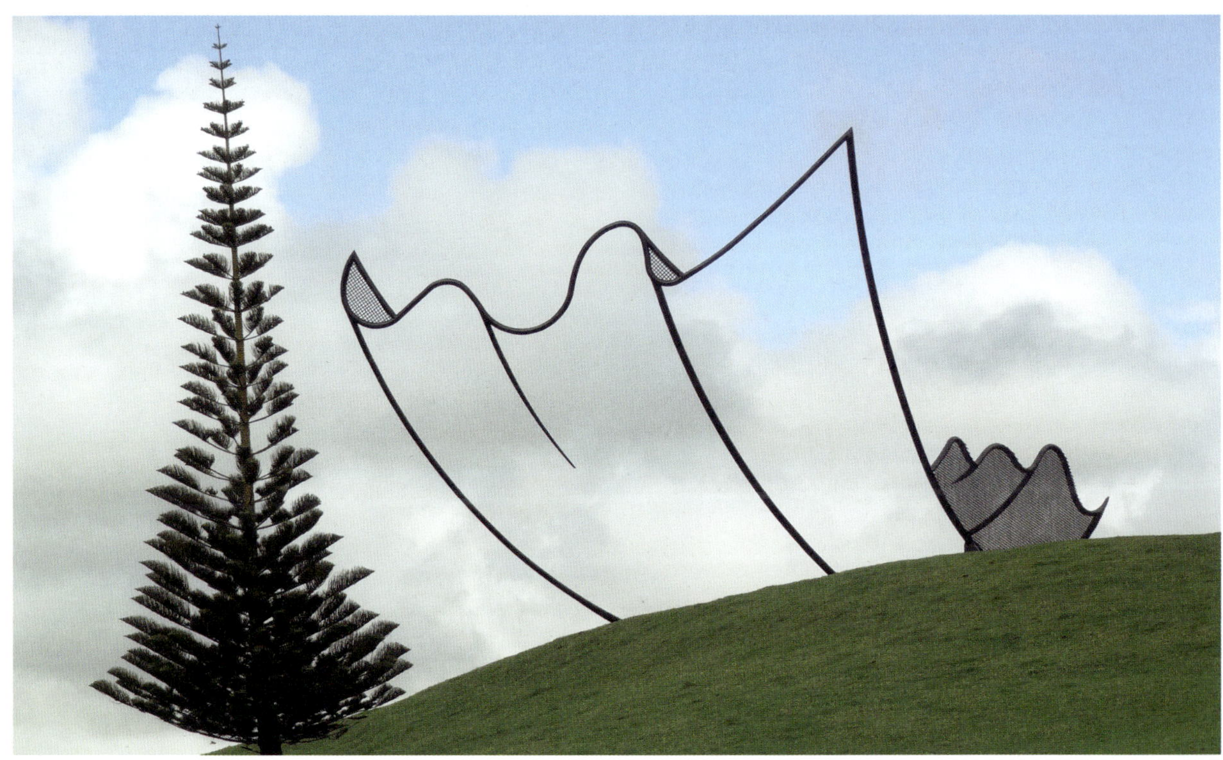

Landscape and sculpture interact in graceful and dramatic ways because of the thoughtfulness with which Gibbs has grown the collection. The silhouette of the pasture is sometimes re-shaped to accommodate an individual artwork. Rarely does one see site and work so perfectly balanced. Each project requires several site visits before a concept is agreed on and developed. During these productive visits, the artists live on the farm with Gibbs and his family. Daughter Amanda and her husband Noel Lane run the estate now that Gibbs is in London for much of each year.

In addition to the most extraordinary sculpture collection, Gibbs Farm is also home to exotic animals such as giraffes, zebras, water buffalo, ostriches and yaks. This makes a visit to the gigantic sculpture park even more surreal.

Alan Gibbs founded Gibbs Amphibians and has been involved in manufacturing, merchant banking, transport and security. He was a key force behind the introduction of Sky television to New Zealand and joint leader of a syndicate that purchased Telecom.

VISITOR INFORMATION

Gibbs Farm is open to the public once a month by prior appointment only. The open days, usually the 3rd or 4th Thursday of each month between 10am and 2pm (other than during school holidays and the winter months), are posted on the website. After filling out the contact form on the website, the applicant will receive an email confirming the visit along with instructions. The dates are booked out quickly and it is necessary to plan ahead well in advance.

**Admission Fees:** Free of charge

**Tours:** Staff members will meet pre-registered visitors at the gate from 10am onwards. Cars must be parked behind the gate as access to all artworks is by foot unless prior arrangements have been made with the farm manager. Good walking shoes are mandatory as the visit to the Gibbs Farm is an intense 3–4 hour walking experience. A comprehensive brochure assists with a self-guided tour. Private buildings are off-limits to visitors.

**Access by car:** Heading north out of Auckland on State Highway 1 to Pine Valley Road, turn right onto Pine Valley Road, turn right onto Kahikatea Flat Road and right again onto State Highway 16. The grey entrance gate to Gibbs Farm can be found on the left-hand side after 14.6 km. The drive will take about 45 to 60 minutes in normal traffic.

**Extra Tip:** Driving from Auckland, one passes Kaipara Coast Sculpture Gardens. As part of this specialist plant nursery and garden centre, the sculpture garden features annually changing, curated exhibitions. Following the 1-km trail through a secluded valley, visitors can enjoy about fifty carefully placed sculptures, as well as picnic spots with nice vistas. The works of art are for sale and the entrance fee is $10 (1481 Kaipara Coast Highway, Kaukapakapa).

**Restaurant Tip:** There are currently no recommended restaurants and coffee shops in the area. It is advisable to bring one's own packed lunch and drinks. A sheltered picnic area and toilet facilities are available at the Barn.

Page 138
Leon van den Eijkel, *Red cloud confrontation in landscape*, 1996
25 cast formed and painted concrete cubes, 1750 x 1750 cm

Pages 140-1
Richard Serra, *Te Tuhirangi contour*, 1999/2001
56 Cor-ten steel plates, 252m x 6m x 50mm

Pages 142-3
Andy Goldsworthy, *Arches*, 2005
Pink Leadhill sandstone blocks stacked into
11 freestanding arches, 70 cm (each arch)

Pages 144-5
Anish Kapoor, *Dismemberment, site 1*, 2009
Mild steel tube, tensioned fabric, west end 250 x 80 cm, east end 80 x 250 cm, length 8500 cm

Page 147
Neil Dawson, *Horizons*, 1994
Welded and painted steel, 1500 x 1000 x 3600 cm

All images courtesy Gibbs Farm

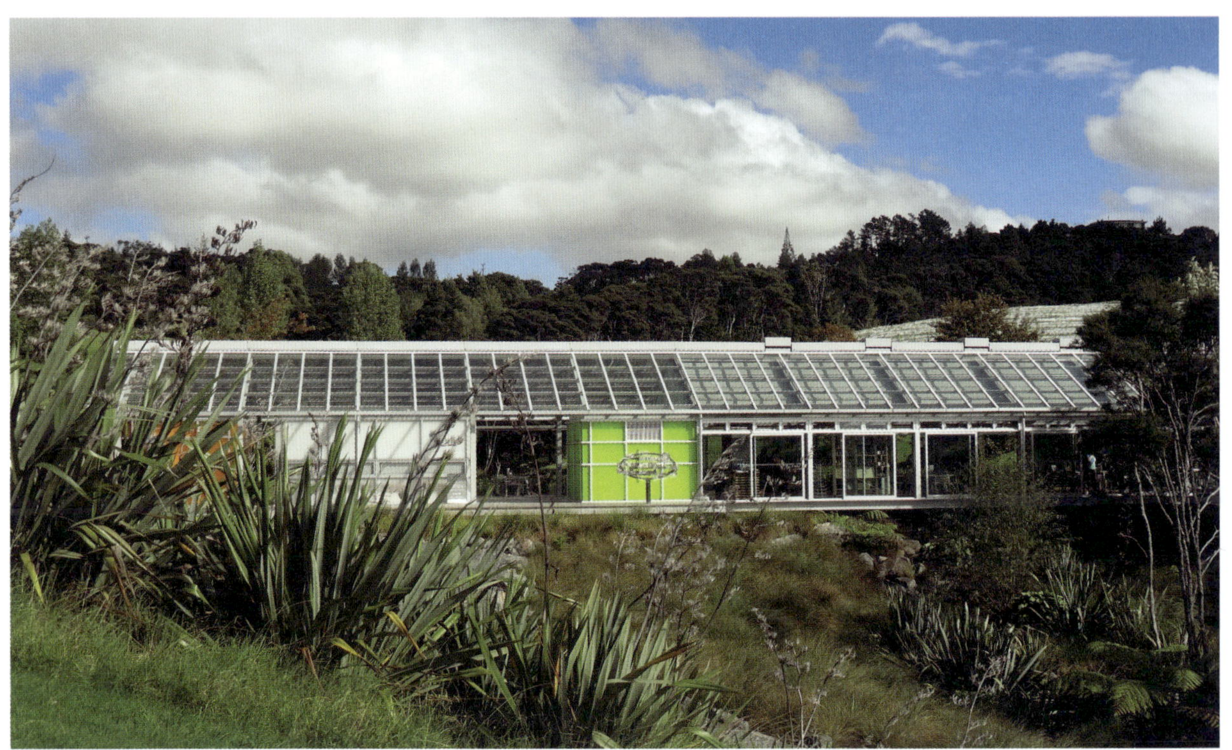

# BRICK BAY SCULPTURE TRAIL

Arabella Lane
Snells Beach
Warkworth

OPENING HOURS
Daily 10am–5pm year around (refer to the website for extended opening hours during the summer months)

Telephone: +64 (9) 425 4690
sculpture@brickbay.co.nz
brickbaysculpture.co.nz

As a wonderful cultural – and viticultural – destination, chic rural Matakana offers a perfect country sojourn for international visitors and New Zealanders alike. At Brick Bay, an enchanting combination of contemporary art, architecture and wine make it a perfect place to experience what New Zealand has to offer in a sophisticated yet casual style.

Christine and Richard Didsbury first came to Matakana from Auckland in 1986 when they bought a coastal farm and slowly changed an old brickworks site with plantings of rare and native trees. The brickworks was originally established in the 1840s in a small bay on the eastern boundary of the property, using the local clay to supply the bricks for the copper mines on nearby Kawau Island. The Didsburys commissioned well-known Auckland architect Noel Lane to design a house, initially intended as a holiday home, around the historic and now iconic brick tower. They added several parcels of land in and around Matakana to their portfolio in the early 1990s and, in 1995, started planting the first Brick Bay Wines vineyards on 4.5 hectares. Being long-time collectors of sculptures and enthusiastic patrons of the arts in general, and having commissioned several site-specific sculptures on their farm, they faced the increasing dilemma of wanting to share their art while retaining their own privacy. A visit to the Cass Sculpture Foundation, a sculpture park based at Goodwood in West Sussex, England, confirmed their initial idea about an outdoor gallery on the property adjacent to their private grounds. Subsequently the Sculpture Trail and Glass House were conceived and built from 2004 to 2006, opening to the public in 2007.

Luminescent green, white and orange cubes glow from within the giant, award winning Glass House. Hovering above a lake on one side and a cascade of rocks on the other, it also serves the purpose of an elegant café/restaurant/wine-tasting area, as well as providing a display room for small-scale indoor sculptures. Noel Lane's highly successful modern design reflects the area's industrial past and present. The slatted timber floors refer to the nearby shearing sheds, and the glass transparency to the horticultural hothouses.

The Sculpture Trail, accessed via the Glass House, offers a selection of ever-changing top calibre New Zealand artists, including Virginia King, Jeff Thomson, Gretchen Albrecht, Paul Dibble, Phil Price, Leon van den Eijkel, Louise Purvis, Gregor Kregar, Terry Stringer and David McCracken. All manner of media are represented. Each sculpture has been carefully sited to interact with the natural surroundings in which it is placed. The landscape is sympathetically used to ensure that the environment is the canvas. The 2-kilometre trail, which covers approximately 8 hectares of land, allows a wonderful mix of walking, contemplation and discovery. Over fifty artworks are installed along the path that winds past two small lakes, swamp, elevated vines, bird-filled forest glades and through the adjacent farmland into the native bush. Here ferns, rimu and kauri trees, nikau groves and creepers thrive. Smaller artworks are to be found in the Shrunk courtyards behind the Glass House, an ideal outdoor setting for their more intimate scale.

Based on the concept of the Cass Sculpture Foundation, the Didsburys have created a charitable trust with a curatorial panel to assess artists' applications for funding large-scale outdoor works. Successful applicants have their completed works installed on the trail and these works are for sale. Only the work *Meteorol* by Mary-Louise Browne and Peter Lange's *Last man down* are owned by the trust and on permanent display. The artists use part of their sale proceeds to repay their loan. The trust recycles these funds to finance new artworks, to manage the trail and to fund the annual Temporary Artist Projects, the Brick Bay Folly (launched in 2015), plus new media, sound and ephemeral works which are not for sale. During the summer months, one artist, or a

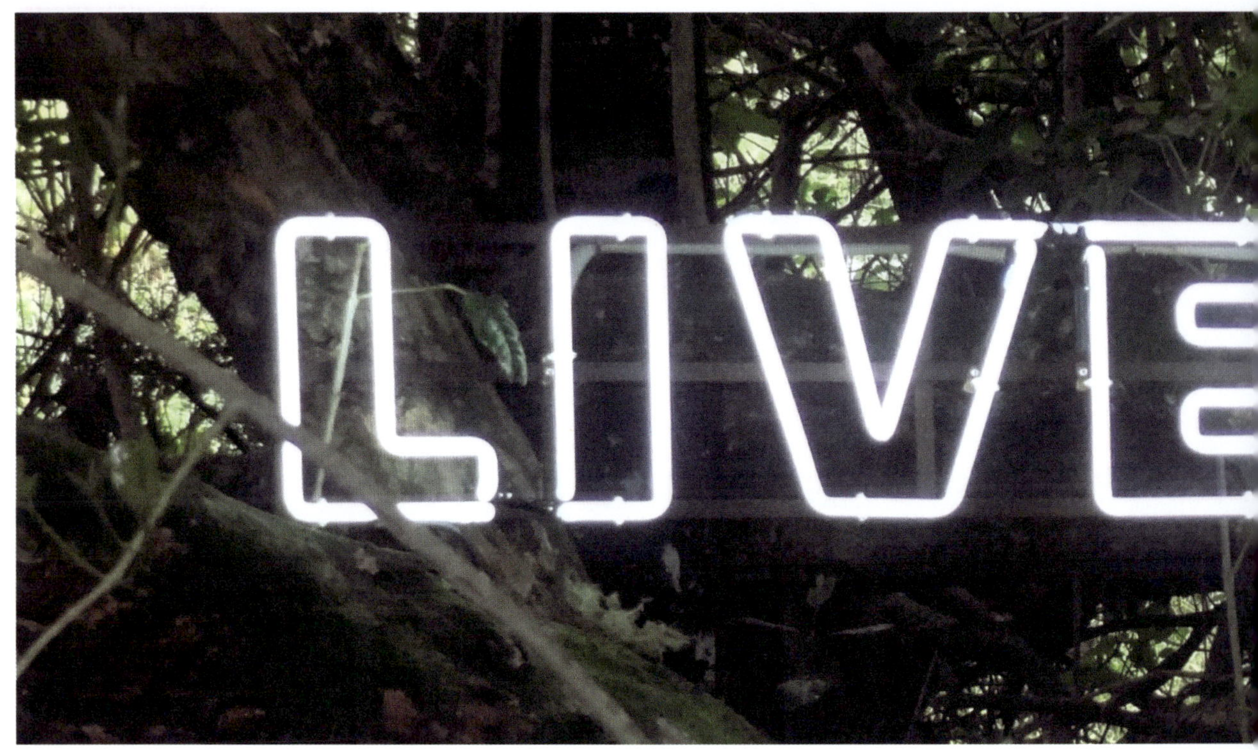


team of artists, are commissioned to install works throughout the park with the brief to broaden the perspective of what sculpture can be. Artists such as Judy Darragh, Tracey Tawhiao and Konstantin Dimopoulos have been part of this stimulating summer exhibition program.

The Brick Bay Folly is based on a project organised by Socrates Sculpture Park and the Architectural League of New York. Emerging New Zealand architects or architecture students are invited to explore the increasing conceptual and technical overlaps between architecture and sculpture, with winning works to be installed on the Sculpture Trail for twelve months, beginning each March. The diverse projects as well as the ongoing exchange of works make frequent visits to Brick Bay worthwhile.

Brick Bay is a great example of a successful family collaboration. Richard was formerly a founding shareholder and director of Kiwi Income Properties Limited and is the overall mentor and ideas man behind the family business. Christine is regarded as wine guru and brand guardian, having enrolled in winemaking and viticulture at EIT (Eastern Institute of Technology), Hawke's Bay. The Didsbury's daughter, Anna, who has a background in both art and viticulture, returned home after working at a biodynamic estate in France to become Brick Bay's general manager.

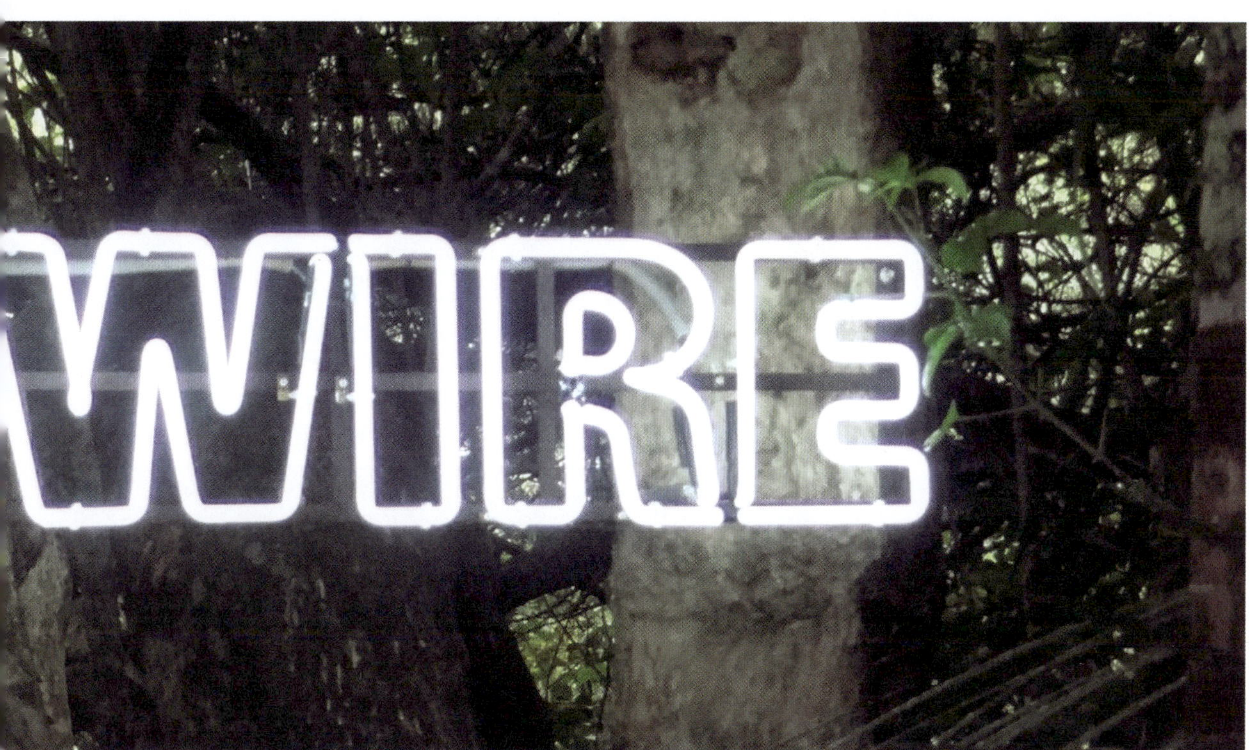


VISITOR INFORMATION

**Admission Fees:** Adult/Concession: $12/$10

**Tours and other Events:** During the summer months, Brick Bay occasionally conducts tours as well as special art and music events. These occasions offer the rare opportunity to experience and view permanent art installations in the private parts of the property.

**Access by car:** Brick Bay is located about 50 minutes north of Auckland city (close to Snells Beach and not to Matakana as the address would suggest). Take the northern motorway (SH1) to Warkworth. At the third set of traffic lights on SH1, turn right and after only 50 m take the right fork to Sandspit/Snells Beach. After 8 km, drivers will see the brown Brick Bay Wines & Sculpture Trail sign. After 1 km, turn left into Arabella Lane and then down the second driveway on the left.

**Access by public transport:** There are frequent coach services to Warkworth by Intercity Coach Lines (+64 (9) 583 5780) and Northliner Express, both leaving from Sky City Coach Terminal, Hobson Street, Auckland City. Services are also operated by Nakedbus, leaving along

Quay Street, across from the ferry building on Auckland's waterfront. To get to Brick Bay from Warkworth (about 10 km), one can either take a taxi (Warkworth Taxi, +64 (9) 425 0000 and Matakabs, +64 (9) 422 2244) or hop on a Kowhai Connection minibus.

**Extra Tips:** On Saturday mornings, visitors can enjoy fresh produce, food and coffee and soak up the colourful atmosphere at the Matakana Farmers Market in Matakana. Richard Didsbury and his wife Christine positively influenced the face and ambience of Matakana forever by asking Noel Lane to design the sophisticated Matakana Village complex that includes art galleries, restaurants and a stunning boutique cinema (the ceiling of one of the theatres is covered with 32,000 handcrafted 'flowers'), and by subsequently donating the land behind the Village Complex for the popular Farmers Market (2 Matakana Valley Road; Saturdays, 8am–1pm). A small detour from Matakana to the magnificently sited Tawharanui Regional Park rewards visitors with stunning beaches, active bird life and great walking tracks (Takatu Road, Warkworth).

Visitors to the region might enjoy a taste of history and some unusual fauna and flora by taking the ferry from Sandspit to Kawau Island, former residence of Governor George Grey.

On the road between Warkworth and Matakana, the Protea Patch Nursery accommodates the charming sculpture garden The Sculptural Habitat (545 Matakana Road, RD5, Warkworth; open daily 9am–4pm except Wednesdays; entrance fee $5).

A visit to Brick Bay during the summer months can be easily combined with a trip to Zealandia (refer to page 150). The Matakana area offers a wide range of accommodation to suit any budget. The exclusive Takatu Lodge and Vineyard provides for a perfect overnight stay in a modern, hacienda-style lodge (518 Whitmore Road, Matakana).

**Restaurant Tips:** The Glass House Kitchen at Brick Bay offers relaxed all-day dining. The menu showcases seasonal produce and locally sourced ingredients, many of which are grown on the property. On the way from Matakana to Brick Bay, the smart vineyard restaurant-cum-cellar door Plume offers international and local cuisine (49a Sharp Road, Matakana RD2, Warkworth; +61 (9) 422 7915; closed Mondays and Tuesdays other than during the high season). The best ice-cream of the region and locally harvested fruits are available daily just a few metres away from Plume at Charlies Gelato Garden (17 Sharp Road). Located in Matakana, Plume Café serves freshly baked patisseries and bread (1335 Leigh Road, Matakana (entrance off Wharf Road); open daily until 3pm).

Page 144
Gretchen Albrecht, *Oceans, islands, sky*, 2006
Stainless steel plate, stainless steel mesh, 170 x 230 x 39 cm

Pages 146-7
Mary-Louise Browne, *Live wire*, 2009
Neon, 25 x 183 x 15 cm

Page 149
Gregor Kregar, *Reflective habitat*, 2013
Stainless steel, dimensions variable

All images courtesy Brick Bay Sculpture Trail

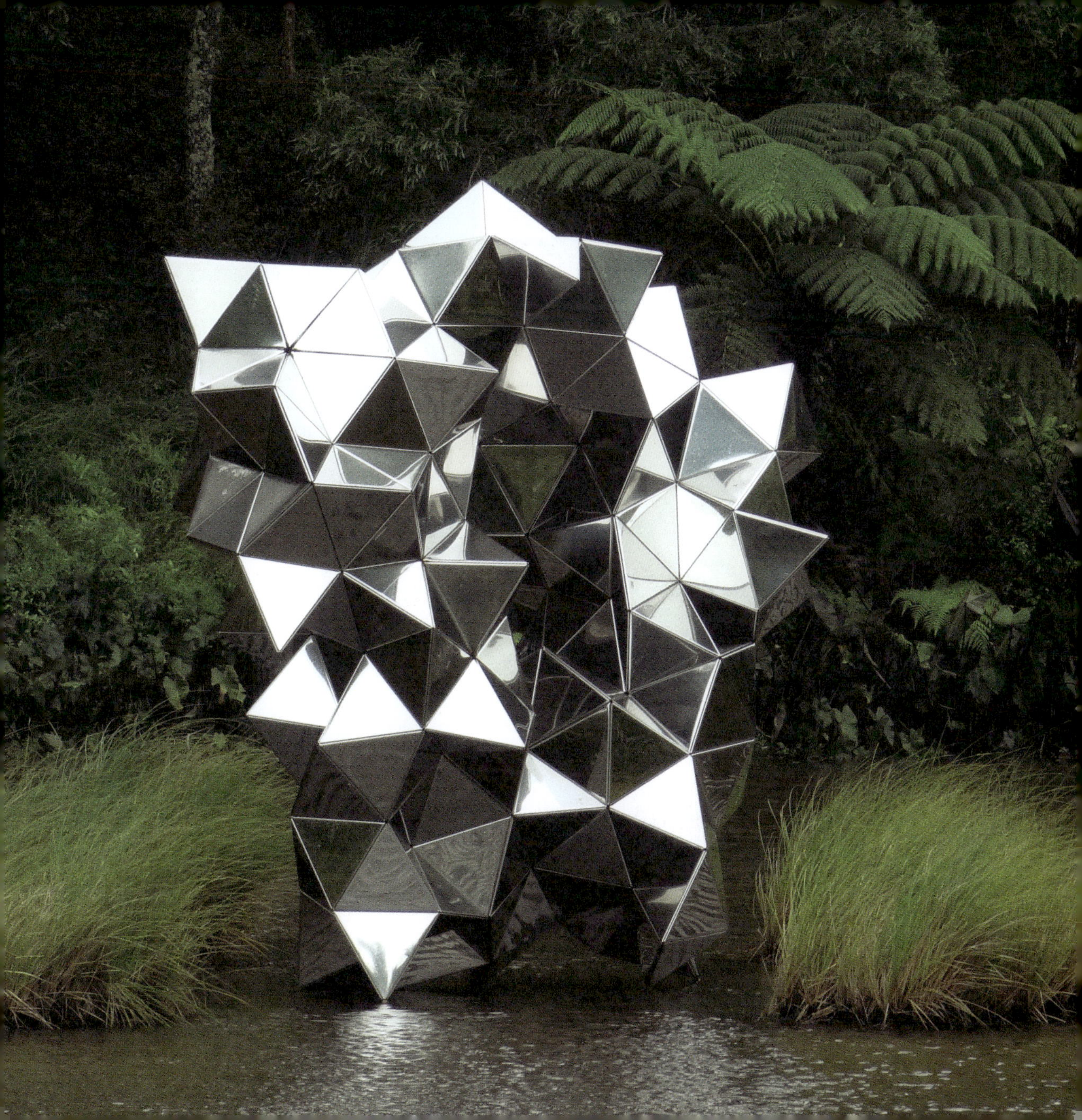

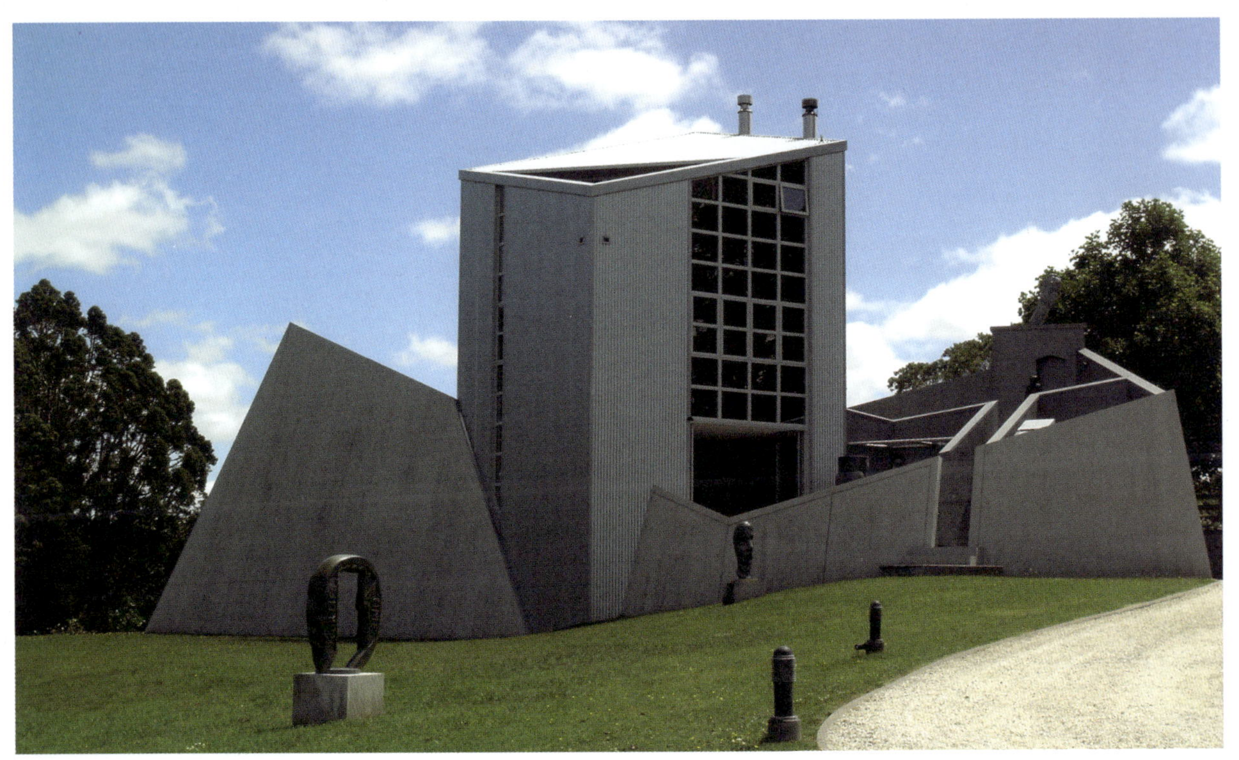

# ZEALANDIA SCULPTURE GARDEN

138 Mahurangi West Road
RD 3, Warkworth

OPENING HOURS
A visit is possible by prior appointment
from November–March

Telephone: 0274 987 987
timmcw@ihug.co.nz
zealandiasculpturegarden.co.nz

Zealandia Sculpture Garden, located about 50 kilometres north of Auckland, also serves as a residence for owners Terry Stringer – one of New Zealand's most acclaimed sculptors – and his partner Tim McWhannell. Opened to the public in 2000, its name refers to the 'daughter' of Britannia depicted on New Zealand's coat of arms. Terry and Tim have created an exquisite space that conveys the essence of the country by engaging the visitor in a symbolic sculptural vision of New Zealand's pastoral landscape.

The site comprises an imposing sculptural building idiomatic of the New Zealand shed, the Gate Gallery (next to the car park) and the Enclosed Garden. From there a steep walkway leads into a small but enchanting Kauri forest and beyond to a vista of large sculptures spread out on manicured lawn. The main building and Gate Gallery were designed by well-known Auckland architect Pip Cheshire in collaboration with Terry Stringer. They house the annual changing exhibitions of art-works from Terry's collection or on loan from guest artists. As a result of Terry's wide-ranging interest in art, exhibitions may include folk art, nineteenth-century Russian icons, small sculptures and a diversity of paintings. Terry Stringer's fascination with riddles is demonstrated on the exhibition level of the main building, where a trapeze-shaped room with plywood panelling and rotating walls reveals a hidden room decorated with his intriguing sculptural illusions.

The Enclosed Garden is a small maze built on the site of the original cattle yards. Works by former tutors Greer Twiss and Molly McAllister, alongside sculptures by Chris Booth, Richard McWhannell and Mary-Louise Brown are displayed here, together with Terry Stringer's references to Lois White and Paul Beadle. The principal focus of this collection is interactivity between the work and the viewer.

A steep walkway leads to a small platform overlooking some lush New Zealand bush that cradles an ancient kauri tree, possibly 1000 years old. It is framed by carefully placed sculptures by Terry Stringer and other artists. On leaving the bush, visitors are encouraged to wander among the sculptures on the lawns. A group of Stringer's outdoor sculptures has as their theme the 'passing of time'. Some start from a conceptual idea. Others reference patterns in nature. The subject matter may derive from classical myth, literature or the Christian religion. An important characteristic of Stringer's work is that the human form is the starting point for most of his sculptures, each having more than one principal viewing point.

This enchanting and diverse park is enhanced by the individual attention given to each visitor. Tim McWhannell welcomes guests with a cup of tea or coffee inside the main building and guides them around different parts of the property and the fifty-six sculptures. For the next few years, visitors will be able to enjoy the sculpture park, as well as having access to Stringer and McWhannell's private museum in Auckland. The new establishment, in a large warehouse in Eden Terrace (Couldry Street), will feature Stringer's works in the context of a collection of pieces by colleagues and teachers, including paintings by A. Lois White and sculptures by Paul Beadle.

VISITOR INFORMATION

**Admission Fees:** $10 per person (15 years and over)

**Access by car:** From Auckland, the drive takes about 45 minutes. Travel on the Northern Motorway towards Warkworth and, 3.5 km after passing the Puhoi turn-off, turn right into Mahurangi West Road (see signage for Mahurangi Regional Park). The signposted car park for Zealandia can be found 1.5 km on the right.

**Access by public transport:** The Northstar Bus 895 and 895X (a faster service) Midtown to Waiwera depart Auckland from Stop 7073 at 13 Albert Street and arrive near 2 Waiwera Road. A prior arrangement for a pick-up by Tim is necessary.

**Extra Tips:** The nearby Mahurangi Regional Park is the perfect spot for a walk and a picnic.

A visit to Zealandia can be easily combined with a trip to the Brick Bay Sculpture Trail (refer to page 144) and the Matakana area.

**Restaurant Tips:** Great pub food is served at the rustic historic Puhoi Pub Hotel & Stables (up from the corner of Puhoi Road and Saleyards, Puhoi). Cheese lovers will enjoy a stop at the Puhoi Valley Café & Cheese Store (275 Ahuroa Road, Puhoi). Wine and sharing platters (served on long wine barrel trays) can be enjoyed during the day at the contemporary Ransom Wines Vineyard (46 Valerie Close, Warkworth, just off State Highway 1; closed Mondays).

Page 150 and right
Courtesy Terry Stringer and Zealandia Sculpture Garden

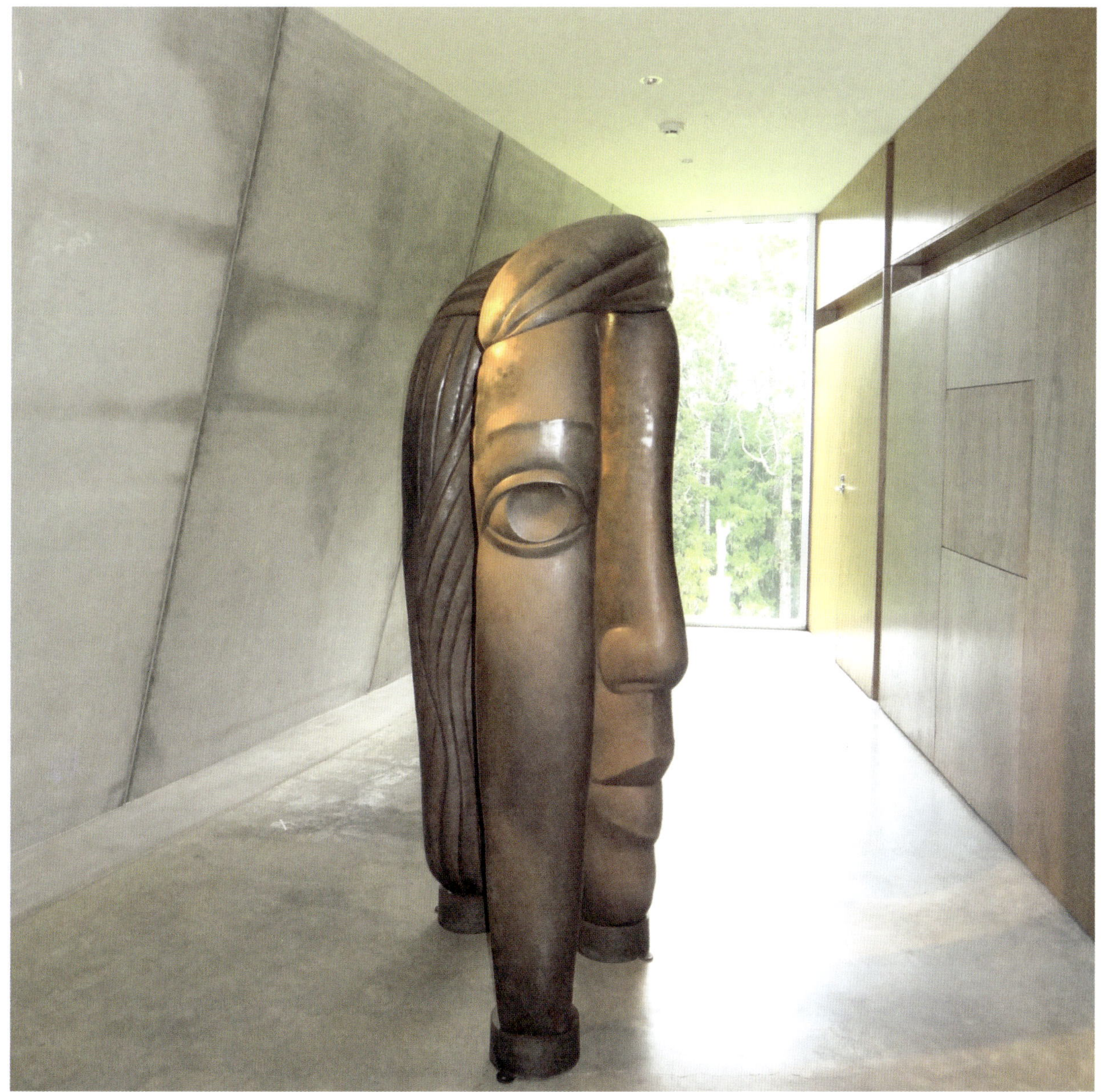

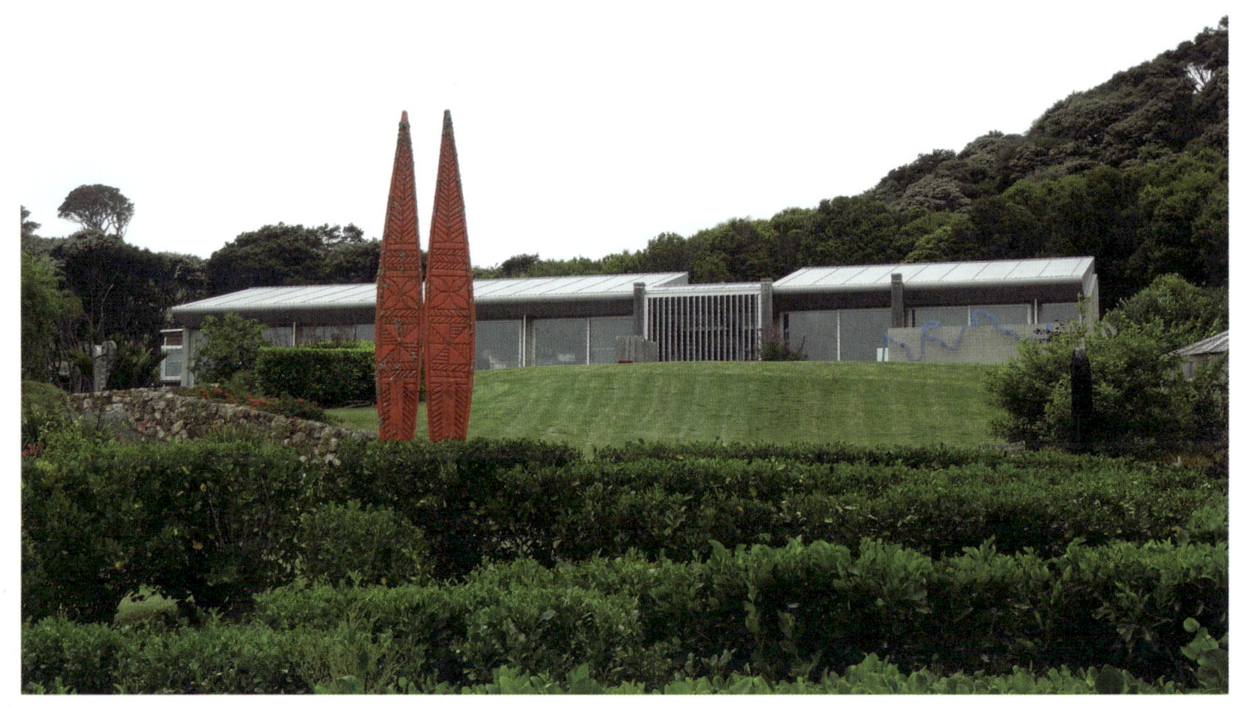

# DEAD DOG BAY WETLAND GARDEN + SCULPTURE

100 Margaret Reeve Lane RD1
Te Whau
Waiheke Island

OPENING HOURS
Daily 10am–5pm

Telephone: +64 (9) 372 6748 or (021) 426290
contact@deaddogbay.co.nz
deaddogbay.co.nz

Hidden in a secluded valley on Waiheke Island, facing Putiki Bay and the Okoka wetland, this property delights both gardening and art enthusiasts alike. The Te Whau Peninsula was subdivided in the 1990s, and what is now colloquially known as Dead Dog Bay was part of the last stage. Kay and Lance Peterson, avid sailors who moved up from Hawke's Bay after their retirement to be closer to one of New Zealand's top sailing destinations, bought the land in 2005. They also owned the neighbouring property, Te Whau Garden, which had been open to the public since 2003. It would take seven more years to develop Dead Dog Bay Wetland Garden & Sculpture. Having planted over 2000 New Zealand natives while mixing in exotic flowering trees, perennials, roses and flowering shrubs to add some colour, the park now incorporates 4 hectares of intensively planted garden and 1.2 hectares of raupo wetland, an area of special ecological significance.

The 'gallery in the garden' grew out of Kay Peterson's active involvement with Headland Sculpture on the Gulf. What began as a small assemblage of works by friends developed into a collection of about 100 ceramic and sculptural artworks, primarily by New Zealand artists. The unique domestic setting offers visitors the rare opportunity to partake in the Petersons' personal journey, which is widely reflected in their collection. Carefully positioned sculptures enhance the intimate and expansive spaces in the park and all around the private dwelling. Visitors are invited to roam through the backyard and even to admire the artworks on the veranda around the house (however, please refrain from entering the building). It is here that one comes across a delightful sculpture by Paul Dibble, an intricate artwork by Virginia King, as well as a large ceramic work by Barry Brickell.

The Petersons designed a concrete wall on the north-western corner of the bungalow to accommodate *Blue scribble*, a bright blue artwork by up-and-coming Auckland artist Louise Purvis. One of the Petersons' favourite artworks, *Heart 'x'* by Paratene Matchitt, is placed nearby. Other favourites include *Va-a-toa*, a fabulous red and yellow work by the well-known Auckland-based Samoan artist Fatu Feu'u, which represents the twin hulls of a Polynesian canoe, as well as the ceramic work *Prow* by Peter Lange (brother of late former prime minister David Lange). Rick Terstappen's rimu sculpture *Titama he taneata (The argument)*, which is based on a drawing by Arnold Wilson, is equally loved. The close associations with artists have also led to several site-specific sculptures. An interesting artwork in this category is Jeff Thomson's *Serpentine gateway*, which is the first sculpture visitors encounter when they walk onto the property. Terstappen, who is widely known for reusing industrial materials in his works, created a cluster of sculptures for Dead Dog Bay. *Tower* is a particularly impressive and personal work made from recycled galvanised steel trays which the Petersons used in their former food-processing business.

A stroll through the delightful property will take about an hour and a-half. Plenty of seats encourage visitors to take in the stunning views and to listen to birdsong.

VISITOR INFORMATION

**Admission Fees:** $10, to be deposited at the garden office, where a map and details for the self-guided tour are available

**How to get there:** By passenger ferry: Take the regular ferries, Fullers or Explore from downtown Auckland to Waiheke's Matiatia Wharf. Book ahead for a taxi (+64 0800 372 200 or +64 (9) 372 4111) or a rental vehicle (+64 (9) 372 8998 or +64 (9) 372 8001). Ananda Tours offer small or large group transport to the garden and guided tours on arrival. It is also easy to hop onto the Waiheke bus towards Rocky Bay, which meets the Fullers ferry in front of the ferry terminal. Ask the driver for a drop-off at the corner of Margaret Reeve Lane and O'Brien Road. Turn into the Margaret Reeve Lane (west) and turn left shortly before the end of the road. Please walk past the gate-chain to the garden office (200 m).

By car ferry from Half Moon Bay to Kennedy Point: Contact Sealink (+64 (9) 300 5900).

Driving from Matiatia: On picking up a rental car at the ferry landing, follow the signs through Oneroa towards Ostend. Follow Ostend Road, turn right into O'Brien Road and right again into Margaret Reeve Lane at the top of the hill. Please park the car on the road at the end of Margaret Reeve Lane, go back a few metres, turn right (south) and walk past the gate-chain to the garden office.

**Extra Tips:** Waiheke is a true paradise for nature and art lovers. The recently opened walking trail Te Ara Hura, which passes through Dead Dog Bay, links 100 km of tracks all around Waiheke Island. Hikers pass a range of sculptures, which are situated on private land, as well as several large public sculptures, which were acquired from previous Headland Sculpture on the Gulf events (refer to Connells Bay Sculpture Park), while taking in the stunning scenery on the west side of the island. The informative Te Ara Hura marker posts help visitors to stay on the trail. Free maps about the trail as well as the Waiheke Art Map, which includes galleries and open studios, are available at the island's information centres. If arranged beforehand, a visit to Dead Dog Bay can be easily combined with a trip to Connells Bay Sculpture Park (refer to page 158) during the summer months.

**Restaurant Tips:** Waiheke is home to many of New Zealand's most celebrated winemakers. Spectacular views and excellent food can be enjoyed at the ultra-modern Te Whau Vineyard & Restaurant (218 Te Whau Drive) as well as at the romantic Mudbrick Vineyard & Restaurant (Church Bay Road, Oneroa). The Shed at Te Motu Vineyard won Metro's Best Rural Restaurant Award 2014 for its outstanding food and unusual setting (76 Onetangi Road, Onetangi). Located in the main strip of the village of Oneroa, the popular and very trendy Oyster Inn serves tasty food in a joyful beach-chic atmosphere (124 Ocean View Road, Oneroa; +64 (9) 372 2222). The artisanal bakery Ringawera sells delicious bread and award-winning Lavash varieties. Located just around the corner from Dead Dog Bay, this quirky Maori enterprise is the perfect place for a coffee fix (104 Te Whau Drive; open daily from 8.30am–1pm during the summer months). Visitors are welcome to bring a picnic to Dead Dog Bay and even to take a swim at the adjacent beach.

Page 154 and right
All images courtesy Dead Dog Bay Wetland Garden & Sculpture

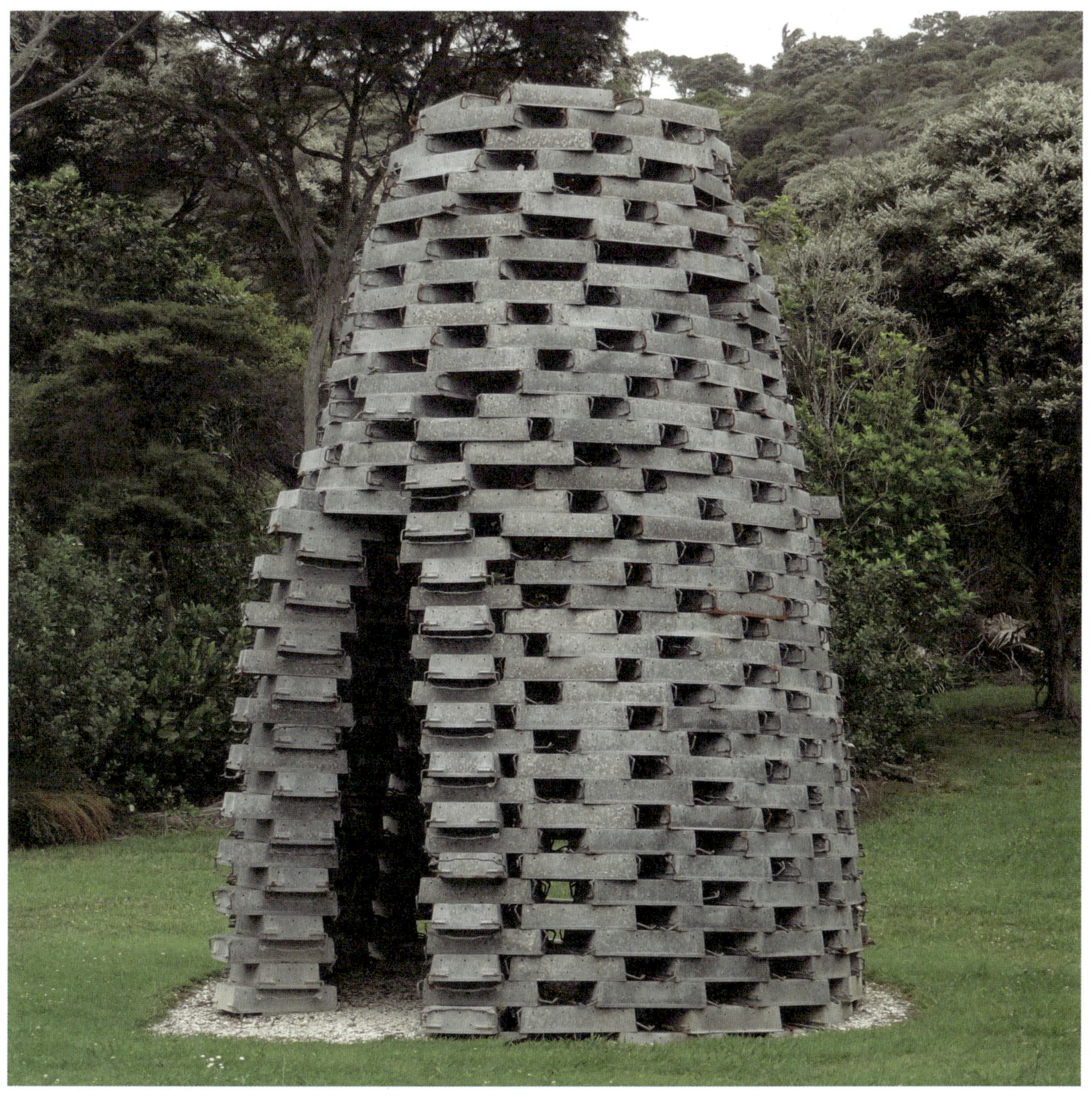

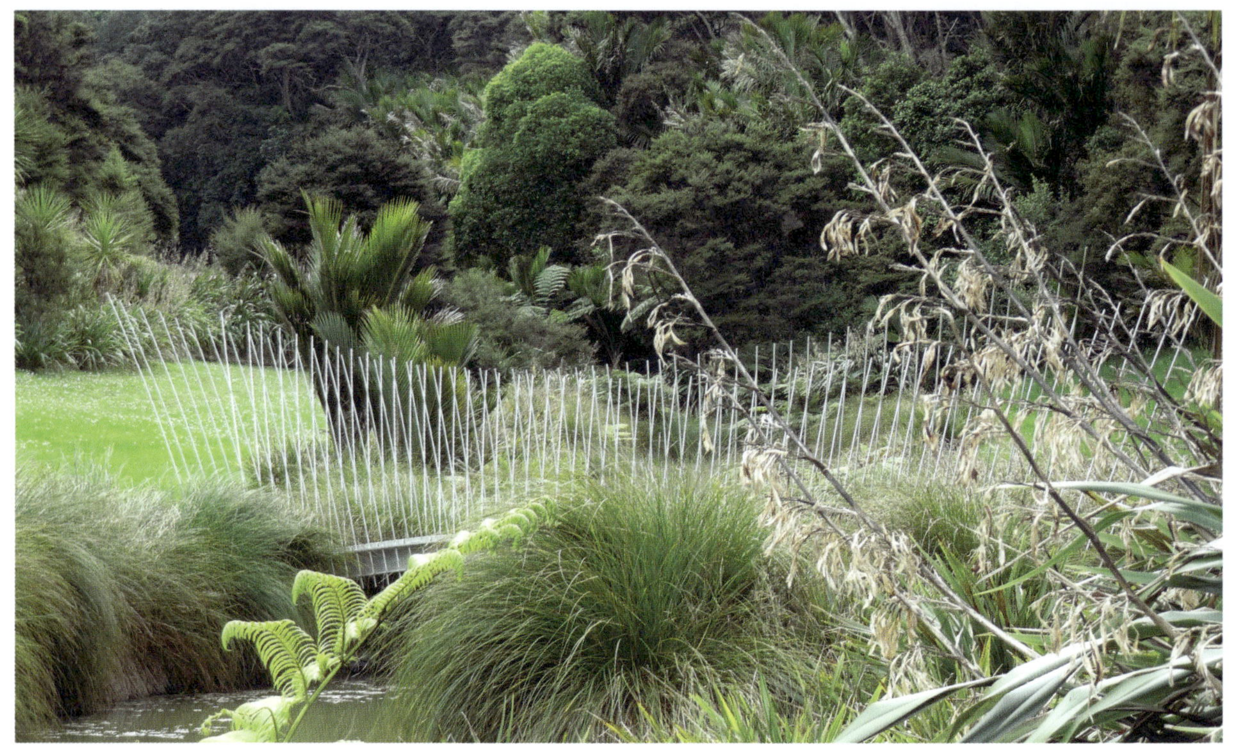

# CONNELLS BAY SCULPTURE PARK

142 Cowes Bay Road
Waiheke Island

OPENING HOURS
By appointment only, late October–late April

Telephone: +64 (9) 372 8957
info@connellsbay.co.nz
connellsbay.co.nz

In a remote and secluded spot on the eastern end of New Zealand's Waiheke Island, art admirers can discover a stunning 'gallery without walls'. Named for William and Jane Connell, who bought the 25-hectare land parcel in 1903, Connells Bay was at some stage not only a farm but also the site of a thriving general store, post office and boat-fuelling depot. It was under the proprietorship of the Connell family until 1980, then sold to Warren Fowler and in 1993 on-sold to John and Jo Gow. Initially set up as a private property for their own enjoyment, the Gows soon envisioned a sculpture park where art and nature are united to create special places to be enjoyed by a wider audience. They planted 20,000 native trees over fifteen years. And while slowly converting the wild and hilly property into a wonderful park with manicured paddocks among native bush areas, they placed majestic New Zealand sculptures throughout the property.

The growing collection currently includes over thirty documented sculptures of various sizes in concrete, ceramic, bronze, steel, aluminium and wood. Some sculptures trace the contour of history; others blend beautifully with the natural surroundings. Many of the commissioned sculptures relate to the owners' life story. Some, for example installations by Cathryn Monro and Chris Booth, are built into the land in such a way that they will be almost impossible to shift to another property at a later stage. Particularly interesting and intriguing is Gregor Kregar's *Vanish*, his final and largest self-portrait work, which comprises 160 colourful ceramic figures. Phil Dadson's *Tenantennae* is a stunning interactive acoustic work designed to engage viewers visually, physically and sonically. Equally involving is Virginia King's *Oioi Bridge*. The collection also includes works by David McCracken, Phil Price, Neil Dawson, Paul Dibble, Fatu Feu'u, Christine Hellyar, Jeff Thomson, Richard Thompson and other senior and emerging New Zealand artists. New works are being added from time to time. Every two years, a carefully selected photographic work is installed for a period of six months. The expectation of pushing boundaries can often be sensed in these finished works. Each unique installation along the 2-kilometre walkway reflects the commitment of all involved. Prior to opening Connells Bay to the public in 2004, John Gow spent twenty years in accounting and investment banking, successfully arranging funding for a number of major musicals in the United States, the United Kingdom and Australia, including *Cats*, *Les Miserables*, *Phantom of the Opera* and *Miss Saigon*. Jo was born in Uganda and, after studying nursing, pursued a number of positions in hospices, counselling, and exchange-student areas. John and Jo are well known in New Zealand as eager and generous benefactors in the arts.

Visitors receive an introduction to the artworks inside a small gallery building where books, artists' documentary photographs, drawings and maquettes are exhibited. A few small sculptures by selected artists whose works have found their permanent home at Connells Bay are on display for sale. All permanent sculptures are owned by the Connells Bay Sculpture Trust, which also leases the property on a long-term basis.

The nearby exquisitely renovated owners' guest cottage is available to visitors who would like to extend their stay at Connells Bay.

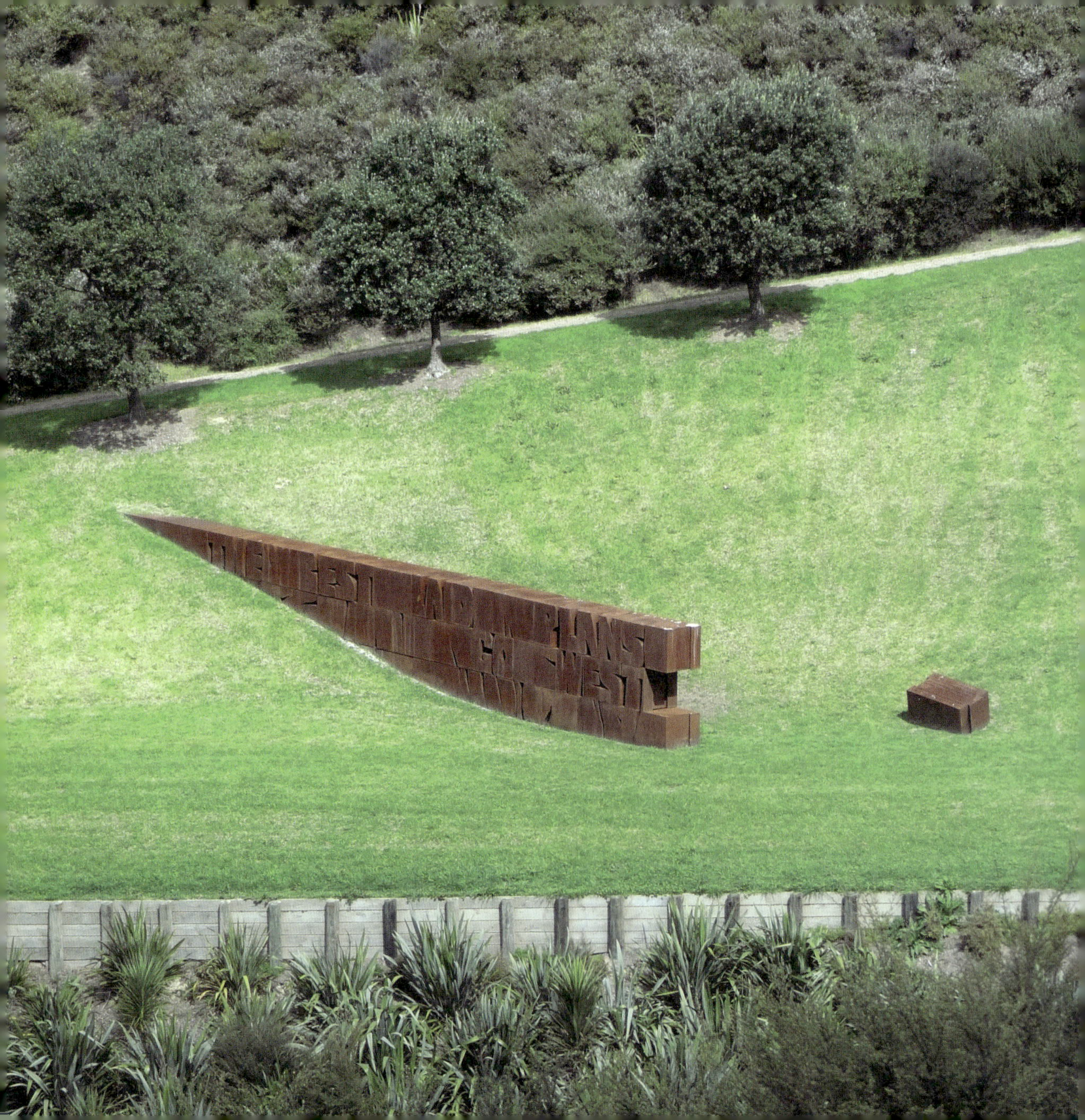
BEST LAID PLANS
GO WEST

VISITOR INFORMATION

A visit is only possible on a guided walk (approx. 2 hours), facilitated by the owners. Bookings can be made for a 10.30am or 3pm tour by completing a form on the website or by phone.

**Admission Fees:** Adults/Students/Child (under 15): $30/$25/$15

**How to get there:** By passenger ferry: Take the regular Fullers ferry from downtown Auckland to Waiheke's Matiatia Wharf. Book ahead for a taxi (+64 (9) 372 200 or +64 (9) 372 4111) or a rental vehicle (+64 (9) 372 8998 or +64 (9) 372 8001).

By car ferry from Half Moon Bay to Kennedy Point: contact Sealink (+64 (9) 732 546).

Driving directions for Connells Bay Sculpture Park will be provided to visitors when the appointment is confirmed.

**Extra Tips:** John Gow's passion for art and land conservation is not limited to Connells Bay. Latterly he was director of the Rotoroa Island Trust. For over 100 years, Rotoroa Island has been owned and used by the Salvation Army as an alcohol and drug rehabilitation centre. Having been off-limits to the general public, it became accessible as a day park in 2011 owing to the generosity of philanthropists Neal and Annette Plowman, as well as the work by John and other trustees. The island's award-winning exhibition centre and museum, walking trails through regenerating native bush, and iconic sculpture by Chris Booth are easily explored on a day trip from Auckland). During the first two weeks of February of every uneven year, Auckland's Waiheke Island showcases one of New Zealand's favourite summer art exhibitions: Headland Sculpture on the Gulf, which features selected large-scale sculptures by some of New Zealand's most respected artists set along a truly spectacular 2-km coastal walkway, starting close to the ferry landing.

Tourists and locals alike enjoy the fantastic opportunity to visit over twenty private gardens open to the public during a weekend in November as part of the Jassy Dean Garden Safari. Spending the Saturday on the island, visitors might enjoy stocking up at the Ostend Market on the way to the sculpture park (open 7.30am–1pm). A visit to Connells Bay can be easily combined with a trip to Dead Dog Bay Wetland Garden & Sculpture (refer to page 154).

**Restaurant Tips:** Man O'War Winery's Tasting Room, just 5 km past Connells Bay, offers a wonderful opportunity for a lunch by the beach (725 Man O'War Bay Road) whereas Passage Rock Winery offers a wine tasting, café menu and wood-fired pizzas on weekends, just 5 km before Connells Bay (438 Orapiu Road).

Visitors to Connells Bay are welcome to bring their own lunch to enjoy on the veranda outside the gallery, which overlooks the park. Please advise at the time of booking if that is the intention.

Page 158
Virginia King, *Oioi bridge*, 2002
Aluminium and silver coins, 700 cm (overall)

Page 161
David McCracken, *The best laid plans go west*, 2010
Welded Cor-ten steel, 1800 x 240 x 80 cm

All images courtesy Connells Bay Sculpture Park

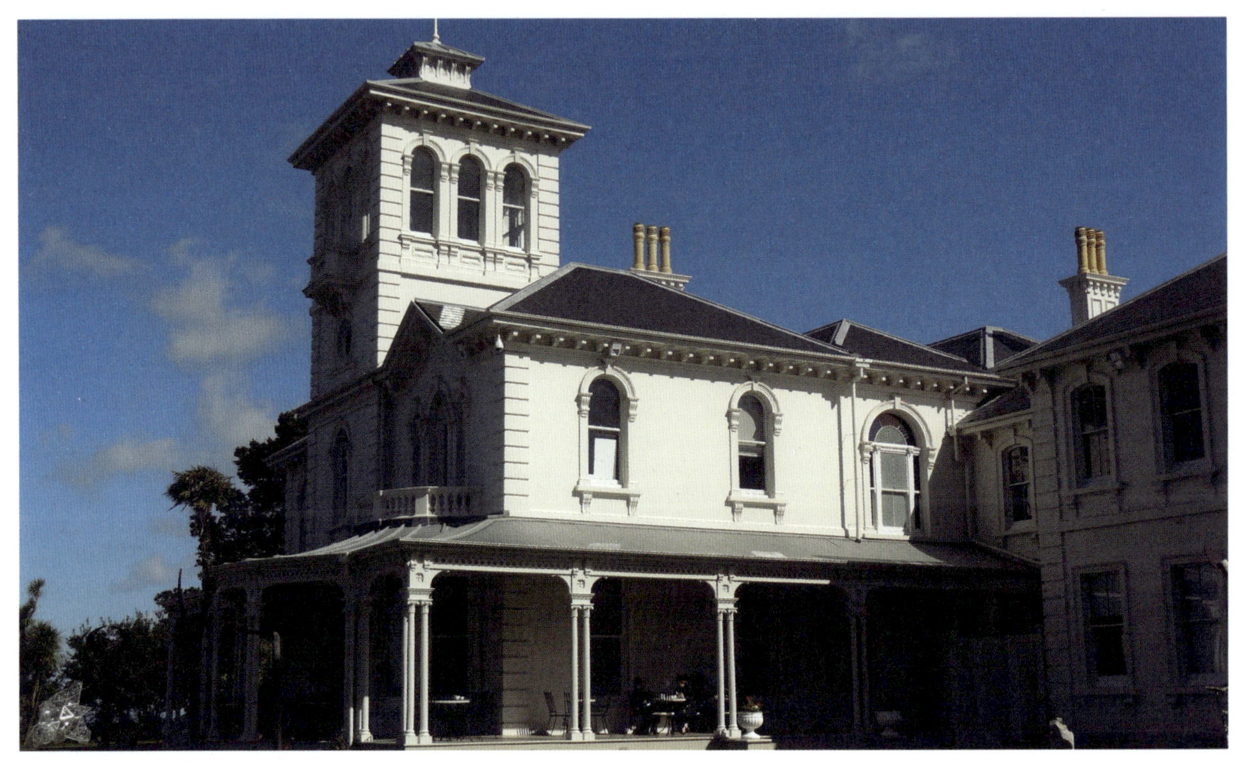

# TSB BANK WALLACE ARTS CENTRE

72 Hillsborough Road
Hillsborough
Auckland

OPENING HOURS
Tuesday–Friday 10am–3pm
Saturdays and Sundays 10am–5pm
Closed every Monday including public holidays

Tel +64 (09) 639 2010
tsbbankwallaceartscentre.org.nz
enquiries@wallaceartstrust.org.nz
wallaceartstrust.org.nz

Located in the beautiful historic Pah Homestead in Auckland's suburb Hillsborough, this exciting, distinctively New Zealand cultural destination can be easily reached from the city and the airport alike. Having opened in August 2010, the colourful Arts Centre is the main home of The Wallace Arts Trust and its epic collection. It is surrounded by Monte Cecilia Park, which offers some of the finest exotic trees in Auckland and magnificent views to Manukau Harbour and One Tree Hill. The original 162-hectare property was purchased from Maori by an early Auckland settler and then resold before James Williamson purchased it and built the Pah Homestead between 1877 and 1879 as his 'gentleman's residence'. Designed by the architect Edward Mahoney, the homestead was the largest house in the Auckland province at that time. It remains largely as it was built, with almost all of its original door and window joinery, parquet floors, marble fireplaces and even the hidden vault intact. At various times it has served as an orphanage, novitiate house, boarding school and emergency housing.

In 2002 the homestead was bought by the then Auckland City Council. Supported with generous contributions from The Wallace Arts Trust and the TSB Bank, Auckland Council extensively and painstakingly restored and adapted the homestead between 2009 and 2010. Mathews & Mathews Architects Ltd subsequently won the NZIA Auckland Architecture Award for Heritage in 2010. The trust has a long-term renewable lease for the homestead from Auckland Council and carries the ongoing operating expense. Helpful volunteer guides assist the trust's small professional administrative team.

Sir James Wallace, the Managing Director and Chairman of Wallace Corporation Ltd, a successful film producer and keen philanthropic arts patron, began collecting New Zealand art in the mid-1960s. He initially focused on the work of emerging artists and in 1992 formed the present charitable trust, transferring his collection to that Trust. He continually financially supports the trust to enable it to buy on average about 500 artworks a year, which he personally selects, and to fund the arts in New Zealand in general. The scope of the Arts Collection has now broadened to include works by 'mid-career' and 'established' New Zealand artists, creating a 'diary collection' and the possibility of presenting entire oeuvres. The collection currently holds over 8000 works of art and is intended to function as a cultural resource for all New Zealanders. The trust owns the strongest collection in any hands of many emerging and mid-career artists, as well as a number of senior artists such as Sir Toss Woollaston, Eion Stevens, Glenn Jowitt, Ian Scott, Terry Stringer, Mary McIntyre, Pete Wheeler, Gary Freemantle, Mark Braunias and Philip Trusttum. Other significant artists represented with a range of work include Dick Frizzell, Colin McCahon, Michael Smither, Don Binney, Richard Killeen, Stephen Bambury, Gretchen Albrecht, Denys Watkins, Peter Robinson, Francis Upritchard, Rohan Wealleans, Andrew McLeod, Peter Gibson Smith, Richard Lewer, Peter Panyoczki, Gregor Kregar and Max Gimblett. The trust has also initiated over eighty commissions ranging from Pat Hanly stained-glass windows to Terry Stringer sculptures.

Solo or themed exhibitions are curated from the Trust Collection about every six to eight weeks by Sir James Wallace and his team. These shows frequently link with other events in the larger Auckland area. The entire collection is catalogued and available on an online database (wallaceartstrust.org.nz). Approximately ten exhibitions annually are passed on to the Wallace Gallery Morrinsville, a community gallery with a permanent Wallace Arts Trust Collection exhibition room. In addition, The Wallace Arts Trust loans artworks to some fifty institutions ranging from schools to universities and hospitals. Occasionally, sections of the 770-square-metre homestead exhibition space are used by other travelling exhibitions as well as by exhibitions curated from the extensive collections of the Hocken Library. The attractive sculpture garden surrounding the Pah Homestead features a number of important sculptures by Gregor Kregar, Mark Hill, Terry Stringer, Jeff Thomson, Paul Dibble and other New Zealand artists.

In 2014 the 23rd Annual Wallace Art Awards were held, consisting principally of four major overseas residencies. These awards are now the longest surviving and richest annual art awards of their kind in New Zealand. The Arts Centre also houses an artist-in-residence program in association with the Otago University, mainly for non-visual artists. The trust gives numbers of other awards and prizes to schools and universities.

VISITOR INFORMATION

**Admission Fees:** Free of charge; a donation towards the operating expenses is appreciated

**Tours and other Events:** Introductory talks about the history of the Pah Homestead, the operations of the James Wallace Arts Trust and current exhibitions are available for groups of over five people. They need to be booked at least three weeks in advance (refer to website for details). Artists' talks about specific works or exhibitions are offered regularly. In addition, the Arts Trust organises various special events and activities throughout the year.

Art enthusiasts who would like to get an even more personal insight into Sir James Wallace's collection, might want to consider booking a tour through Rannoch, Sir James's private residence and garden. Originally named 'Moose Lodge', the architect James Lloyd built the four-storey arts-and-crafts house for a Canadian dental surgeon and his wife between 1913 and 1915. Sir James had the basement extended and the upper floor modified so that the whole house can function as a living museum of modern art. The ancient Mt Eden lava forest surrounding Rannoch is alive with architectural obscurities and curious forms, amounting to over a hundred sculptures from New Zealand's leading artists. Guided tours of Rannoch house and the enchanting Sculpture Forest can be arranged for groups between 10.30am and 4.30pm Monday to Friday and some Saturdays.

**Access by car:** Starting in downtown Auckland, head east on Custom Street, which changes into Beach Street, Parnell Rise, Parnell Road, Broadway, Manukau Road/Urban Route 12 (follow signs for Royal Oak/Onehunga). Turn right onto Mount Albert Road/Urban Route 10 (signs for Mt Albert Road/Route 10). Take the first left onto Hillsborough Road/

Urban Route 15 and then left again onto Delargey Avenue (which looks more like a driveway). The car park for the Arts Centre is on the left-hand side.

**Access by public transport:** There are several different bus companies leaving from midtown and downtown Auckland which pass Hillsborough Road. A direct bus is the infrequent Civic Centre to Lynfield Metrolink Bus 299. Leaving Queens Street (Stop 7055, opposite the Civic Theatre), it reaches the 'Opposite 67 Hillsborough Road' bus stop in about 30 minutes. The Airbus Express sets down passengers close to the Pah Homestead if drivers are alerted.

**Extra Tips:** The newly extended and fabulously refurbished Auckland Art Gallery, located in Auckland's CBD, is a must-see for every art addict visiting the city. The gallery's permanent collection showcases New Zealand art from the 1600s to the present day along with outstanding examples of international art. It is also the home of the privately owned Chartwell Collection, which is one of the best collections of contemporary art in New Zealand (corner Kitchener and Wellesley streets, Auckland).

Visitors who are looking for authentic and original contemporary New Zealand jewellery, might want to stop by at Fingers, an artists' initiative which is located across the road from the Art Gallery (2 Kitchener Street, Auckland).

The temple-like Auckland Museum comprehensively displays stunning authentic Pacific Island and Maori artefacts. The daily Maori Culture Performance provides an insightful introduction to Maori customs (The Auckland Domain, Parnell). Nearby, the beautiful Wintergarden displays a great overview of local bush vegetation and international flora.

**Restaurant Tips:** During the opening hours of the Arts Centre, the particularly atmospheric Pah Café, which is operated by renowned caterer Dawsons, serves great café-style food both inside and outside on the ground floor of the villa.

On the way back to town, several great coffee shops can be found in Mount Eden Village along Mt Eden Road. Also located in Mount Eden is Merediths, one of New Zealand's leading and most inventive restaurants (365 Dominion Road, Mt Eden; dinner only). The industrial area of Kingsland features several new additions to Auckland's lively coffee shop scene. The cheerful community café Crave serves great coffee and slices (25 McDonald Street, Kingsland).

Page 162
Courtesy TSB Bank Wallace Arts Centre

# SOUTH ISLAND

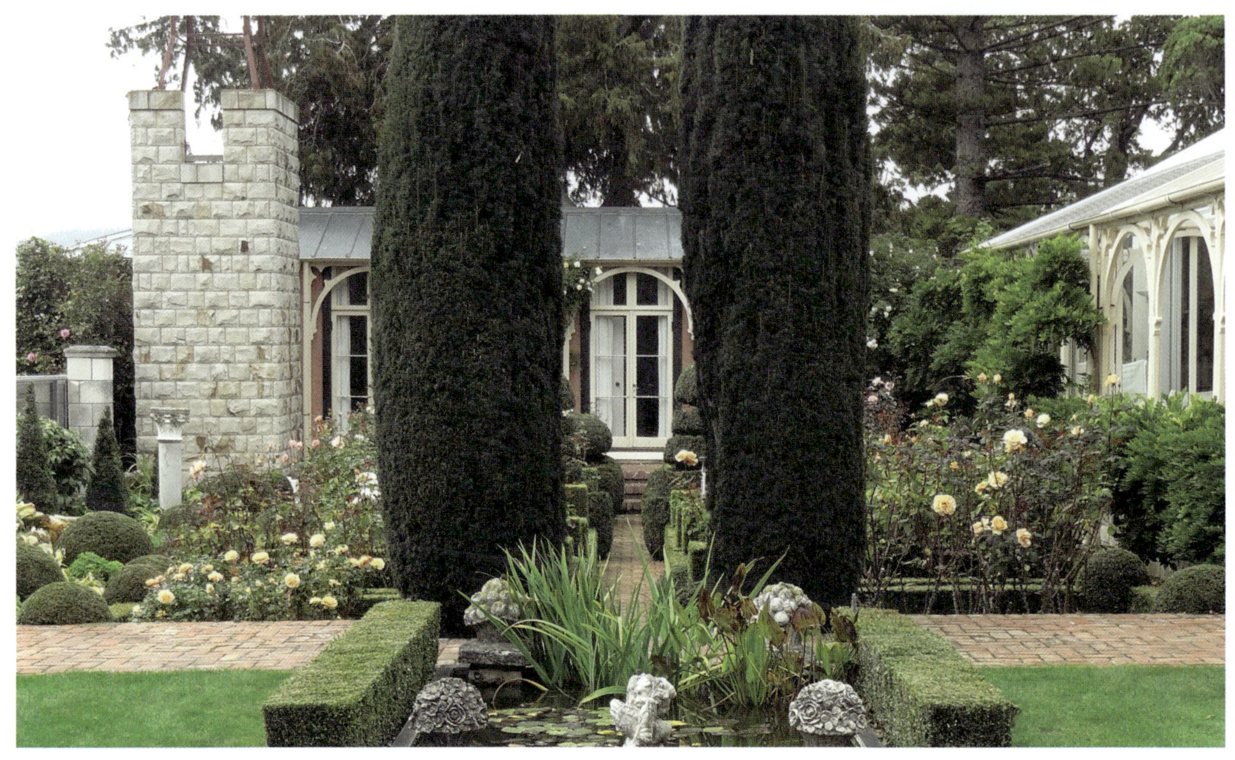

# OHINETAHI

31 Teddington Road
RD1 Governors Bay
Lyttelton

OPENING HOURS
Open September–April
Weekdays 10am–4pm, weekends by appointment

Telephone: +64 (03) 329 9852
smilesw@xtra.co.nz

It might come as a surprise that one of New Zealand's best formal gardens is equally adelight for the creatively minded. Ohinetahi is a 1.8-hectare property sheltered by Lyttelton's volcanic crater rim. As well as being a category-1 heritage house, it is the residence of one of New Zealand's foremost modern architects, Sir Miles Warren.

When Sir Miles bought Ohinetahi, meaning 'The Place of One Daughter', in 1977 with his artist sister Pauline Trengrove and her husband, architect John Trengrove, it was little more than a rundown house surrounded by an unkempt lawn. However, it featured mature specimen trees and shrubs of exotic varieties planted by early owner Thomas Potts, a wealthy amateur botanist, who had acquired the property in 1858. Sir Miles and the Trengroves restored the house and travelled to England to gather inspiration from famous gardens. Instead of opting for a romantic Victorian garden, they painstakingly designed and implemented a garden in the arts-and-crafts style with a number of separate 'rooms'. The north-south and east-west axes provide a bounty of botanical and spatial surprises. The garden nowadays boasts numerous statues, granite Corinthian columns, stone and block towers, various follies and architectural fragments (including finials from Dunedin's first church, a deconsecrated baptismal font, and decorative features from Christchurch's Regent Theatre dome). Most importantly for art enthusiasts, there are about ten impressive metal and stone sculptures, including early works by Phil Price, as well as artworks by Paul Dibble, Neil Dawson, Graham Bennett, Andrew Drummond and other New Zealand artists, all cleverly integrated into the garden.

The grand home, was badly affected by the September 2010 earthquake. The stone gables of the top storey collapsed through the roof. After recovering from the initial shock, Sir Miles – together with family and friends – removed the valuable contents and managed to stabilise the remainder of the building before city officials could classify it as unsalvageable. The two top floors were removed altogether. A large portion of the 140 tonnes of stone was later reused for the curved terracing of the amphitheatre. It is doubtful that the house would have survived the second earthquake in 2011 were it not for the strengthening that had been put in place a few months earlier.

The restorations have since been completed and visitors fortunate enough to be invited by Sir Miles into the main house will be treated to an exquisitely decorated interior. The library, with Sir Miles's vast collection of architectural volumes, the collection of fine bone china, as well the art-filled walls, including many watercolours completed by Sir Miles on numerous excursions, invokes a feeling of visiting a lived-in, historic museum. However, walking down brick steps, one is instantly transported back to the present. The modern art gallery, which is open to the general public, is a gentle reminder of the owner's foremost vocation. The right wing of the building features examples from Sir Miles's collection of artworks on canvas and paper by renowned New Zealand artists such as Ralph Hotere, Pat Hanly, Shane Cotton, Milan Mrkusich, Stephen Bambury and Peter Robinson. The smaller gallery on the left-hand side displays architectural models of projects as well as photographs of buildings that Warren & Mahoney designed over nearly four decades. Having formed the practice Warren & Mahoney in 1958, Sir Miles was instrumental in developing the 'Christchurch School' of architecture, and it is very interesting to see a selection of his best-known constructions, particularly since many of these buildings were demolished after the 2011 earthquake.

Sir Miles, who was knighted in 1985, gifted his home and garden to the Ohinetahi Charitable Trust, which oversees the maintenance of the property for the ongoing enjoyment of the public. Sir Miles remains at Ohinetahi as a watchful tenant, a principal trustee and a fascinating host.

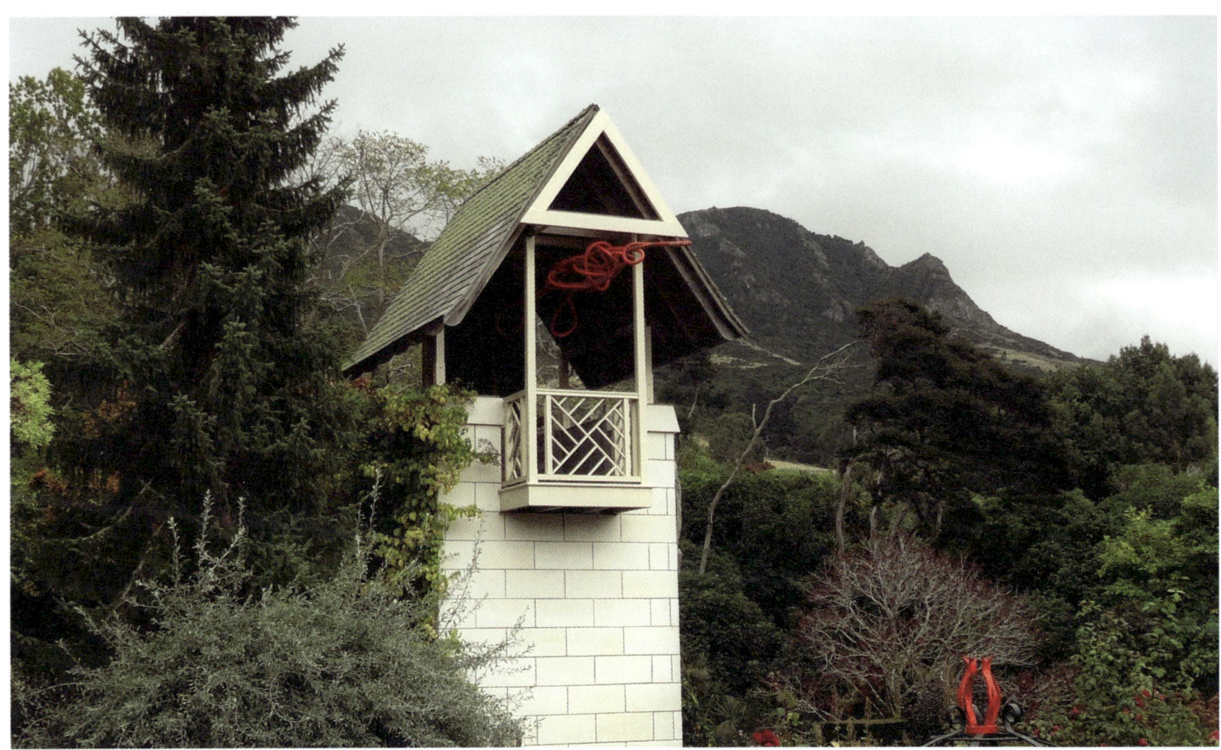

VISITOR INFORMATION

**Admission Fees:** $15

**Access by car:** Leaving Christchurch, head south on Colombo Street, continue on Dyers Pass Road to Governors Bay, then continue on Main Road, which becomes Teddington Road. You will find the sign for Ohinetahi on the left about 1.5 km past the Governors Bay Hotel.

**Extra Tips:** Despite having been badly damaged during the earthquake in 2011, the small township of Lyttelton is worth a stroll. The drive there from Ohinetahi offers some stunning views towards Governors Bay.

**Restaurant Tips:** Coffee, homemade food and great views can be enjoyed on the way to Ohinetahi at Cup Coffee, (corner Dyers Pass and Hackthorne Roads, Cashmere, Christchurch, on the right-hand side). Chocoholics will be in heaven at She Universe Café & Chocolaterie (79 Main Road, Governors Bay).

Pages 168 and 170-1
All images courtesy Ohinetahi

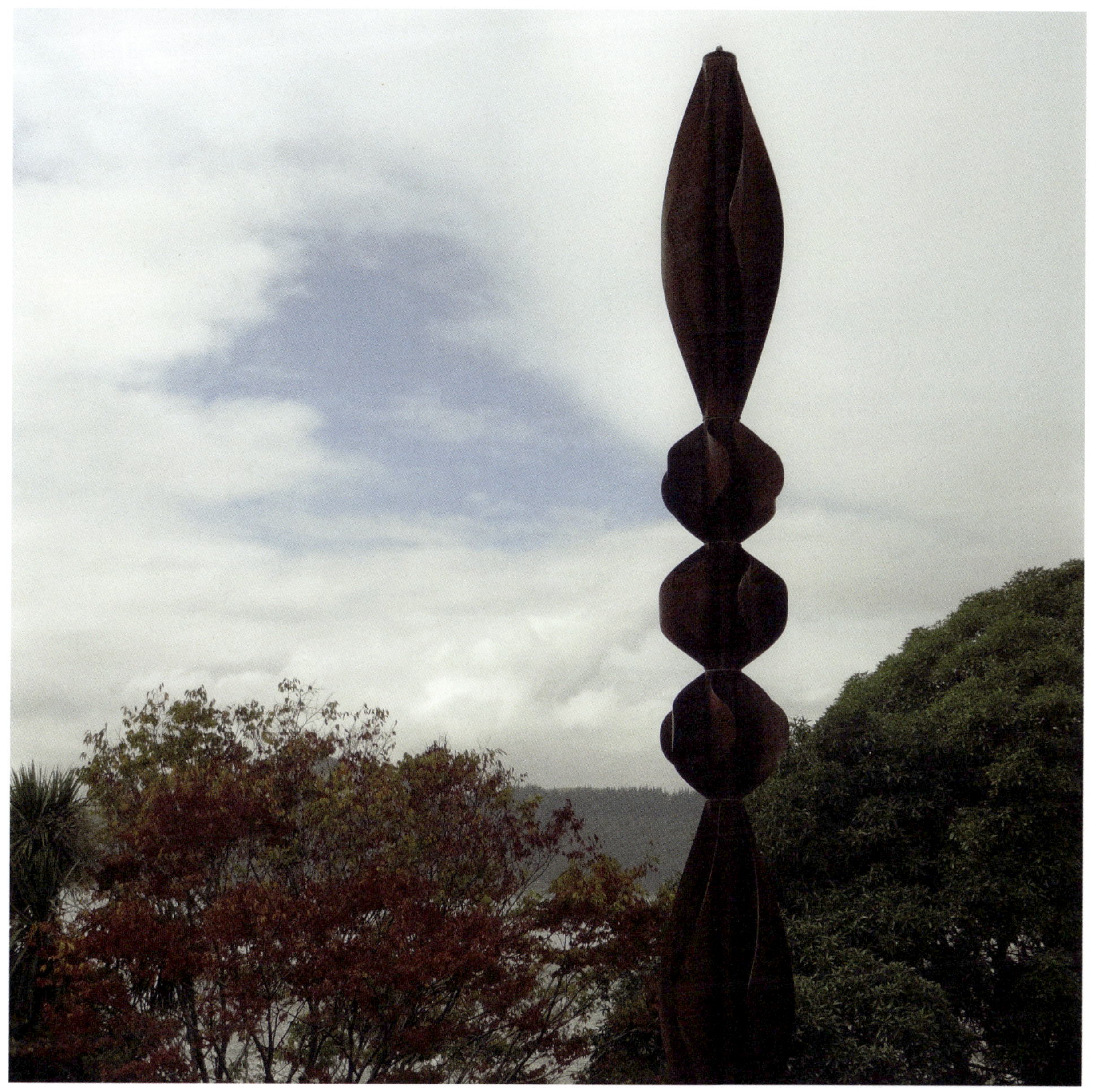

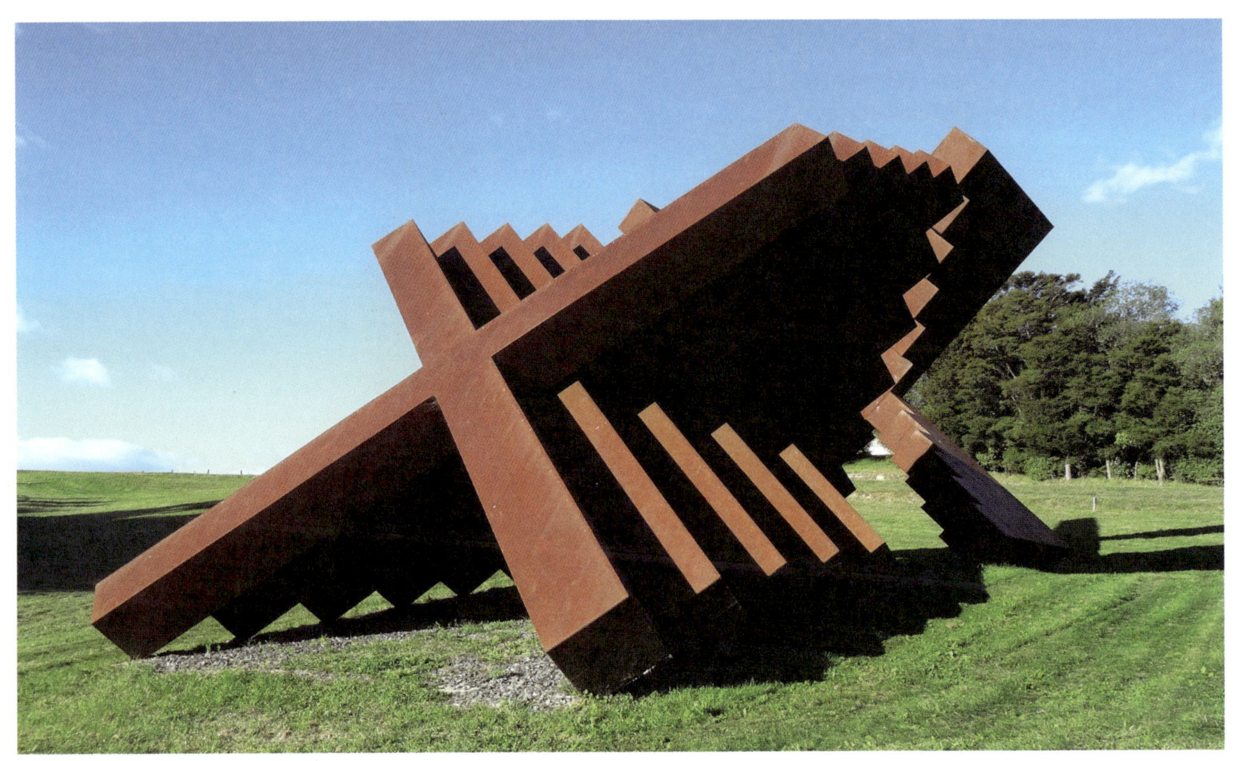

# WOOLLASTON AT MAHANA

243 Old Coach Road
Upper Moutere
Nelson

OPENING HOURS
7 days, 11am–4.30pm

Telephone: +64 (3) 543 2817
mail@woollaston.co.nz
woollaston.co.nz

Located near Nelson, in New Zealand's sunniest region, this scenic and innovative winery is a beautiful place to visit. Mainly known for its organic wines and interesting buildings, it is also home to a significant collection of art, heralded by a bold sculpture by Marté Szirmay which greets visitors at the gateway.

Philip Woollaston, the youngest child of renowned New Zealand artist Sir Toss Woollaston, entered the wine industry in 1993, developing a small vineyard with his wife Chan. Originally intended as a retirement hobby after a twenty-two-year 'second career' in politics (he was a Labour MP for Nelson, a cabinet minister, worked for the UN Environment Program and was the mayor of Nelson), his interest grew into passion and he developed a vision to produce top quality wines. The concept of Woollaston at Mahana was formulated in 2000 after a serendipitous meeting with Glenn Schaeffer, an American business leader and philanthropist, who has a strong affection for New Zealand. Both men discovered they shared a love of wine, art, literature and the Nelson landscape, so their dream was to develop a winery that was not only highly functional, but was also sensitive to the natural aesthetic of the area. With developing expertise and additional vineyards, a sophisticated winery was established and officially opened in 2007 by Helen Clark, New Zealand's then prime minister.

The unique four-level gravity-fed winery was designed by Oregon winery architect Larry Ferar (supported by Arthouse Architecture of Nelson) to incorporate the best of traditional wine-making practices with state-of-the-art modern equipment. Built into the hillside and blending into the environment with its native tussock-covered roof, the concrete edifice itself is a work of art. Gabion retaining walls hem the pathways throughout the property, referencing New Zealand's early development when gabions were used to support roads and railways alongside the country's many fast-flowing rivers.

Philip Woollaston and Glenn Schaeffer's adoration of art is seen and felt throughout the estate. Commissioned by Woollaston at Mahana and constructed on the vineyard property, the site-specific 7.5-metre tall sculpture *Yantra for Mahana* is aligned with Mt Arthur (Wharepapa, the sacred mountain of local iwi). The magnificent 40-tonne Cor-ten steel sculpture by the Hungarian-born New Zealand artist Marté Szirmay incorporates Buddhist and Christian symbolism. The elegant 'fountain' sculpture in the courtyard outside the Cellar Door was made by Nelson-born sculptor Andrew Drummond, while his wind-powered *Vertical form, counter rotation* – and Christine Boswijk's *Totems for a vineyard* – are visible from the courtyard. These works are from Glenn Schaeffer's private collection, one of the most extensive collections of minimal art on the South Island. Standing in the private grounds adjoining the strikingly modernist Mahana House, a luxury lodge which was the Schaeffers' residence until recently, they can only be enjoyed from a distance. The ground-floor winery cellars contain Bill Culbert's neon installation *Seven cs*, Neil Dawson's *Mahana dome* and two superb tapestries by American artist Ed Moses as well as several pieces by Auckland painter Noel Ivanoff. These works are accessible to the public only when the cellars are open for special events or on pre-arranged tours. Bill Culbert, who represented New Zealand at the 55th Venice Biennale, based this artwork on his own drawings of items from his collection of antique French corkscrews.
The site-specific installation fuses two significant elements of Culbert's oeuvre – the use of 'found art', and experimentation with light and colour. Deep within the winery cellars, Neil Dawson's stunning site-specific sculpture is suspended from an invisible ceiling. This intricate work is Dawson's homage to the elements, which are the ultimate source of the wine.

The two large tapestries, designed by American abstract artist Ed Moses are, like Noel Ivanoff's four 'pallet paintings', part of Schaeffer's personal collection on loan to the winery. Adjoining the newly renovated Cellar Door, the gallery (Mahana Art) has visiting exhibitions alternating with selected works from the Schaeffer art collection, and the Woollaston Room shows oils and works on paper by Toss Woollaston while the dining room features artworks in all media by New Zealand and American artists. With a few exceptions the works exhibited are available for purchase.

VISITOR INFORMATION

**Admission Fees:** Admission to the Cellar Door and gallery is free. A small charge may be made for wine tasting

**Tours and other Events:** The winery and cellars are not open to the public but, subject to winemaking operations, group tours (which could include visiting the artworks located in the winery cellar) may be arranged by appointment. Please email for details of availability and price.

**Access by car:** Woollaston at Mahana is a scenic 30-minute drive from Nelson. Leave the city south-west on State Highway 6, turn right onto Coastal Highway 60 after Richmond, follow for about 15 km, turn left onto Dominion Road and turn left again onto Old Coach Road.

**Extra Tips:** Mahana House, Glenn and Renée Schaeffer's former private residence, nowadays provides luxury accommodation, amenities and service alongside the Schaeffers' private art collection.

The World of WearableArt™ and Classic Cars Museum celebrates two distinctly different visions. An interesting collection of classic cars can be viewed alongside sixty wearable works of art from all around the globe (Cadillac Way off Quarantine Road, Annesbrook, Nelson). The Nelson region features one of the most stunning national parks in New Zealand. The Abel Tasman Park is a coastal paradise, which can be explored on foot, by boat or by sea kayak.

**Restaurant Tips:** Excellent á la carte lunches with beautiful views over the vineyard can be enjoyed at the Cellar Door of the Woollaston Estates during the day. Visitors who are taking the short drive to the Mapua Wharf are rewarded with yummy smoked seafood at The Smokehouse (Shed 2 Mapua Wharf, Mapua), with healthy, homemade meals at the Apple Shed (Shed 3) and great food with a Mediterranean influence in a picturesque yet casual setting at The Jelly Fish Café and Bar (Shed 1). Craft beer and typical pub food can be enjoyed at The Moutere Inn (1406 Moutere Highway, Upper Moutere, Nelson), New Zealand's oldest pub. Heritage apples can be picked up at Richards' Orchard street stall (Coastal Highway; near Bronte Road; from mid January to the end of August).

Page 172 and right
All images courtesy Woollaston at Mahana

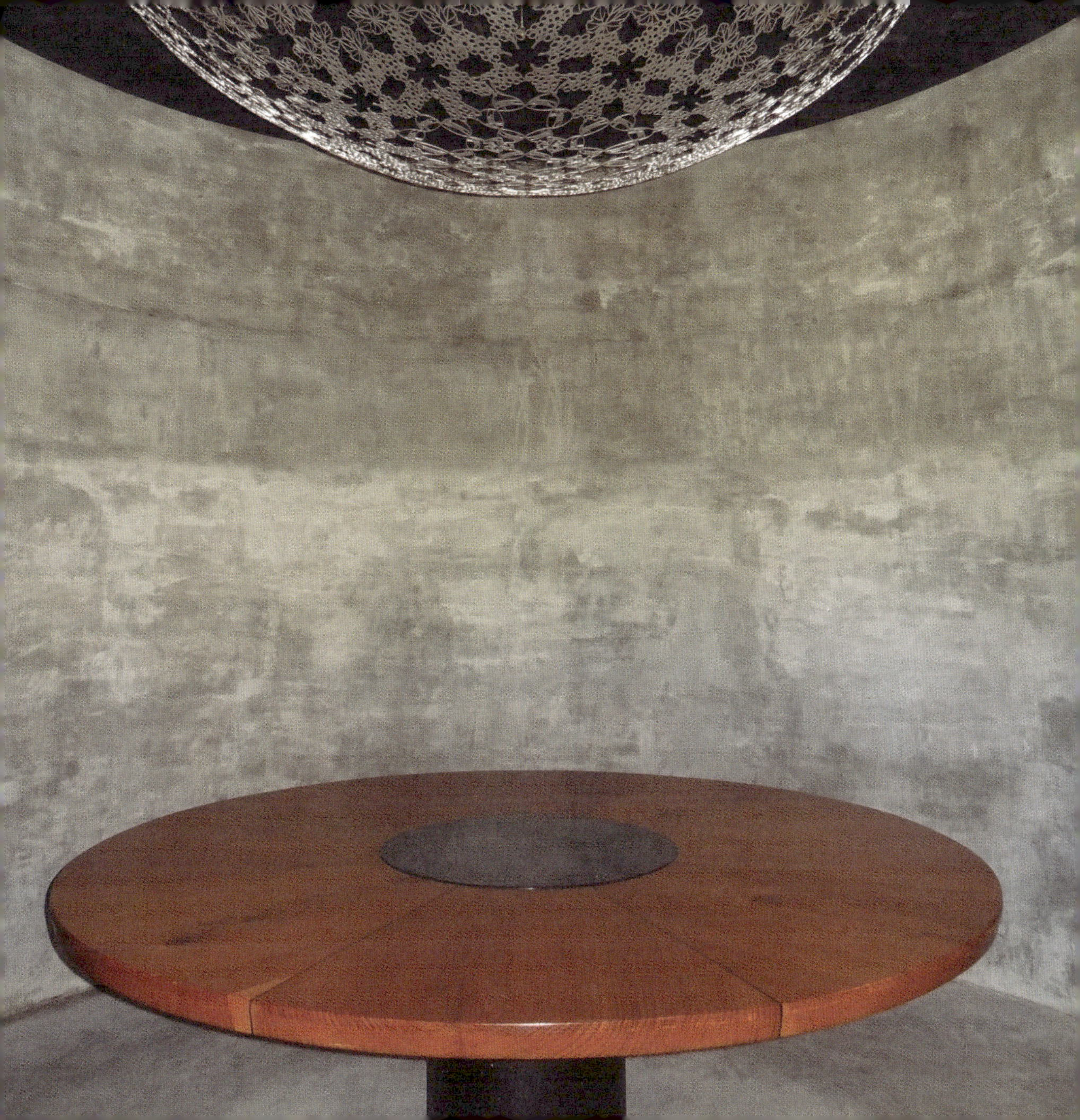

## ACKNOWLEDGMENTS

Firstly, I would like to extend my gratitude to the collectors who are included in this book. The art scenes in Australia and New Zealand would be far less innovative and diverse had it not been for their personal commitment to individual artists and their philanthropy towards the arts and culture in general. I admire and salute the collectors for their courageous decision to make their collections accessible to the public. By doing so, they allow visitors a deep insight into their soul – which, in my opinion, is mirrored in these carefully compiled collections. I would also like to thank the collections' staff members, who have supported my project and, in particular, my friends who have been so generous with their time and invaluable assistance.

Skadi Heckmueller has a degree in business and economics.
She has previously written *Privatzugang*, a German guidebook on private art collections in Germany, Austria and Switzerland, in co-operation with the publishing house Distanz Verlag, Berlin. Skadi is currently living in Sydney.